SUSTAINABLE WORLD SOURCEBOOK

CRITICAL ISSUES • VIABLE SOLUTIONS • RESOURCES FOR ACTION

Compiled by Sustainable World Coalition
dedicated to the children of all species

"Every few hundred years in Western history there occurs a sharp transformation. Within a few short decades, society—its world view, its basic values, its social and political structures, its arts, its key institutions—rearranges itself. And the people born then cannot even imagine a world in which their grandparents lived and into which their own parents were born. We are currently living through such a transformation."

—*Peter Drucker, author,* Post-Capitalist Society

TABLE OF CONTENTS

INTRODUCTION

Publisher's Preface: *LIVING AS IF OUR WORLD DEPENDS ON IT*

For me, the *Sustainable World SourceBook* and the corresponding website are a "pay it forward" endeavor. While attending the UN World Summit in Johannesburg, South Africa, in 2002, I ran across a book much like this one. It gave a broad, concise overview of the big global issues, the proposed solutions and strategies, and ways I could make a difference personally. As I grasped the severity of the threats and the enormity of the challenges facing us, I felt stunned and devastated. I had a life-changing epiphany that led to my changing careers, from graphic designer to sustainability educator. I created a nonprofit organization and immediately began producing events and materials that were—and are—intended to catalyze a widespread shift in awareness and action.

This *SourceBook* is designed to similarly inspire YOU to gain an essential understanding of the challenges facing humanity, and to make the connection between your daily life choices and your impact on the world. The *SourceBook* brings clarity to the major issues of our time, presents some of the best solutions, and provides guidelines for effective personal and collective action. Our purpose is to contribute to the creation of an environmentally sustainable, spiritually fulfilling, and socially just human presence on the planet.

Humanity as a whole faces daunting challenges that put our own survival into question. Recent years have seen increasing numbers of people and organizations addressing environmental devastation, resource depletion, species extinction, and extreme wealth inequity by exposing the truth, advocating for change, and implementing solutions.

Many of these organizations have invested a great deal of time and expertise to come up with innovative strategies and potential remedies, leading to working models now in practice or in the pipeline. We do have reason to believe we can turn things around, but time is short to do so.

It is a fact that those of us in the wealthy countries must share much responsibility for the crises, given our high per-capita consumption, and that those in poorer countries often bear the brunt of those excesses. Until we are willing to look squarely at our situation, we remain largely unmoved by its realities. Yet once we summon the courage to confront our predicament, we find that indeed there is much we can do on levels big and small, and many signs of hope and possibility that this book portrays in broad strokes.

According to current data, we are rapidly nearing a point of no return for saving much of what we know and love on our beautiful planet. There is no time to wait! Restoring balance and sustainability across the globe will take our best minds and a critical mass of citizens who are not just concerned but committed to making the changes required.

We know from past crises that as things continue to heat up and get worse, we will begin to experience real humility, rethink what's important, and mobilize for action. We will find ourselves working together for the common good in ways we only now dream of. That vision gives me great hope.

So where do we begin?

STEP 1: GET INFORMED. Find out about the issues both global and local, the proposed solutions, and how we as individuals can contribute to creating a healthy and just world.

STEP 2: GET ENGAGED. Open your heart. Engage your creativity, your passion, your dreams. Deepen your connections to the Earth and one another. Act on what you know and learn. Get involved with improving your community. Challenge your friends to do the same—we're all in this together.

Thank you for reading this book—please pay it forward.

Vinit Allen – *Director, Sustainable World Coalition*

A World of Thanks

Claus Wawrzinek

We appreciate the networks, interwoven relationships, and the multitude of organizations doing the important, leading-edge work that inspired and informed the process of compiling the *SourceBook*. Our gratitude goes to all the people whose advice, assistance, talents, and commitment to creating a better world made this book possible. Kudos to all readers who join the movement or become reinvigorated in their hopes and efforts—we need and thank you all!

We modeled a bottom-up collaborative approach exemplary of the movement itself, and the following people are among those who helped co-create the *SourceBook*.

RESEARCHERS, EDITORS, WRITERS, PROOFERS, AND ASSISTANTS: Alexandra Hart, Anita Sanchez, Anjee Lang, Ann West, Bruce Erickson, Cheryl Fralick, Claire Borgeson, Ellen Augustine, Ellen Hong, Gary Hughes, Jackie Braun, Jewel Snavely, Jim Embry, Joan Olawski-Steiner, Juan Pablo Obando, Rev. Kelly Isola, Kevin Danaher, Kit Tennis, Laura Baker, Lawrence Wallersheim, Leslie Mezei, Linda Delair, Linda Foster, Marianne Williamson, Marn-Yee Lee, Meredith Stechbart, Michele Drivon, Michele Mahoney, Michele Perrault, Nicole Freeling, Paul Gilbert, Paula Morrison, Peter Galvin, Rajyo Markman, Randy Hayes, Rebecca Strong, Rebecca Wait, Robert Bostick, Romola Georgia, Rua Necaise, Sarah Wechsberg, Shera Sever, Susan Thomas, Suzie Mummé, Stephanie "Slim" Russell, Steven Goldfinger, Susan Burns, Southern Oregon University Sustainability Leadership Class (2009), Tewa Heartsong, Tom Christopher, Trathen Heckman PUBLICATION SUPPORT: Lyndie Kahanek VIDEO: Celestine Star PHOTOS: Claus Wawrzinek, Connie Barlow, Frank Taylor, Jessica Ayala, Jim Embry, John Story, June Holte, Karen Clawson, Kelly Slocum, Leah Beck, Lizzy Ziogas, Marva Weigelt, Roberta Vogel, Vicki Walker CARTOONS: Brian Narelle FUNDING: David and Shirley Allen.

"Spiritual practice is really about weaving a network of good relationships."
—*Dhyani Ywahoo*

From the Editors

Pachamama Alliance

Dear Reader,

We consider this book to be a tool to support you in your personal journey of contributing to the creation of a just, sustainable human presence on Earth—portable, skimmable, gift-worthy—one to which you will return again and again. This is a living, breathing document; its online component is a searchable database, where the book itself can be found as a free downloadable PDF, replete with hotlinks. The book is a forum rather than a definitive treatment or position. Errors or omissions—well, please help us fix them! We sincerely hope you will visit our website, www.swcoalition.org, to collaborate and interact with us via this newly expanding platform.

Although we provide a global context, the primary distribution of the *SourceBook* will be in the United States—the country with the largest ecological footprint and largest economy, and thus the country with the largest responsibility to address our collective challenges. In attempting the audacious task of summarizing all of the world's major issues and their solutions in just 100 pages, we were not able to cover many important areas, and we hope you will follow the many links to useful organizations and networks (such as WiserEarth.org). To cover our topics comprehensively, we often wrote "long," later trimming sections into nutshell summaries for the book, and cutting some altogether—saving the longer versions for our website, where you can go for more depth of information.

We aimed to find the most credible sources and to document them all, hence we've created an extensive *Endnotes* section and *Resource Directory*, which is even more robust online. Contributors listed above are not responsible for the content of this collaborative project, the compilation of information, or views expressed. Innumerable people and organizations are contributing to a sustainable world, directly and indirectly, each unique and valuable. We found it amazing to witness the vast number of organizations and people—from all walks of life, professions, and sectors—on board and contributing to the Great Turning. Millions are heeding the wake-up call and rising to the occasion. We urge you to explore the articles, major documents, and links to respected organizations doing this important work. The Web's potential to disseminate information and organize people around the world is truly phenomenal.

This *SourceBook* is a labor of love! Many people volunteered untold hours, riding the waves of continuously morphing content as the sustainability movement expands exponentially around us. The writers, researchers, editors, and reviewers include both established and emerging leaders and experts. Volunteers include practitioners, graduate students from sustainability/green institutions, and Awakening the Dreamer, Changing the Dream Symposium facilitators, hailing from diverse disciplines and residing in all time zones of the US, as well as India and the UK. Our gratitude extends to Vinit Allen, for his vision, funding, distribution, and editorial partnership in this project.

Sincerely,
Jude Wait, Kathy Glass, June Holte, Karen Chaffraix

Creative Commons/itza fine day

FOREWORD BY PAUL HAWKEN

There is a possibility that the world will see again. At this moment, global civilization is blind to the peril and possibility that resides in forces at play in society and the environment. To rectify that, there is an essential and indispensable course of action, a systematic call from each village and neighborhood and family to others, to become literate in the social and environmental challenges we face.

Aristotle said that genius is metaphor, but there is as yet no metaphor (or genius) that can adequately describe or encompass this moment in time because there is no precedent. The terms crossroads, turning point, watershed, and moment of truth do not address this juncture for these are civilizational times and they require each of us to reimagine what it means to be a human being. Critical to this act of newly conceiving who we are and what we should be doing is literacy. The *Sustainable World SourceBook* is a door to a newly born and critically important literacy of the world around us.

Literacy is the first step to dialogue, conversation, and collaboration. If you cannot read, books look like cooking fuel. You may see a bird as gossamer and feathers, but it is also a creator of forests and meadows, flying with its small sac of undigested seeds. We can see the world as doomed and fatally flawed, or we can see every trend and statistic as the possibility of transformation. We can see ourselves as fortunate and separate from the suffering of others, or we can see that our bounty rests heavily on the shoulders of unknown people. Concomitant to our good fortune is the responsibility to create a world of equals, not just a nation of equals.

As stunning and paralyzing as is the data about climate change, the possibilities that are emerging from the imagination and concerns of humankind are equally stunning. In energy alone, we are tasked with reducing carbon-based energy by 80% in the next 25 years if we are to prevent temperature from rising more than 2 degrees Centigrade.

Yes, the world uses 84 million barrels of oil per day. But, a square meter of the Earth receives in one year the same amount of energy as a barrel of oil. The US, a profligate user of energy, has about 4,000 times more solar energy than its annual electricity use. For the world, that figure is 10,000 times, which means that if 1% of the world's land were used for solar photovoltaics, we would have 10 times the amount of energy needed. And a new branch of thin-film solar technology is nearly at grid parity, meaning that a solar panel can produce electricity at costs commensurate with coal and gas. This example is repeated in hundreds of areas of social and technical innovation. Humanity knows what to do, once it knows what needs to be done.

To make a change this broadly this quickly is unheralded. It calls for a mobilization where human beings are not rallying to defeat an enemy, but organizing to support each other. It is not just our energy and resource profligacy that is devastatingly expensive; our divisions, dislikes, and antagonisms are equally unaffordable. Coming together in communities of empowered people, to quote former President Clinton, is the work at hand, and this book and the extraordinary experience of the Awakening the Dreamer Symposium are critical tools in humankind's journey to a world that is conducive to and protective of all life.

Paul Hawken is an environmentalist, entrepreneur, journalist, and best-selling author. He has dedicated his life to sustainability and changing the relationship between business and the environment. Paul resides in Northern California.

Part One
SETTING THE CONTEXT

Now you begin to see that

your dream is a nightmare...

All you have to do is

change the dream...

You need only

plant a different seed,

teach your children to dream

new dreams.

—Elder of Ecuador's
Shuar tribe

I n the summer of 1995, a small group of people answered a call for partnership from one of the world's most remote, indigenous dream cultures, the Achuar of the Ecuadorian rainforest. Thus was born The Pachamama Alliance. (*Pachamama* is from the Andean language *Quechua;* its meaning encompasses the sacred presence of the Earth, the sky, the Universe, and all time, although it is often translated as "Mother Earth.") This partnership supports a federation of tribes working together to protect over two million acres of pristine rainforest, with achievements that include something unprecedented: Nature has been granted rights in Ecuador's constitution. Yet, all along, the Achuar had pointed to another aspect of the work to be done: changing the "dream" of the modern world.

Thus, in partnership with dozens of organizations and individuals, The Pachamama Alliance created the *Awakening the Dreamer, Changing the Dream Symposium.*[1] Since 2006, a growing number of over 2000 trained volunteer facilitators are taking the symposium around the world—sharing it with groups large and small, currently in 40 countries on six continents.

"From the very beginning, our indigenous partners told us that...if we really wanted to protect their lands permanently, we would need to go to work in our *part of the world, and, as they put it, we would need to change the dream of the North, the dream of the modern world, a dream rooted in consumption and acquisition, without any regard to the consequences of the natural world, or even our own future."*
—Lynne Twist, co-founder, The Pachamama Alliance

The *SourceBook* opens with a summary of the Awakening the Dreamer Symposium, in order to set the context for what follows. We will discover that the big global issues we face are symptoms of our consciousness, rooted in our cultural story, so this is the place to start.

CHANGING THE STORY, AWAKENING THE DREAMER

"The most remarkable feature of this historical moment on Earth is not that we are on the way to destroying the world—we've actually been on the way for quite a while. It is that we are beginning to wake up, as from a millennia-long sleep, to a whole new relationship to our world, to ourselves and each other."
—Joanna Macy, eco-philosopher

The journey of life has brought many of us to want to better understand the crises we now face on planet Earth—ecological, social, economic, spiritual—and what we can do about it. We are embarking on what Joanna Macy points to—creating a new relationship with life, our world, and the others who share this planet with us. We are, in fact, part of changing the "dream of the modern world."

The global overview here is offered as an exploration of the root causes of our global crises, providing hopeful possibilities for the future.

The *SourceBook* and Awakening the Dreamer share a common purpose: *to bring forth an environmentally sustainable, spiritually fulfilling, socially just human presence on this planet.* Although this mission seems to be three separate issues, they are actually three facets of one interconnected whole.

WHERE ARE WE?
A status report on the health of our planet

Environmental Sustainability

Since 1972, the UN Environment Programme has been reporting on the Earth's vital signs. More than 1,360 experts worldwide participated in the most recent state-of-the-art scientific appraisal of the condition and trends in the world's ecosystems, from 2001 to 2005. They conclude that, in every natural domain, the Earth is under very severe stress.

- 60% of the ozone layer has been lost in 50 years.
- 70% of the world's original forests have been eliminated.
- 30% of the world's arable land has been lost in the last 40 years.
- 90% of all large fish are gone from the oceans.[2]

"Sustainability is the ability of the current generation to meet its needs, without compromising the ability of future generations to meet theirs."
— *United Nations, 1987*[3]

The chart below illustrates one measure of humanity's impact on Earth.[4] We are now using 30% more of nature than it can regenerate—called "global overshoot"—eroding the natural capital that life depends on. If everyone lived as North Americans do, we would need five Earths; as Europeans do, three Earths. China and India are just under the one-Earth level, but that is increasing steadily. Moderate projections from the UN show that, by 2050, we will be using about twice the carrying capacity of Earth. This is accompanied by a catastrophic loss of much of Earth's unique biodiversity. Although the news hasn't reached the general public, we are in the midst of a mass extinction crisis: Half the species on Earth are in danger of becoming extinct in 50 years.[5]

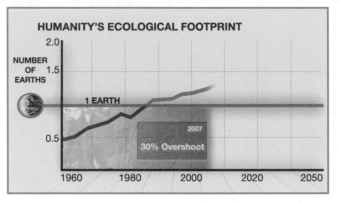

HUMANITY'S ECOLOGICAL FOOTPRINT

NUMBER OF EARTHS

2.0
1.5
1 EARTH
0.5

2007
30% Overshoot

1960   1980   2000   2020   2050

"We lament the passing of the people we love, and our pets...but how to lament the permanent loss of a mode of life? I think that's beyond most of us, because we haven't deepened our hearts in a way that would make possible the grief that is wanting to be felt."
— *Brian Swimme, author, professor, cosmologist*

Social Justice

Most people who are aware of the environmental crises are worried that climate destabilization, resource depletion, pollution, and habitat destruction will soon have a major impact on their lives. For many, it already has. Environmental degradation is profoundly affecting millions. The movement to address this disparity in who is affected the most is called "Environmental Justice." It reflects a deep, innate human longing for justice and equity.

"Environmental Justice is the belief that no community should have to bear the brunt of a disproportionate amount of environmental burdens and not enjoy any environmental benefits. But right now race and class are the best indicators as to where you'll find the good stuff— like parks and trees—and where you'll find the bad stuff—like waste facilities or power plants."
— *Majora Carter, founder, Sustainable South Bronx*

No one would assert that we have achieved a socially just human presence on the planet. Globally 200,000 people a day are moving to cities from environments that have sustained them for generations, many to live in slums where they have very few options for work.[6] Almost half the world—over three billion people—live on less than $2 a day.[7] The gap between rich and poor is widening rapidly everywhere, which exacerbates many social problems.

If you have food in a refrigerator, clothes in your closet, a bed to sleep in, and a roof over your head, you are better off, materially, than 75% of people on this planet.[8]

Spiritual, Psychological and Emotional Impact

What about our personal sense of wholeness and fulfillment? The costs resulting from our modern worldview are evident. Study after study shows that material gains do not lead to greater happiness or spiritual fulfillment. Our belongings are scant comfort when we lack a sense of belonging.

Jessica Ayala

"There is a great loneliness of spirit today. "We're trying to...cope in the face of what seems to be overwhelming evidence that who we are doesn't matter; that there is no real hope for enough change; that the environment and human experience is deteriorating rapidly, and increasingly, and massively. This is the context, psychically and spiritually, in which we are working today. This is how our lives are reflected to us. Meanwhile, we're yearning for connection with each other, with ourselves, with the powers of nature, the possibilities of being alive.

"When that tension arises, we feel pain, we feel anguish at the very root of ourselves, and then we cover that over, that grief, that horror, with all kinds of distraction—with consumerism, with addictions, with anything that we can use to disconnect. We've been opening ourselves to the grief, to the knowing of what's taking place—the loss of species, the destruction of the natural world, unimaginable levels of social injustice and economic injustice that deprive so many human beings of basic opportunities. And as we open to the pain of that, there's a possibility of embracing that pain and that grief in a way that it becomes a strength, a power to respond."

—John Robbins, author,
Diet for a New America

HOW DID WE GET HERE?
Cultural Drivers and Unexamined Assumptions

It's important to recognize that human decisions and human behavior created our current challenging situation. We did this to ourselves! This is good news—if our actions created this outcome, then different actions can create a different outcome.

It could be said that we in the modern world are living in a kind of "trance"—what some indigenous people would call the "dream of the modern world." The late Thomas Berry referred to our industrial age as a period of "technological entrancement" in which we think we're headed toward some ill-defined "dream of progress." Berry scholar and poet Drew Dellinger describes it like this: "We think we're behaving

rationally—creating jobs, gross domestic product is rising, thinking we're on a kind of logical economic course—but actually we're heading toward our destruction. Western civilization creates and perpetuates a radical separation between the human world and the natural world. We give all rights to humans and none to the natural world."

This "trance" is our current worldview—a point of view so pervasive that it is invisible to us. As the saying goes, "If you were a fish, the last thing you would discover is water." Our worldview is held in place by a set of beliefs and unexamined assumptions that we're completely unaware of—like glasses we've worn so long, we're unaware we're looking through them. People take actions appropriate to how they see the world. Thus, if our actions are producing outcomes we are not intending, it's useful to explore the unconscious, unexamined assumptions that generated those actions. Here are some examples of unexamined assumptions widely held in the modern world:

- We humans are separate from one another and the rest of creation.
- Nature is a resource for our human use, and it is unlimited.
- A healthy society depends on a growing economy.
- When we buy something, the price we pay reflects the full cost of making it.
- There is a place called "away" where we can throw things. (Where is "away"?)
- We have disposable resources, disposable species, and disposable people.
- One individual can't make a difference.

Other Worldviews

There are many other people on this planet not caught in the "dream of progress," people who have a very different way of seeing the world and their place in it. These include many indigenous cultures who have lived sustainably on Earth for thousands of years. Recognizing other worldviews can help us gain perspective on the trance that our modern worldview has generated, and on what else is possible.

"We use another terminology, called 'Mitakuye Oyasin,' which is, 'All My Relations.' We recognize that we are related to everything...We have a rela-

tionship here, human being to human being. And I'm also related to the animals, to the plants, even the micro-organisms...Somehow, industrialized society has not caught up with itself to really appreciate and respect what indigenous peoples have to offer, but it's something that's very important, I think, that's going to save the planet."

—Tom Goldtooth, executive director,
Indigenous Environmental Network

The contrast here is striking and informative: The worldview that has come to prominence over recent centuries in the modern world holds that the world is like a huge machine made up of separate parts, like a big clock—a mechanical, rather than organic, model of life. But this worldview is missing something profound.

No wonder we've been creating such havoc—our destructive behavior and its unintended consequences are the result of an inaccurate worldview. Our actions have resulted from a cultural perspective we can now see as misguided, limited. We are mistaken, not somehow innately flawed. We can now see that most of the unintended consequences can be traced to one central unexamined assumption: believing we are separate, from the world and from each other. This assumption shapes virtually all of our perceptions and our actions.

But this worldview is shifting. We in the modern world are just now coming back around to what indigenous cultures have known all along: The world is totally connected and interrelated. We have begun to recognize, and are waking up from the "trance" of believing that we are separate.

Jessica Ayala

Roberta Vogel

Transforming the Cultural Story—A New Story for All of Humanity

One way to describe our shared world-view—and the myriad of unexamined assumptions that comprise it—would be to call it our cultural "story." At this time in history, our story is transforming, going through a process no less profound than the change in our Western cultural story during the profound shift—from assuming that the Earth was at the center of the Universe to eventually knowing that the Earth actually revolves around the sun. Imagine the clash between those who adopted the new system of understanding—that the sun is the center of the solar system—with those who held on dearly to believing that the Earth was the stationary center of everything.

What is now emerging in the modern world is a transformation of our way of seeing and experiencing the world. This new story is consistent both with modern science and with the understanding of the world that indigenous people have always had, and it is beginning to shape the consciousness on our planet. It opens the possibility for a future that is not merely an extension of the past.

"It suggests that a profound wisdom is at work in the Universe…As we move into this understanding, we have a new identity of ourselves as cosmological beings. We're not just Americans, we're not just French, we're not any small category. We are the Universe in the form of a human. And it is true of everyone. It's an amazing new understanding of

ourselves that is so profoundly inclusive, and everyone is part of this. Everything is part of this. And we discover, as well, a profound kinship, that no matter what being we're talking about on the planet, we are related. We're related in terms of energy. We're related in terms of genetics. We're all like a form of kin. …It is a massive change in human consciousness."

—Brian Swimme

The fact that this new understanding exists—and is becoming embedded in modern cultures—changes everything. In an emerging story of connection and the understanding that we're all part of one unified whole, behaviors that before would have been considered to be an assault on the Earth can now be seen as an assault on ourselves, because we're part of—not separate from—the web of life. This opens up enormous new possibilities for the future.

WHAT'S POSSIBLE FOR THE FUTURE?
The Great Turning

Clearly something fundamental has to change. Our current path is unsustainable on virtually all levels. But changing the dream of the modern world, changing the course of history? Is it possible?

When we look at great social change in history—like the British leaving India, the end of the Cold War, and of South African apartheid—there seems to be a pattern: After many years or decades of what appears to be business as usual, at some point there is an unpredicted shift in society, and

dramatic results show up in a very short period of time. When we look deeper, though, we find that the time before such sudden shifts was a kind of incubation period of background work, often marked by the blood, sweat, and tears of those involved. Many small actions by many people over time create the environment in which a rapid turnabout becomes possible. This means that *any day can be a tipping point.*

"Can we change? Absolutely. Our species changes when it has to. And that's where I find hope in the despair of the situation…There's a driven-ness in our species and a creativity…a capacity to let go, to start over, to forgive…that we've barely begun to tap."

—Matthew Fox, Episcopal priest, founder, Wisdom University

Clearly something *is* happening on Earth—virtually everywhere people are creating solutions that can lead to a sustainable, just, and fulfilling world. Are these random isolated occurrences, or are they signs of an emerging global phenomenon? Paul Hawken has concluded that the largest social movement in history is arising—over 1.2 million organizations—that doesn't yet know itself as a "movement."

"There is another superpower here on Earth that is an unnamed movement…far different and bigger and more unique than anything we have ever seen…non-violent…grassroots… no central ideology…The very word 'movement' is too small to describe it. No one started this worldview, no one

is in charge of it...it is global, classless, unquenchable and tireless...arising spontaneously from different economic sectors, cultures, regions and cohorts... growing and spreading worldwide...It has many roots, but primarily the origins are indigenous culture, the environment and social justice movements. This is humanity's immune response to resist and heal political disease, economic infection, and ecological corruption caused by ideologies. This is fundamentally a civil rights movement, a human rights movement; this is a democracy movement; it is the coming world."

—Paul Hawken, author, environmentalist, entrepreneur

This movement encompasses a resurgence of interest in personal spiritual growth, in the guiding wisdom of indigenous cultures, and in bringing together the faithful of all religions to create peace in the world. The New Dream isn't something that is yet to come—it's emerging already. Once you become aware of this movement, you will see it everywhere!

WHERE DO WE GO FROM HERE?

Getting Engaged, Taking a Personal Stand

If you're alive today, you have a role to play. What there is for each of us to do at this remarkable time in history is to discover and act upon *what is ours to do*—and to find others to work with who share our vision.

The power of one individual acting on their vision, from their passion, cannot be overemphasized. The Green Belt movement is a perfect example of the way in which many innovations and movements start with one committed person. What began with Wangari Maathai working with a few women on Kenyan hillsides has grown to impact the soil, climate, and local economies all across Africa. More than 600 community groups have planted over 30 million trees, and the movement is now spreading to other regions of the world. For this, Ms. Maathai became the first African woman to receive the Nobel Peace Prize, in 2004.

Coming Together in Community

"My great-great-grandchildren ask me, in dreams, 'What did you do while the planet was plundered? What did you do when the Earth was unraveling? Surely you did something when the seasons started failing, as the mammals, reptiles, birds were all dying. Did you fill the streets with protest when democracy was stolen? What did you do once you knew?'"

—Drew Dellinger, poet

The story of the monarch butterfly, from evolutionary biologist Elisabet Sahtouris, offers a powerful metaphor for the process of the transformation our world is undergoing at this time.

A caterpillar consumes hundreds of times its own weight before it enters the cocoon stage, when *imaginal cells* begin to emerge. Initially, the dissolving structures interpret this emergence as a threat, and kill off the first imaginal cells. In time, these cells begin to find one another and bond together. When enough of them cluster, they form imaginal buds that can resist the attack. Even though they are not in the majority, the buds become the genetic directors of the future. The other cells continue to dissolve and feed the growing structures of the butterfly—unpredictable from its consumptive predecessor—a creature of great beauty, which travels great distances catalyzing life.

What's possible is that we who are working to heal the web of life are the imaginal cells on the planet right now. Another metaphor for this is that we are part of the Earth's immune system. We are here to *hospice* the old, resistant, dying structures, while catalyzing and *midwifing* the new,

Earth-honoring systems, structures, ways of seeing and ways of being.

As we realize that we're already interconnected, changing the world comes about by working together, in and as community. Our individual actions are essential, but only within the larger context of "all my relations."

We are part of a cadre of global citizens who are emerging from the dream of the modern world, able to embrace the crisis in which we're living, and able to see that the possibilities are greater than the magnitude of the crisis.

"There's an old African proverb that some of you know that says: 'If you want to go quickly, go alone—if you want to go far, go together.' We have to go far, quickly! So we have to have a change in consciousness, a change in commitment, a new sense of urgency, a new appreciation for the privilege that we have of undertaking this challenge."

—Al Gore, former US Vice President, author of **An Inconvenient Truth**

Our work together is to contribute to the creation of a global movement of engaged people—global citizens—who are informed and compassionate; people who are able to see, embrace, and create a new possibility for the future, and who are continually learning and growing, to ensure that their actions will be as effective as possible in bringing needed change during these challenging times. We invite you to stay in a state of what modern dance pioneer Martha Graham called *blessed unrest*—a vibrant, active state of agitation and empathy with those in need which fuels creativity and committed action.

John Story

Part Two ENVIRONMENT

Healing the Web of Life

CLIMATE CHANGE
Life in a Warming World

Our culture is based on a principle that directs us to constantly think about the welfare of seven generations into the future.

—Iroquois Confederacy

"It is not the strongest of the species that survives, nor the most intelligent, but the one most responsive to change."

—*Charles Darwin,*
19th-century English naturalist

The human race may one day deeply regret its slow response to the millennial challenge of climate change facing us right now. While paid-off politicians dither so that sectors of the oil and energy industry can protect their profits—and a complacent, confused, and argument-wary public lets them—the actions we must take to reverse the crisis languish on someone's desk. With 5% of the world's population, the US is responsible for at least 18% of global greenhouse gas emissions (GHGs).[1] That this country lags so far behind on this issue is unconscionable.

Humans' impact on the Earth's climate is everywhere, if you look, and increasingly severe changes are predicted for the future. If the increase in human-made GHG emissions continues unabated, temperatures will rise even more than they have, and the damage will be irreversible. Water table levels will continue to dwindle while snow evaporates and ice and glaciers melt into oceans. Sea levels are already on the rise. Adapting to unavoidable climate change while simultaneously reducing emissions requires unprecedented global cooperation. Many aspects of climate change are happening earlier and more rapidly than climate models and experts initially predicted.

It's no longer appropriate to keep one's head in the sand by claiming that there is not yet scientific consensus on the existence or causes of global climate change. Scientists have called the warming trend "unequivocal" on the basis of multiple lines of physical evidence, including the obvious melting of ice caps and glaciers and the rising sea level.[2]

Among those who understand the science of long-term climate processes, this is not a debate. The challenge apparently lies in convincing the public of this, since confusion and wild claims seem to be a common mischaracterization of serious efforts to rein in global

"So *that's* where they're all going!"

warming. Such inaccurate perceptions are no doubt fueled by vocal opponents from a scientific and political fringe group backed by industries with the most to lose by mandated emissions reductions and appropriately allocated responsibility for them.

The Verdict Is In: *We* Are the Source of Global Warming

Various factors cause climate to change over the millennia; some are natural, some human-caused. Experts generally agree now that recent increases in global temperatures result mostly from higher levels of heat-trapping gases in the atmosphere, which have been increasing because of human activities since roughly 1750, or the dawn of the Industrial Revolution. Scientists have demonstrated that the primary human source (80%) is the burning of coal, oil, and natural gas (fossil fuels), and the second human source implicated (20%) is deforestation and other land use changes.[3]

The ten warmest years in the 150-year thermometer record have all occurred in the twelve years between 1997 and 2008; thus none of the previous fifteen decades have been as warm on average as this one.[4] 2005 was one of the hottest years in more than a century.

In January 2008 scientists indicated that recent warm summers have caused the most extreme glacial melting in Greenland in 50 years.[5] The US West is apparently warming at nearly twice the rate of the rest of the world and is likely to face more drought conditions in many of its fast-growing cities.[6]

Among these serious concerns is the fact that global ecosystems have feedback loops and *tipping points*, not all of which we understand (to say the least). It is now clear that several phenomena are self-sustaining, amplifying cycles—for example, melting ice and glaciers, melting tundra and other methane sources, and increasing ocean saturation with CO_2, which leads to increases in atmospheric CO_2. Once a tipping point or change state is reached, climate feedback mechanisms rapidly speed warming. These processes are non-linear and largely unpredictable. For all we know, tipping points may be long past or just around the corner. We are unable to accurately specify what quantity of GHGs will be dangerous, though many agree it is much lower than commonly assumed.

According to models, global temperatures could rise by 4 degrees C (7.2 degrees F) by 2100. Some scientists fear that we may get there as soon as 2050. If we continue on our current trajectory of rapid fossil-fuel growth, over the next century the "perfect storm" of population growth, resource depletion, and climate change will have catastrophic results. Even in the most optimistic scenario (assuming rapid and deep changes in our economic structure), temperatures are likely to increase by 1.1 to 2.9 degrees C by 2100, according to the International Panel on Climate Change (IPCC).[7]

There is a time lag in seeing the effects of our actions in regard to global warming. Even if we ended all emissions tomorrow, additional warming is on the way thanks to the momentum built into the Earth's intricate climate system. The oceans, for example, have yet to come into equilibrium with the extra heat-trapping capacity of the atmosphere. As the oceans continue to warm, so will the land around them. The velocity and extent of recent changes inform us that our "climate models" are much more conservative than nature itself. Thus this is truly a millennial challenge!

Addressing Climate Change: An Urgent Imperative

Government Action Needed Now!

Given the uncertainties, a public response has been difficult to formulate. The US has a duty to provide leadership on policy shifts because it bears considerable historical responsibility for the problem and has the capability for action. The lack of leadership on the part of the US, the world's top emitter of greenhouse gases, has hampered global progress on all fronts; plus, the oil and coal industries, among other parties, are actively working to defeat effective climate change legislation because it threatens business as usual. Yet the US must be held accountable for emissions, which are double the per-capita level in Europe. The European Union has made a much stronger stand in its commitment to reduce total greenhouse gas emissions (80% by 2050). US carbon emissions continue to increase as you read this, albeit not as rapidly as in China, India, and other parts of Asia. Of course, without a US commitment to curbing emissions, persuading China and India to reduce their levels is unlikely.

"Weaker targets for 2020 increase the risk of crossing tipping points and make the task of meeting 2050 targets more difficult. Delay in initiating effective mitigation action increases significantly the long-term social and economic costs of both adaptation and mitigation."
—*Rainforest Action Network, Climate Change Action Manifesto*

Understanding the Greenhouse Effect

A fortuitous (for life as we know it) mix of naturally present gases in the Earth's atmosphere has historically kept this upper part of our ecosystem in equilibrium and the planet habitable by trapping heat in the thin blanket of air surrounding us. The gases (with sources both natural and human-caused) absorb and re-emit radiation from the sun. This interplay of natural forces that result in warming is called the *greenhouse effect*. The substances now popularized as *greenhouse gases (GHGs)* include carbon dioxide, methane, nitrous oxide, ozone, and CFCs (chlorofluorocarbons, including aerosols). As one of the consequences of increased GHGs, water vapor increases in the atmosphere in response to rising CO_2 concentrations, and this greatly heightens the warming effect of manmade CO_2 emissions.

The greenhouse effect has been conducive to life on Earth, and for millennia the amount of the main GHG, carbon dioxide, remained fairly constant at about 280 parts per million (ppm). But since the Industrial

Revolution, beginning around 1750, the quantity of carbon dioxide and other gases being released into the air by human activity has greatly increased. These *emissions* from cars, jets, power plants, industry, etc., remain in the atmosphere for many decades, so they are sure to affect the climate far into the future. Today's level of carbon dioxide (CO_2) is 394 ppm—a 40% rise from pre-industrial times, in only a fraction of the time of humans on Earth! When the amount of GHGs exceeds the capacity of the ocean, forests, and soil to absorb it (these are our "carbon sinks"), more heat is retained in the atmosphere; then air, ocean, and land temperatures rise and *global warming* is said to occur. Climate change is a result.

The farming of animals produces GHGs that are more harmful than carbon dioxide, generating 65% of nitrous oxide (296 times as warming as carbon dioxide), as well as 37% of methane (23 times as warming as carbon dioxide); the latter is largely produced by the digestive system of the animals.

One-third of all the raw materials and fossil fuels used in the US go to raising animals for food. Worldwide petroleum reserves would be exhausted in 11 years if the rest of the world ate like the US. A nationwide switch to a vegetarian diet would allow the US to cut its oil imports by 60%.[8]

Go Climate-Neutral: How One Group Did It

The Center for Biological Diversity (CBD) chose to become climate-neutral with a program to explicitly track and then maximally reduce GHGs. They also purchased "carbon offsets" equal to the amount of all past emissions since the organization's inception in 1989. These offsets, which support forest conservation in Madagascar, produce many direct additional benefits to biodiver-

---

TERMINOLOGY FOR THE 21ST CENTURY

Global Warming: As more greenhouse gases are released into the atmosphere from the burning of fossil fuels than are trapped by ocean, forest, and soil sinks, more heat is trapped there, and the average global atmospheric temperature increases, a condition known as "global warming."

Climate Change/Global Warming: Climate change results directly or indirectly from human activity that changes the composition of the global atmosphere; this is in addition to natural climate variability. The more popular term "global warming" recognizes that global temperatures overall have been increasing since the Industrial Revolution.

Intergovernmental Panel on Climate Change (IPCC): A large, global scientific body tasked to evaluate the risk of climate change caused by human activity.

Kyoto Protocol: This international agreement is a protocol to the United Nations (UN) Framework Convention on Climate Change, an environmental treaty produced at the 1992 UN Conference on Environment and Development, informally known as the Earth Summit, held in Rio de Janeiro, Brazil. The treaty is intended to achieve "stabilization of greenhouse gas concentrations in the atmosphere at a level that would prevent dangerous anthropogenic interference with the climate system." The Kyoto Protocol establishes legally binding commitments for the reduction of six greenhouse gases produced by industrialized nations, as well as general commitments for all member countries. It was to be updated in Copenhagen in December 2009 after this book went to press.

Fossil Fuels: Also known as mineral fuels, these fuel sources are derived from fossils, or hydrocarbons found within the top layer of the Earth's crust. Examples include coal, petroleum, and methane. Fossil fuels are non-renewable resources because they take millions of years to form, and fossil fuel reserves are being depleted far faster than new ones are being formed.

Carbon Dioxide (CO_2): The main greenhouse gas is released into the atmosphere largely through the combustion of fossil fuels. Atmospheric concentrations of CO_2 are estimated to be at their highest level in at least 800,000 years.

Methane (CH_4): This chemical compound is the principal component of natural gas. Burning methane in the presence of oxygen produces CO_2 and water. The relative abundance of methane and its clean burning process makes it an attractive fuel. However, methane's high global-warming potential puts a damper on its use: over time, a methane emission has 23 times the impact of a CO_2 emission of the same mass.

sity and local communities. CBD used the Corporate Greenhouse Gas Accounting and Reporting Standard developed by the World Resources Institute and others to create an inventory of sources including all electricity and heating fuel used in offices, and all automobile and airplane travel on CBD business. They then calculated average emissions per staff member and multiplied this by the number of staff members in previous years to obtain an estimate of total emissions since 1989. This total is relatively small, about 480 tons of CO_2. After extensively researching carbon offset purchasing options, CBD chose to purchase 500 tons of CO_2 credits in the Makira Forest Conservation Project, Madagascar.

Notes Peter Galvin of CBD, "It needs to be pointed out that the entire offset concept is a controversial one. The key issue here is something called verifiable 'additionality'—or removal of GHGs in ways that would not otherwise occur."[9]

The island of Madagascar off the east coast of Africa is one of the world's biodiversity hotspots. The Makira Forest Conservation Project, a joint project of Conservation International, the Wildlife Conservation Society, and the government of Madagascar, will mitigate 9.5 million tons of CO_2 emissions over the next 30 years through forest conservation, including replanting of cleared areas.

WHAT YOU CAN DO

Increasing awareness of the greenhouse gas consequences of our energy use, travel, food, and other choices is the first step toward reducing our own emissions. The average American generates approximately 24 tons of CO^2 annually, but this number can be drastically reduced with simple changes, many of which will also save you money. There are many resources available to further reduce your emissions. See "Getting Personal" for footprint information.

Once you have reduced your emissions as much as possible, you can go even further by supporting organizations working for policy change and purchasing offsets. Lend your vocal political and financial support to organizations that are serious, committed advocates for policies involving *mandatory reductions* in GHG emissions. Investing your offset dollars to sue polluters is dollar for dollar, GHG pound for pound, quite

arguably the most effective offset strategy to achieve the urgently needed massive GHG reductions the US must make.

Every individual's footprint on the environment must be greatly reduced through conservation, improvements in technology, and potentially challenging changes in lifestyle. Start with the simple acts of energy conservation suggested in these pages. Electricity, natural gas, propane, and all forms of energy are as valuable as water and must not be wasted. There are environmental costs to their production, transport, and combustion. Be aware and conserve.

Think about your personal "carbon footprint" on the Earth: How much generated "juice" do you burn during your day? How much embodied energy goes into each product you buy? How much do you drive or fly in a given week? Try to carpool or use public transit at least part of the time!

Be active in the public dialogue, and talk about this problem to your friends. Help clear up public misperceptions that "no one really knows anything for sure; the Earth changes all the time." Educate others that cutting or reducing emissions of GHGs is a change we all must support now.

Urge local, state, and federal government bodies to make appropriate legislation a priority. Tell your representatives at both federal and local government levels the following:

- Act now to limit potential damage from climate change rather than waiting and having to take more costly, reactive measures in the future. Timely action could ease the coming impacts of hotter weather, rising sea levels, and bigger storms.
- Adopt federal policies that establish mandatory limits on GHG emissions. Adhere to international agreements such as the Kyoto Protocol.
- Harness the power of markets to drive innovation and protect the climate. Subsidize renewable energy investments.
- Don't make carbon-intensive investments in developing countries.
- Climate protection in developing countries must be supportive of economic and social development; foster technical cooperation programs.
- Financiers must devise new ways of investing in the needed global transition to a low-carbon "re-industrialization."[10]

Many important decisions are made at local, state, and regional levels on the issues that most affect you. In fact, many cities and localities have begun to take action, not waiting for the federal government to do it for them. Locals can make the best local plans of action.[11]

ARE YOU IN THE KNOW ABOUT 350?

Renowned American environmental activist and writer Bill McKibben is building a global-scale climate change movement, focused on the significance of the number 350. The 350.org campaign aims to involve everyone in realizing our collective effect on global warming.

According to McKibben, "350 is the most important number in the world"—the number determined to be the safe upper limit for carbon dioxide measured in parts per million in our atmosphere. "If we can make this number known across the planet, that mere fact will exert some real pressure on negotiators. We need people to understand that 350 marks either success or failure for climate negotiations."

With CO_2 levels already exceeding 350 parts per million, McKibben is traveling the world to awaken people to the dire threat of global warming and create a powerful and unified call to action. On October 24, 2009, people in 181 countries came together for one of the most widespread environmental action events ever.

THE OCEANS
Deep Problems on the Water Planet

"The frog does not drink up the pond in which s/he lives."

—*oral tradition, Teton Sioux*

Vast as they are, covering three-quarters of the globe, the world's oceans are not infinite. We are pushing up against limits by overfishing, as well as by polluting and dumping waste into waterways and seas, including non-biodegradable plastic. Current problems of acidification, pollution, and threats to fisheries stem from cumulative abuse. And only a serious culture-wide reduction in both pollutants generated and carbon dioxide (CO_2) emitted will stem this rising tide of death.

All life on Earth is connected to the oceans. They are our life support systems, from the food chain to the water cycle. Yet human activities are collectively driving the health of the world's oceans down a rapid spiral.[12]

Global Warming

As a major carbon sink, or absorber of CO_2 and other greenhouse gases, the ocean is ultimately limited in this capacity. Though the response takes decades, the ocean's average surface temperature and acidity are now rising, thereby contributing to weather changes, higher sea levels, current shifts, coastal erosion, and altered fish migration routes. The oceans have absorbed about half of the CO_2 we've emitted in the last 200 years as it accumulates in the atmosphere;[13] this load is currently estimated at about

22 million tons per day.[14] The CO_2 reacts in the oceans to form carbonic acid, which has greatly increased in concentration (by 30%) in the last two centuries.[15] This is how higher levels of greenhouse gases acidify the oceans' pH balance and threaten marine life, which is unable to adapt so quickly.

Ocean acidification has been called global warming's evil twin.

Ocean acidification depletes seawater of compounds that organisms need to build shells and skeletons, impairing the calcium-building capacity of coral-forming polyps, crabs, seastars, sea urchins, plankton, and other marine creatures. In what could be one of the first indicators of an industry-wide if not ocean-wide effect, the Pacific Northwest oyster industry is collapsing because

the hatcheries can't grow larvae anymore.[16] Acidic waters may prevent coral reefs from surviving in most regions by mid-century if current GHG emissions trends continue, an international panel of marine scientists said in early 2009. The ripple effect throughout marine ecosystems could be disastrous, according to the Monaco Declaration, the science panel's joint statement, which added: "The current increase in ocean acidity is a hundred times faster than any previous natural change that has occurred over the last many millions of years."[17]

In one of the many *feedback loops* we are witnessing in this time of rapid environmental change, the rising ocean temperature interferes with established ocean currents that move vital nutrients upward from deep regions. Without these nutrients in abundance, the plankton do not thrive at the foundation of the ocean food chain. Furthermore, abundant plankton actually helps store CO_2 in the ocean floor as they die and decompose.[18]

Overfishing

The booming population of humans with our growing appetite for seafood is pushing many ocean species toward extinction. Global seafood consumption (per person average) has tripled since the 1950s,[19] and fish stocks are already collapsing worldwide. Most of the ocean changes observable today—as well as immediate threats to marine species—are the result of unsustainable fishing. Scientists project that at today's rates of withdrawal, all currently fished species of wild seafood could collapse (experiencing 90% depletion) by 2050.[20] This will not only affect the entire food chain, it will decimate the livelihood and sustenance of millions of people who depend directly on the ocean's bounty, including some 100

Creative Commons/webzer

million people in Southeast Asia[21] and as many as 3 billion worldwide.[22]

Fisheries have had many catastrophic effects on the oceans—disrupting the food chain, diminishing water quality, destroying habitat, harassing and displacing wildlife, and otherwise altering the overall marine ecosystem. And wherever there's fishing, there's *bycatch*—fisheries' wasteful and unintentional capture of unwanted species. Commercial fishing creates millions of tons of discarded catch annually, including not just fish species but turtles, marine mammals, sharks, and even seabirds.

Pollution

Wastes carried in the world's rivers and streams ends up in coastal waterways and oceans, including sewage, industrial dumping, and agricultural run-off. Industrial pollutants like mercury or PCBs that end up in streams and oceans are absorbed by fish we

cat, thus adding to our toxic load.

The oceans' ability to dilute these substances is declining, but the amount of contaminants is not. In places like the Mississippi delta, the waters are **dead zones** for miles—uninhabitable for fish and shellfish. Nitrogen, phosphorus, and other nutrients from fertilizers, large livestock farms, and septic systems provoke explosive blooms of tiny plants known as phytoplankton, which die and sink to the bottom and then are eaten by bacteria that use up the oxygen in the water. This oxygen starvation makes it difficult for fish, oysters, sea grass beds, etc., to survive—hence the dead zones.[23] There are now at least 200 of these zones around the world, and they are increasing rapidly.[24] The most severe cases exceed 20,000 square kilometers.[25]

More than 1.2 trillion gallons of sewage (including human waste, excreted pharmaceuticals, detergents, and household

chemicals) and polluted storm water are discharged into American waters annually.[26] Around 60% of the wastewater discharged into the Caspian Sea is untreated, while in Latin America and the Caribbean the figure is close to 80%, and in large parts of Africa and the Indo-Pacific region it's as high as 90%.[27]

WHAT WE CAN DO

- Use a lot less fossil fuel-based energy. Use as little plastic as possible. Don't eat endangered or threatened species. Limit your consumption of seafood in general, and learn which species concentrate toxins and thus toxify you.

- International laws are drastically inadequate to address threats like large-scale commercial fishing, which sweeps life out of the seas at unprecedented rates—often only to discard the unusable "bycatch," an unacceptable waste of life.

- Urge the US Congress to increase government protection of fish stocks. Existing regulations and controls on overfishing must be enforced, primarily targeting those fisheries with the highest rate of bycatch.

- Join a beach clean-up. Since 1986, the Ocean Conservancy organizes shoreline cleanups each fall. To date, 6.2 million volunteers in International Coastal Cleanups have removed 49 million kilograms of debris from nearly 288,000 kilometers of coasts in 127 nations.[28]

CORAL REEFS
Colorful "Rainforests of the Sea"

Degraded for decades by toxic run-off, bleached coral reefs are now viewed as early indicators of global warming.

Coral reefs are among Earth's most diverse, exquisite, and fragile ecosystems, essential to the web of life. They have been vanishing at alarming rates for the last 40 years, mainly from run-off of agricultural (including lawn) chemicals and waste. Now the rapid pace of environmental change threatens to overwhelm the reef species' ability to adapt. Coral reefs appear particularly vulnerable to even the most modest climate-change scenarios, as they are unable to adjust to rapid changes in temperature and ocean acidity, and we may be approaching a tipping point that will wipe out entire bio-regions.

While these changes are likely to exceed the capacities of many species to adapt, elkhorn and staghorn corals gained US federal legal protection in 2006, becoming the first species listed under the Endangered Species Act because of vulnerability to global warming. Coral reefs throughout the Caribbean and along the coast of Florida are vanishing at unprecedented rates.[29] Protection under the ESA creates greater opportunities for coral reef conservation.

The 2008 report, released by the Global Coral Reef Monitoring Network, predicts that many of the remaining reefs may disappear within the next 40 years if current emission trends continue; 19% are already dead.[30] A third of reef-building corals are threatened.[31] The demise of coral reefs affects the entire ocean ecosystem—a quarter of all marine fish species reside in the reefs, according to The Nature Conservancy. The International Union for the Conservation of Nature (IUCN) estimates that 500 million people depend on coral reefs for their livelihoods.[32]

The coral reef assessment found that 45% of the world's reefs are healthy, providing hope that some species may be able to endure the changes expected from global warming. Marine biologists are now attempting to understand how certain coral reef species can better survive warmer, more acidic ocean waters.

In addition to climate change with its warming sea-surface temperatures and acidification, other factors affecting the health of coral reefs are overfishing (including the technique of dynamiting reefs to catch fish), pollution, and invasive species such as crown-of-thorns starfish.

WHAT WE CAN DO

- The area of coral reefs under protection needs to be increased globally from the current level of 15% to 30%. Within these protected regions there need to be clear areas where human uses are significantly limited so that already-stressed marine species can recover.[33]
- Don't touch delicate corals with swim fins. Learn to enjoy snorkeling without touching or breaking the corals, or keep a safe distance.
- Don't buy coral jewelry, and inform those selling it about the threats to coral.

If nothing is done to substantially cut CO_2 emissions, coral reefs as we know them will no longer exist.

Creative Commons/rhoth 1888

FRESH WATER
Using Water Wisely

We all know that most life on Earth is impossible without water, so why would we pollute and waste this priceless substance? Water bodies are assumed to have endless capacity to "disappear" toxins, trash, and wastes (industrial, sewage, agricultural, to name a few). But Earth's rivers, lakes, and oceans have suffered so much dumping that their ability to support life is lost, compromised, or disappearing fast. There isn't enough anymore, with our increasing population, to waste another drop. With global warming drying out much of the planet, this will only get worse.

Nearly 97% of the world's water is salty or otherwise undrinkable. Another 2% is locked in ice caps and glaciers. *Only 1% can be used for all agricultural, residential, manufacturing, community and personal needs, and much of that is polluted.*[34]

About 20% of the world's fresh water (one-fifth of the 1%) is in the Great Lakes.[35] Humans currently consume 50% of the Earth's available fresh water, leaving what's left over for all other species.[36]

"What you people call your natural resources our people call our relatives."
—*Oren Lyons, faith keeper of the Onondaga*

Climate change will exacerbate water shortages. The Intergovernmental Panel on Climate Change (IPCC) predicted that melting alpine glaciers and evaporating snow cover will accelerate during the 21st century, which it has steadily been doing. As a result, many regions will likely experience a decline in freshwater resources and hydropower potential, with redirected seasonal water flows.[37] Water security in a warming world will require major improvements in water use efficiency (especially in the agricultural and industrial sectors) and in techniques such as rainwater harvesting and groundwater management and use.

It may be that investing in renewable energy sources enables us to conserve water. According to *Harper's* magazine, half of all fresh water drawn from US sources each year is used to cool power plants.

According to the *Washington Post* in 2005, just one flush of a toilet in the West uses more water than most Africans have to perform an entire day's washing, cleaning, cooking, and drinking.[a]

Water: A Basic Right Not Yet Available to Everyone

Ensuring access to safe water for all people has long been a humanitarian goal, but this has yet to be accomplished. It's already clear that the UN's Millennium Development Goal will not be met in this area: "Halve by 2015 the proportion of people without sustainable access to safe drinking water and basic sanitation."

In addition to the existing shortages, strife, and distribution problems around clean drinking water, we are facing an enormous crisis of increasingly degraded water quality and diminishing quantity. The world's population is growing rapidly while freshwater sources are drying up or polluted—from overdrafted aquifers to shrinking glaciers to toxic urban rivers.

More than a billion people today lack access to potable water, and 2.4 billion are without sanitation services.[38] That's one out of six people worldwide. The United Nations projects there will be more than four billion people living in nations defined as water-scarce or water-stressed by 2050, up from half a billion in 1995.[39] How to ensure that all people will have access to this vital, limited resource? Conservation and wise usage is the only answer.

Transnational corporations are viewing investments in water as potentially lucrative—in fact, water is being called "the oil of the 21st century." *Yet water should not be a profitable industry.* Concerned organizations are working to protect universal access to safe and affordable drinking water by keeping it in public hands.[40] In short, the sale of public works to private companies can foster corruption and result in higher rates, inadequate customer service, and a loss of local control and accountability, as many privatization efforts have shown.

Historically, governments have been responsible for public water systems, but with the high cost of development and upkeep along with the moral imperative to extend systems to the billion people worldwide who lack access to clean drinking water and sanitation, the private sector has entered the picture. Institutions like the World Bank and Inter-American Development Bank often require privatization of utilities as a condition of making loans to governments. The idea is that the public sector is failing to deliver; and the private sector, which is presumed to be more efficient and cost-effective, can pick up the slack. However, in countries with heavy debt loads and desirable natural resources, "Privatization World Bank-style becomes a feeding frenzy for foreign multinational corporations, eager to scoop up struggling enterprises at bargain prices."[41]

The social and environmental impacts of water privatization have caused fresh waves of protest as communities all over the world have organized, and in some cases shed blood[42] to regain control of their water resources. This growing social movement stands in firm opposition to the privatization of our most essential natural resource.[43] Let's face it: Private-sector companies are organized to make profit, not to fulfill socially responsible objectives.

No Profits from Water!

WHAT YOU CAN DO

Support Public Water!
Ensure that a public resource stays in public hands

- If your utility is publicly owned, ask if privatization is being considered. Get involved. Food & Water Watch can help provide information on fighting privatization—email cleanwater@fwwatch.org.
- Advocate for democratic control and protection of public water resources in the face of international corporate strategies to privatize ownership and distribution.
- Public funding for infrastructure improvements is the answer, not privatization!
- World Health Organization's website is a great educational resource to learn more about the water crisis. You can contribute to this cause through organizations like World Water Council; Charity: Water; and End Water Poverty.
- To raise awareness, the US Fund for UNICEF has initiated the **Tap Project** (www.tapproject.org): Various restaurants pledge a certain amount of money and then offer diners the option of paying a nominal fee for their usually free tap water. Funds provide drinking water to children around the world who lack access. As the website tell us, "Just $1

TRUE THIRST

- 40% of the world's population carries their water from wells.
- 50% of India's morbidity is because of poor water quality.
- In Nigeria, impoverished households spend almost 20% of their income on water.
- By 2050, more than 523 million people in Africa will not have access to clean water, and famine will be even more rampant as the arid landscape increases.
- Forty of the 50 countries on the critical list for water scarcity are located in the Middle East, and in north and sub-Saharan Africa.
- 60% of the world's population lives in Asia, which has only 36% of the Earth's renewable fresh water.
- 90% of wastewater of developing nations is discharged untreated into local waterways.
- Between 1.8 and 3.5 million Americans get sick from tainted water annually.[b]

THE FOLLY OF BOTTLED WATER

Consumers waste billions of dollars a year on billions of gallons of bottled water. With these unnecessary purchases, we are creating trash and financing the corporate takeover of water supplies. Bottled water can cost up to a thousand times more than tap water and funnels the profits from the sale of water, a public resource, to private companies.[45]

As much as 40% of bottled water comes from a municipal tap![46]

Production, transportation, and disposal of bottled water consume large quantities of water and energy. You can actually conserve water (and spare yourself the carcinogenic leaching of plastic chemicals into the liquid) by switching from the bottle to the tap.

BOTTLED WATER CONSUMPTION IN THE UNITED STATES

- 1978: 415 million gallons.
- 2001: 5.4 billion gallons.
- That's a rise of 1,300%, equaling about 43 billion 16-oz plastic bottles.
- Bottled water is now the fastest growing product among the top 50 supermarket categories.
- *National Geographic* estimates that more than 85 million plastic water bottles are used every three minutes.

can supply a child with safe drinking water for 40 days."

- Techniques for water retention and improved technology allow simple practices such as solar water heating, rainwater harvest and storage, stormwater management (bioswales, sediment traps, rolling dips), micro-hydro electricity generation, and biofiltration ("living machines")— all of which help replenish groundwater resources, conserve water, and use it wisely. The Internet offers many options and resources.

- Rainwater harvesting can take place anywhere there is a roof by gathering rainwater in do-it-yourself systems (such as plastic barrels) or commercial systems (for irrigation and livestock). This traditional practice is just as appropriate today, if not more so![44]

- Water is a public trust. It is time for a water trust fund, a long-term solution to provide all US communities safe and affordable water for the future—not just those that can afford sharp rate increases. Support clean and safe tap water—tell Congress to make clean water a priority and to increase funding for it.

- Download and share the **Smart Water Guide** from Food and Water Watch, filled with facts and helpful tips.

- Host a movie screening of **FLOW, Blue Gold,** or **The Water Front**, powerful

Creative Commons/Matthieu: giik.net/blog

documentaries sure to get the message across.

- **Curb your own water use!** Calculate your water footprint using an online water calculator: www.h2oconserve.org (part of foodandwaterwatch.org).

FORESTS

Forests have long been valued and exploited for timber products, leading to the loss of the great majority of global primary forest ecosystems. According to one estimate, stands of century-old forest now account for only 7% of forest cover in the US.[47] But lately trees are being looked at a little differently because of their ability to suck carbon out of the atmosphere and sequester it in their biomass. Climate change might finally be the catalyst to economically value standing forests more than lumber. The global money machine is even beginning to work out a process for giving *carbon credits* to businesses that leave trees standing and storing carbon. This also spares the air the effects of burning the wood that is cut down—a massive contributor to global warming that has put Indonesia and Brazil third and fourth, respectively, on the list of top GHG contributor nations (with the US and China topping everyone).

Home to countless creatures, forests are the lungs of the Earth, arbiters of weather patterns, major storehouses of carbon, and our original cathedrals.

Scientists agree that the world's rainforests are the best natural defense against climate change because they are *carbon sinks*. For example, Indonesian old-growth rainforests store almost 750 tons of carbon dioxide—the equivalent of 620 flights between New York and London—per acre. When cleared, rainforests release that carbon into the atmosphere, furthering global warming rather than curbing it.[48]

Halting new deforestation is as powerful a way to combat warming as closing the world's coal-burning plants.[49] But until now, there has been no financial reward for keeping the trees standing. That's what may change: A growing number of experts is saying that cash payments are the only way to end tropical forest destruction and "provide a game-changing strategy in efforts to limit global warming."[50]

Carbon Offsets

This emerging (and controversial) trade seeks to enable industrialized nations and wealthy corporations to "offset" their GHG emissions by paying developing nations to protect their forests and/or replant new ones—Reducing Emissions from Deforestation and forest Degradation, aka REDD. Forests were not considered as carbon sinks in the Kyoto Protocol, but later realization that deforestation accounts for roughly 20% of global greenhouse gas emissions has led to their reevaluation. Meanwhile, the buyer of the offset can keep polluting (theoretically until he can afford to make deep changes in his business).

Not all offsets are equal. Poorly designed programs to pay for forest conservation can end up financially rewarding the very people who are destroying them! Verifying the efficacy of an offset is a key issue, and the details have yet to be determined. Already many people are lining up to get "carbon credit" for some dubious activity.

Vinit Allen

For example, California issued rules allowing offset credit for logging that can include clearcutting![51] A major criterion is that GHGs be removed from the atmosphere in ways that would not have occurred otherwise—such as replanting denuded areas.

The Plight of the Tropical Rainforests

Home to more biodiversity than any ecosystem on Earth, the magnificent rainforests are falling daily, often for rapidly proliferating palm oil and soy plantations. Largely owned by US agribusinesses, these plantations and the rapid expansion of industrial agriculture constitute one of the fastest-growing threats to the world's great tropical forests: in the Amazon and Indonesia, Malaysia, and Papua New Guinea. Spurred in part by the growing demand for biofuels, US agribusiness giants Archer Daniels Midland, Bunge, and Cargill are establishing soy and palm oil operations in some of the planet's most biodiverse and virginal forests.

WARNING: MAY CONTAIN RAINFOREST DESTRUCTION

Tropical rainforests are disappearing at a rate of 100,000 acres per day. That's an area larger than the state of West Virginia.[52]

Meat consumption is one of several factors driving soybean demand and production. Brazilian beef is surging in global popularity, and soybean prices are on the rise due to global meat consumption and biofuels production. However, biofuels made from recycled waste products differ greatly from "first-generation" agrifuels—agribusinesses' industrial alternative. Agrofuels are not low-carbon. Because of their impacts on climate change, direct and indirect land use impacts, fossil fuel inputs, and the investments they may draw away from real solutions, agrofuels will not solve the twin crises of climate change and our dependence on oil.[53]

Every blade of grass has its angel that bends over and whispers, "Grow! Grow!"
—The Talmud

The Palm Oil Takeover

Palm oil, found in food products, soaps, and cosmetics, could well be the most widely traded vegetable oil in the world today, seemingly a part of everything tasty. It is the controversial link that connects your cookies, climate change, and disappearing rainforests. Demand for palm oil has more than doubled in the last decade as worldwide food consumption soars. And now that palm oil is being used for biofuel, the problems are magnified.[54] Farmers are expanding existing palm oil plantations and burning primary forests to plant more. Nearly all palm oil imported to the US originates in Indonesia.

Rainforests shouldn't be open for agribusiness.

"Biofuels began with a great dream: making fuel from oil or plant waste. But when agribusinesses got involved, the dream went bad."
—Rainforest Action Network

WHAT WE CAN DO

- Don't destroy pristine ecosystems to make way for plantation farming.
- Consumer power can be directed to seek out responsible sources of palm oil and to avoid products derived from recently cleared land and other unsustainable agribusiness practices. Companies providing palm oil need to improve techniques and sourcing to be part of the solution.
- Instead of cutting and burning forests to make way for palm plantations, farmers should be encouraged to grow the crop on already cleared land. "Global production could be doubled by planting palm trees on degraded areas of Borneo. The advantage is that not a tree would have to be cut."[55]
- Go vegetarian, or at the very least, source your meat responsibly. Beef production is ruining the planet.
- Rather than continuing to pursue agrofuels policies and increasing the global marketplace for agrofuels, decision-makers in the corporate and political arenas should prioritize proven, true solutions that halt the expansion of carbon-intensive industries. Policies and investments that support mass transit, bike transit, and plug-in vehicles recharged by a green grid

are far more efficient and cost-effective means to reduce our dependence on oil. Agrofuels are not low carbon, and we can't afford to lose any more time pursuing false solutions. It's time for a real transportation revolution.[56]

■ Wood and paper buyers should endeavor to understand the origin of the products they buy.[57] Look for the Forest Stewardship Council (FSC) logo as a tool to promote environmentally, socially, and economically responsible management of the world's forests. Beware of imitations such as the Sustainable Forestry Initiative (SFI), designed to evade higher standards and mislead consumers. Learn more about certification standards at these links: **www.credibleforestcertification.org** and **www.buygoodwood.com**. The trees thank you!

BIODIVERSITY
Every Species Matters

"This we know. All things are connected like the blood that unites one family. Whatever befalls the Earth befalls the sons and daughters of the Earth. Man did not weave the web of life; he is merely a strand in it. Whatever he does to the web, he does to himself."
— attributed to Chief Seattle

This is the sixth great extinction documented on Earth, and the largest since the dinosaur exodus 65 million years ago. A 2008 study in the *Proceedings of the National Academies of Science* said the current extinction period, known as the Holocene extinction event, may be the greatest event in the Earth's history and the first due to human actions.

Our impacts are undeniable in regard to the current extinction crisis, including our relentless pressure to accommodate the exploding human population, obtain essential forest and ocean resources, and convert native ecosystems to arable land (in large part to raise soybeans to feed cattle to make burgers). Land use changes such as deforestation and conversion to cropland contribute to global warming emissions as well as species loss.

Extinction is accelerating all around

us, in myriad large and small ways. Although extinction is a natural phenomenon, its "background" rate is about one to five species per year. Scientists estimate that presently dozens are going extinct every day.[58] According to biologist E.O. Wilson, we are experiencing this catastrophic extinction "at 100 times the normal rate of extinctions, and this rate is expected to rise to 1,000 or higher. In each of the prior extinction spasms, it took about 10 million years for evolution to regain the amount of biodiversity lost."[59] If present trends of human consumption continue, half of all species of life on Earth could be extinct in less than a century "as a result of habitat destruction, pollution, invasive species, and climate change."[60]

Species loss weakens the web of biodiversity. Given our interrelatedness here on spaceship Earth, the extinction numbers are likely to snowball in coming decades if ecosystems continue to unravel. We don't know what the major tipping points will be.

Every 10 or 20 minutes—the time it may take you to read a few pages—the last individual of a unique species has taken its last breath and has gone extinct forever.[61]

Major Causes of Extinction

Habitat Loss
Habitat alteration and loss is the main force driving species extinction. As human populations increase exponentially, more land is deforested or otherwise altered for housing,

---

CRIES OF THE WILD

- 50% of all primates and 100% of great apes are threatened with extinction.

- Three of the world's eight tiger subspecies became extinct in the past 60 years; the remaining five are endangered.

- Humans have already driven 20% of all birds to extinction.

- 12% of mammals, 12% of remaining birds, 31% of reptiles, 30% of amphibians, and 37% of fish are threatened with extinction.[c]

---

farming, livestock, fuel, roads, and other uses. Species previously living on that land either move and adapt or die. Worldwide' deforestation is occurring at record rates.[62] Efforts to reestablish habitat seldom work and are less stable than the natural systems that evolve over time.

The extinction of species has reached crisis proportions with the collapse of the diversity of life that sustains both ecosystems and human cultures *Extinction is forever.*

Invasive Species
The second leading cause of extinction is the presence of invasive species, brought to a new habitat by humans. Not all transplanted species adapt well, but some can take over habitat of indigenous species, often driving them to extinction. Humans can be viewed as the number-one invasive species, since we use 40% of net primary productivity—all organic matter produced by photosynthesis on Earth—leaving what's left over for other species.[63]

Pesticides and Toxic Pollution
After World War II, the use of new synthetic chemicals as pesticides and herbicides became widespread and began to bioaccumulate in plants and animals, including humans. Rachel Carson's ground-breaking book *Silent Spring* (1962) brought our attention to negative effects on wildlife.[64] Additional sources of potentially lethal pollution include lawn chemicals, human medications, and other synthetic chemicals flushed into surface water. Mercury from coal-fired power plants is found in fish throughout the US.[65]

Global Warming
The warming climate is undermining biodiversity by accelerating habitat loss, altering the timing of animal migrations and plant flowerings, and forcing some species toward the poles and to higher altitudes. Major alterations to the complex and delicately balanced food chain will have significant and often unpredictable impacts, including the domino effect. Scientists warn that just ten more years of our current GHG pollution trajectory may commit the planet to devastating warming trends,

Vicki Walker

sea-level rise, and species extinction. Many species such as polar bears and penguins are already suffering and severely threatened by the effects of climate change.[66]

Overexploitation and Poaching

Overhunting by humans has caused many species to go extinct. "Sport" hunting of tigers and other large mammals has contributed to the demise of many of the planet's most majestic creatures. Poaching, such as the elephant deaths that the illegal ivory trade propagates, undermines global conservation efforts and must be opposed with all legal means.

Solutions

Many concerned nonprofit organizations assist countries with purchasing and managing refuges for endangered wildlife while simultaneously educating people about the importance of biodiversity, rainforests, and sustainability. See the *Resources* section for a complete list, and give these groups your support!

In recent years innovative debt-for-nature swaps give poorer nations a chance to wipe out some of their international financial burden by protecting vital habitat from degradation or loss. Even more recently, intact forest ecosystems are being accorded a different value on the world market—that of *carbon credits*—in recognition of their important natural functions, which include carbon storage and climate moderation. This trade-off has yet to be refined to avoid corruption, but it holds some potential for

protecting valuable wildlife habitat.

Tourism is a vital component of many national economies, bringing in foreign exchange and ideally creating minimal negative impacts on a protected area. If enough travelers pay to visit botanically interesting and/or wildlife-rich areas, this is a strong incentive for local communities to value and protect habitat. Obviously, the local people must be direct economic beneficiaries of tourism to be inspired to maintain natural qualities for long-term motives rather than short-term gain.

Ecuador has recently taken a mighty step by passing an amendment to its constitution stating that nature has the right to exist, persist, maintain, and regenerate its vital cycles, structure, functions, and its processes in evolution.[67]

Finally, only a concerted international effort to slow greenhouse gas emissions and maintain as much biodiversity as possible will give any of Earth's wild species a hope of surviving the coming decades, much less centuries.

WHAT YOU CAN DO

- Never buy products made of endangered species' parts, e.g., ivory, turtle shells, coral, etc.
- Travel with responsible eco-tour groups, and carbon-offset your travel.
- Grow a wildlife garden, not a lawn.
- Eat less meat and fish, and if you wish, go vegetarian or vegan.
- Support animal rehabilitation centers.

- Support conservation groups locally and worldwide.
- Educate your friends and family about these issues.
- Don't buy wood unless it is certified "green." Purchasing power can stop the destructive logging of endangered forests around the world.[68] Read and follow the guidelines in *Green America's Guide to Woodwise Purchasing*. Urge government representatives to enter into and support treaties to protect wildlife and preserve ecological "hot spots." Encourage creation of jobs that will help achieve these goals.
- Demand elimination of subsidies that promote destruction of habitats (forests, wetlands, oceans, etc.).
- Eat lower on the food chain: a plant-based diet respects the lives of animals as well as the sustainability of the planet.
- Work for a strong climate bill. Become an advocate for legislation to cap and rapidly reduce GHG emissions. Encourage the enforcement of existing laws like the Clean Air Act that already address GHG pollution.
- Write to companies that have an obvious negative impact on species, e.g., those that promote operations that cut down rainforests or pollute.
- Continue to educate yourself. Documentary videos, in particular, are a powerful experiential way to stay informed.
- See The Center for Biological Diversity's "toolboxes" for more ideas for action, including advice on writing letters and speaking out: www.biologicaldiversity.org.

"Pollution not only is destroying the global commons worldwide but also is 'trespassing' onto the local commons and private property. I say trespassing advisedly because loud noises, the unwanted glare of lights at night...the stench from a nearby factory, and industrial chemicals fouling water in a private well are all examples of pollution caused by someone else, somewhere else—pollution that crossed the boundary into such commons as the seven seas, national parks, city parks, as well as private property, all without the owner's permission."

—*Chris Maser,*
author, **Earth in Our Care**

WASTE, POLLUTION, AND TOXICS
Fouling Our Own Nest

As a species we've created a lot of pollution on Earth, far more than anyone wants to really know. That fact is not news if you have read about or even experienced poisoned produce, toxic tuna, birth defects, or asthma induced from particulates in the dirty air. Yet the work of reducing waste and pollution at its source remains to be tackled with resolve. Excess consumption, wasteful practices, and the ongoing manufacture of deadly toxins are at the core of many of our environmental problems. They need to be comprehensively addressed at the industrial level as well as the personal. Fouling one's own nest is a sign of a sick animal.

While we can lobby our political representatives to enact or enforce laws reining in industrial-scale pollution, most people feel powerless to alleviate these serious problems. Yet there are multiple personal actions that we can each take to reduce not only climate pollution (those darn greenhouse gases) but plastic and paper trash, cumulative effects from "mildly toxic" home and yard products, and many other pernicious forms of pollution. More importantly, you might finally be inspired to tackle the consumption disease—*affluenza*—at its core and create a simpler life, thereby inspiring others around you to do the same. Just stop buying and using most of this stuff! That alone will help curtail its production. See "Getting Personal" for details on how to clean up your own act.

The Plastic Vortices

With all the plastic we produce, use, and toss, it was inevitable that the oceans would eventually teem with windblown and drifting debris. Durable and lightweight, buoyant and persistent, plastic travels over vast distances. The majority of marine debris is plastic. A plastic "vortex" north of Hawaii has been the subject of recent study and news reports, but as it turns out, this North Pacific Gyre is not the only one in our oceans. And while the main known part of this particular gyre is stated to be twice the size of Texas, this particular vast eddy of plastic refuse is now known to be a sub-gyre of a much larger area (approx. 10 million sq. miles!) stretching from the equator to about 54 degrees N latitude.[69]

Plastic debris doesn't just look bad—it behaves abominably.

A plastic vortex, or *gyre*, gets its name from the dynamics of its formation: ocean currents and winds create pools or eddies where things can gather. And gather they have—about threefold since the 1960s. The North Pacific Gyre (also known as the Great Pacific Garbage Patch) contains at least 4 million tons of plastic litter, including bits of packaging, plastic bags, cigarette lighters, and diapers. Broken, degraded plastic pieces outweigh surface zooplankton here by a factor of 6 to 1. That means six pounds of plastic for every single pound of zooplankton.[70] The UN Environment Programme estimates that 46,000 pieces of plastic litter are floating on every square mile of the oceans.[71] The gyre continues to increase due to poor waste management practices on land and sea. Estimates for the total quantity of plastic at sea exceed 100 million tons, with only 20% from ocean sources (like lost or tossed fishing gear) and 80% from land-based sources. Much of the plastic is single-use disposable consumer items like bottle caps, wrappers, and plastic bags.

The tragedy of plastic is that it doesn't biodegrade—no naturally occurring organisms can break it down. But it does photodegrade (breaks down from the effects of sunlight) into ever tinier bits, each of which remains a plastic polymer for centuries that can resemble seaweed or plankton. Most

plastic floats near the sea surface where it is mistaken for food by birds, fish, and other marine life. Marine conservation groups estimate that more than a million seabirds and 100,000 mammals and sea turtles die globally each year by getting tangled in or ingesting plastics.[72]

Although plastic products are of great convenience, plastic dust never fully degrades, even the process of photodegradation can take a long time: Estimates include 500 years for a disposable diaper and 450 for a plastic bottle. The more we produce, the more we have to live with forever! Just say no to plastics!

Project Kaisei, which is surveying the area and gathering data, is attempting to find ways to clean up and recycle plastic into useful commodities, such as clothing, construction materials, and diesel fuel.[73]

"Instead of having sand made out of coral and lava rocks and other rocks and shells, now we are having beaches made out of broken-down plastics."
—*Captain Charles Moore, scientific researcher*

Creative Commons/kqedquest

Mushrooms as Planetary Healer

"War against nature is war against our own biology...It's time for environmentalists to come to the forefront of business."
  — *Paul Stamets, mycologist*

Nature's solutions to pollution, evolution, and other daunting processes surpass our conception of what's possible. This is primarily why preserving biodiversity (especially in highly diverse areas such as complex old-growth forest ecosystems) is a matter of human survival and future security. There is too much to lose that we don't even understand yet.

Creative Commons/photogirl7

Mycologist and author Paul Stamets is an advocate of **bioremediation,** or cleaning up contaminated areas with natural processes such as mycelium breakdown of stubborn toxins. To be exposed to his research and insights is to have hope again that our mess may yet get cleaned up properly. Stamets is utilizing mushroom mycelia to break down hydrocarbon-based contaminants such as gasoline, diesel, and PAHs (polycyclic aromatic hydrocarbons); to clean up dioxin at lumber mill sites; to degrade and disappear PCBs, PCPs, pesticides, herbicides, and other toxins; to work as an antimicrobial and anti-viral agent; and even to be active against insects such as the carpenter ants destroying his Washington-state home. Different fungi strains overcome different contaminants or pests, and Stamets has received many patents, including a ground-breaking one for a strain that can work against more than 200,000 different insects and which has the potential to revolutionize the entire pesticide industry.

Mycelium (*plural* mycelia) is the vegetative part of a fungus, vital in terrestrial and aquatic ecosystems for its role in the decomposition of plant material. It contributes to the organic fraction of soil and can also confer resistance to some plant pathogens. The sciences of mycofiltration, mycoremediation, mycoforestry, etc., are part of an emerging field of study with great potential for repairing many forms of environmental damage.[74]

Various forms of *living machines* can create soils, purify water, and break down contaminants utilizing carefully selected grasses, plants, bacteria, etc.[75]

POLLUTION—WHAT WE CAN DO

- Raise the price of what harms the environment. This will help reduce consumption of unnecessary items as well as trigger efficiency improvements in businesses.
- Agencies at all levels of government need to mandate and enforce emissions reduction targets and pollution limits for cars and trucks, industry and agriculture. Penalties must be stiff.
- Eliminate subsidies that go to polluting businesses.
- Institute an environmental tariff: an import or export tax placed on products imported from or being sent to countries with substandard pollution controls. This helps avoid "environmental races to the bottom" and eco-dumping.
- Ideally governments would reward or subsidize low consumption through tax deductions and credits.
- Legislatively require recycled content in containers. Post-consumer material reduces the amount of virgin material consumed.
- Let's move on to a new paradigm that "liberates us from this rat race of cheap replacements for cheap products that pollute and don't work for very long."[76]
- Unfortunately, much "recycling" of electronic waste (old equipment) translates into dumping overseas. It is currently unlikely that you will be able to responsibly recycle your e-waste without paying for the service. For information on recycling electronic waste, go the US Environmental Protection Agency's website at www.epa.gov/osw/conserve/materials/ecycling/index.htm or www.ban.org.
- Products must be easy to recycle, the least toxic, and the most cradle-to-cradle in terms of raw materials. Our calculus must take into account the lifecycle of the product and its true value; we must reject cheap products that don't last.
- Get plastic manufacturers directly involved with plastic disposal and closing the material loop. Container and resin makers can help develop the reprocessing infrastructure by taking back plastic from consumers.
- Standardize labeling and inform consumers: The "chasing arrows" symbol is ambiguous and misleading. We need significantly different labels for "recycled," "recyclable," and "made of plastic type X."
- Reduce, Reduce, Reduce—then offset and reduce some more!
- We need to take the slogan "Yes, we can" seriously and develop alternative strategies—the tepid solutions often proposed are not going to work in the long term.

Jim Embry

Part Three ENERGY

SMART POWER: Toward a More Energy-Efficient and Eco-Friendly Future

Welcome to the dream of renewable energy— a future where our energy consumption doesn't harm the environment.

The fossil-fuel era is coming to an end. Cheap energy has fueled the economic system at the cost of our environment, and reversing course requires changing almost everything. We citizens will have to brace for this change—from the convenience of cars to the level of our utility rates. Some might call it "sacrifice," but we can achieve similar standards along with a healthy environment if we shift our practices away from fossil-fuel dependency. Almost every modern human activity is dependent on oil, and this cannot go on.

The good news is that an array of options exists. We know how to make energy efficiency and renewable power a reality. The bad news is that it is taking us far too long to identify, agree upon, and implement the best alternatives, and to turn our practices around. We are far behind in these efforts. What should have been stepped up with the environmental momentum of the 1960s and '70s ended when Ronald Reagan took office after Jimmy Carter and removed the solar panels from the White House roof.

"Peak Oil" is a term given to the impending scenario in which the supply of oil declines rapidly as demand increases, both in the US and from rising consumption giants such as China, India, and Brazil. (The US currently consumes about 25% of the Earth's oil supply.[1]) The phrase can include all fossil fuels—for example, coal and natural gas, all hydrocarbon-based—which when burned produce carbon dioxide, the principal greenhouse gas and "climate pollutant."

In 2007, Portland, Oregon, became the first city to develop an official strategy for the impending decline of the oil age. Regardless of when the peak in oil production actually occurs, their report notes, the changes required will be so immense that immediate action is necessary to prepare for it.[2]

istock Photo/Plainview

Rather than waiting for government action, many communities are considering proactive strategies based on *relocalization*—meeting more community needs from local sources, and fewer from distant ones. Such arrangements reduce both vulnerability to unstable oil prices and the CO_2 pollution of long-haul transport. Relocalization increases community independence, enhances energy and food security, strengthens local economies, and dramatically improves environmental conditions. Communities can and should set energy usage and water consumption goals. To learn more about this process, check out Transition Towns on the Internet.[3]

HARNESSING RENEWABLE ENERGY

According to Worldwatch Institute and other research centers, solar and wind energy sources are already sufficient to provide for all of the world's energy use today, using available technology (if we had the money to implement systems everywhere). A resource qualifies as "renewable" if it is replenished by natural processes at a rate comparable to or faster than its rate of consumption. Solar radiation, tides, and winds are perpetual resources that are in no danger of running out—for the lifetime of the sun.

Such estimates indicate that renewable energy is more abundant (about 6,000 times greater on an annual basis) than all fossil fuel supplies, and that well before mid-century it will be possible to run most national electricity systems with minimal fossil fuels and only 10% of the carbon emissions they produce today.[4] Solar, wind, and geothermal power, hybrid and electric cars, and aggressive energy efficiency are climate-repairing solutions that are safer, cheaper, faster, more secure, and less wasteful than nuclear power and our ongoing oil addiction. Growing our capacity to make use of renewable energy can alleviate strife, competition, and war over limited fossil fuels; diversify each nation's energy supply and enhance national security; help preserve water and air quality; and create green jobs and a new economy on both supply and demand sides, benefiting millions of energy consumers.

More than $100 billion annually is now being invested in new renewable energy systems, manufacturing plants, and research and development.[5] Yet the output of sustainably produced energy remains a small fraction of global energy production as a whole—supplying only 2 to 3% despite being among the lowest-cost options for reducing CO_2 emissions and fossil-fuel dependency.[6] Increased investment in renewable energy has been spurred by climate change concerns, greater government support, and high oil prices. However, the level of investment needs to grow much more rapidly to meet even the most minimal targets for climate protection.

The Smart Grid

One of the obstacles to utilizing renewable energy on a large scale is the construction and maintenance of new transmission lines for the power produced at remote sites such as the desert Southwest for solar and the Dakotas for wind power. Not only is this a massive financial investment; the power lines often pass indiscriminately through sensitive ecosystems and valuable wilderness habitat. Given appropriate siting of power plants and transmission lines (if possible), and ideally, burial of lines underground, what might a *Smart Grid* or advanced energy-transmission system of the future do?

It will be extremely efficient, non-polluting, and decentralized or "distributed." In the US this unified Smart Grid or "Transmission Superhighway" would serve as a modern upgrade to a national electric power grid that was designed in the 1930s. According to many estimates, the Smart Grid could be built for about $400 billion. Through its increased efficiencies, savings, and reliability improvements, this vital upgrade will be paid in full in fewer than four years.[7]

Policymakers have long known about transmission problems and limitations of the existing grid, but the Feds yield to state governments, which exercise authority over the grid. In Texas, T. Boone Pickens, the oilman building the world's largest wind farm, plans to use a right of way he is developing for water pipelines for a 250-mile power transmission line from the Panhandle to the Dallas market. "If you want to do it on a national scale, where the transmission line distances will be much longer, and utility regulations are different, Congress must act," he said in testimony on Capitol Hill.[8]

States (including California) with aggressive goals for renewable energy are being forced to deal with the grid's inadequacies by adding power lines, but these piecemeal efforts are insufficient to tap the nation's potential for renewable energy.

Solar Power

The energy generated from the sun is thousands of times greater than our energy needs, and its potential for power generation eclipses that of all other renewable energy sources. This, the cleanest and most abundant renewable energy source available, can be actively captured to generate electricity, or passively harnessed to heat water and buildings. Yet at present solar power accounts for only a fraction of a percent of total electrical output—much less than hydropower or wind energy, which are cheaper to produce.[9]

Why? For starters, sunshine is inconsistent and certainly not abundant at every locale on Earth. For small-scale applications such as hot water and household electricity, solar panels work great (and take up no extra space on roofs), but they are expensive. For larger applications, in addition to limitations of the transmission grid, mass collection technology is still being optimized, and (of course) lots of money is needed. Building the infrastructure to switch to solar would cost much more at current prices than continuing to burn fossil fuels. Costs are falling steadily, however, and the abundant sunshine in the tropical and subtropical regions means investment in solar could pay off more quickly there. In a few sunny places where electricity rates are high, such as Italy and Hawaii, sun-generated electricity is closer to competitive.

China is planning a huge new solar project, with US developer First Solar providing the panels. The 2,000-megawatt photovoltaic farm is to be built in the Mongolian desert.[10]

In 2007 the first solar-powered boat crossed the Atlantic in a five-month trip to demonstrate the feasibility of clean energy vessels on the open seas.[11]

Common devices to harness the sun's energy include:

- Solar or photovoltaic (PV) cells made primarily of silicon, the same material used in computer semiconductor chips.
- Concentration systems that use mirrors to focus the sun's energy onto a PV cell or heat-transferring fluid to generate steam which spins a turbine and generates electricity. These can be large enough to replace a coal-fired power plant.
- Windows, sunrooms, and skylights that allow the sun to passively heat and light buildings.[12]

Wind Power

Wind power is the most widely developed aspect of renewable energy, created through the conversion of mechanical wind energy into useful form (such as electricity) using wind turbines. Wind energy has long been used to grind grain or pump water via traditional windmills. While the down side of wind power includes the need to transmit it long distances on an outdated system, and the death of tens of thousands of raptors and other birds who fly into transmission lines and support wires, the potential of this clean energy source is great indeed. Wind energy can compete with coal-powered energy in terms of cost, at around 4 cents per kilowatt-hour. The federal government's National Renewable Energy Laboratory projects that the price of wind energy will fall even further over the next decade, making it the most economically competitive renewable energy technology of them all.[13]

Many modern wind farms are already operational in the US Midwest. In 2008 the US surpassed Germany—the world's leader in renewable energy R&D—to top the list in installed wind capacity. The Department of Energy has stated that the nation can get 20% of its power from wind energy alone by 2030. According to the DOE and the

---

Using solar technology alone, one-fifth of US electricity needs could be produced on a 1,500-square-kilometer plot of land slightly larger than the city of Phoenix, Arizona. An area covering less than 4% of the Sahara Desert could produce enough solar power to equal global electricity demand.[b]

If photovoltaic panels covered just three-tenths of a percent of the US, a 100-by-100 mile square, they could power the entire country.[c]

Creative Commons/Green For All

Solar panel installation, part of Green For All's Green Jobs Now Program.

National Renewable Energy Lab, there will be more than $500 billion of new wind turbine generators added to the US wind turbine fleet between now and 2020.[14] *Job Alert!* There is a huge demand for certified windsmiths, the technicians that keep the wind turbine generators maintained and operating at peak efficiency.

Denmark gets the greatest percentage of its national energy from wind (approx. 19%), and three north German states in 2007 got upwards of 30% of their electricity from wind power—39% in Schleswig-Holstein, whose goal is 100% by 2020.[15] California has the most wind power development in the US, followed by Texas, with the capacity to power approximately 750,000 homes annually.[16]

Geothermal Energy

Talk about a power source! Geothermal potential defies imagination. There is 50,000 times more heat energy contained in the first six miles of the Earth's crust than in all the planet's oil and natural gas resources, according to the USGS.[17]

The most common form of geothermal power plant, a flash steam plant, uses water at temperatures greater than 360°F (182°C) that is pumped under high pressure to electricity generation equipment (turbine generators) at the surface. Geothermal resources are considered "base load," meaning they are available 24 hours a day, 365 days a year.[18]

Other benefits of geothermal include reliability and a cost of about 4 to 7 cents a kilowatt-hour that is competitive with wind power and significantly cheaper than solar. Geothermal facilities occupy a fraction of the space required by wind and solar farms. Although the supply of geothermal energy is virtually unlimited, there are large upfront costs to extract it. According to the USGS, "The amount of heat that flows annually from the Earth into the atmosphere is enormous—equivalent to ten times the annual energy consumption of the United States and more than that needed to power all nations of the world, if it could be fully harnessed."[19]

"This is deeper than a solar panel. I want you to have a clean energy revolution. That's beautiful. But I'm gonna tell you the truth about it. If you stop there, if all you do is have a clean energy revolution, you won't have done anything. I'm gonna tell you why.

"If all we do is take out the dirty power system, the dirty power generation in a system, and just replace it with some clean stuff, put a solar panel on top of this system, but we don't deal with how we're consuming water, we don't deal with how we're treating our other sister-and-brother species, we don't deal with toxins, we don't deal with the way we treat each other…If that's not a part of this movement, let me tell you what you'll have; you'll have solar-powered bulldozers, solar-powered buzz-saws, and bio-fueled bombers, and we'll be fighting wars over lithium for the batteries instead of oil for the engines, and we'll still have a dead planet.

"This movement is deeper than a solar panel. Don't stop there! We're gonna change the whole thing. We're not gonna put a new battery in a broken system. We want a new system! We're gonna change the whole thing."

—Van Jones, author,
The Green Collar Economy,
speaking at the PowerShift '09 conference for youth

THE MICROPOWER REVOLUTION

While nuclear power struggles to attract private capital, investors have switched to cheaper, faster, less risky alternatives that *The Economist* calls *"micropower"*—distributed turbines and generators in factories or buildings (usually cogenerating useful heat), and all renewable sources of electricity except big hydro dams (over ten megawatts).

An even cheaper competitor is end-use efficiency *("negawatts")*—saving electricity by using it more efficiently or at smarter times. Despite relatively small subsidies and many barriers to fair market entry and competition, negawatts and micropower have lately turned in a stunning global market performance, with electrical savings already adding up to huge totals. Indeed, over decades, negawatts and micropower can shoulder the entire burden of powering the economy.

This section condensed from information available from the **Rocky Mountain Institute.**

RENEWABLE ENERGY DIY (Do It Yourself)[d]

Turn the sun, wind, or rain into on-demand power at your home!

Assessing the potential:

- If you have a spot on your roof or within a few hundred feet of your house that sees sun from 9 a.m. to 3 p.m. most months of the year, you have excellent solar potential.

- If your site has an annual average wind speed of 12 mph, you are in a good area for a wind turbine.

- If you can divert 40 gallons of water per minute (7.5 seconds to fill a 5-gallon bucket) into a pipe and run it downhill/downstream 100 feet, you can potentially have 400 watts of hydropower, 24 hours a day.

Available technologies to use and store renewable resources:

- ***Photovoltaic modules (PV)*** use semiconductor technology to convert sunlight into electricity, which can be used in an off-grid system to charge batteries, or in a grid-connected system to directly feed the grid, offsetting part or all of the energy consumed on site.

- ***Solar water heating systems*** are a logical way to meet part of your energy demand. Contemporary systems are well-designed, reliable, and efficient.

- ***Wind turbines*** can charge batteries or directly feed the grid (like PV). They are usually designed to make the best use of the available resource, considering variables such as wind speed and turbulence.

- On or off the grid, appropriately sized small ***hydroelectric generators*** (aka "micro-hydro" systems) can operate seasonally or year round. They can work 24 hours a day (unlike solar and wind) and are capable of generating high-voltage power, which can be sent thousands of feet, enabling you to access a more distant water resource.

- Inverters change the direct current (DC) power from a battery bank or directly from the renewable source to alternating current (AC), a more common and usable form of electricity.

- ***Batteries*** are essential to an off-grid system, for storing energy when it's available and accessing it later. However, their production and disposal remain weak links in the alternative energy reality.

Remember, if you are investing now in alternative energy, you can receive a federal tax credit of 30% of the price of the installed system. California residents can receive a rebate for the installation of grid-connected PV and wind systems.

Biofuels, Biomass, and Biomethane

All these green options can get a little confusing, so here is the lowdown on these up and coming energy sources that can often utilize waste products.

Biofuels are developed from crops such as corn (ethanol), soy, and palm oil. For all the hype about biofuel, its net benefit to the global warming crisis remains uncertain. When the expansion of biofuel crops forces food production to move elsewhere or releases carbon from the soil or vegetation through clearing and deforestation, it makes the world's climate problem worse because forests, peatlands, and grasslands are nature's premier method of carbon capture. In this case, biofuels can actually produce more CO_2 than they save, negating any biofuel-related benefit for decades.[20]

Prioritizing fuel crops can also exacerbate hunger issues. For example, in the US nearly one-third of all corn planted will be used to create biofuels rather than food.[21] New biofuel studies tell us in yet another way that the current world agricultural system, like the world energy system, is unsustainable. And unless it's fixed, increasing production of both fuels and food will contribute to global warming.

As biofuel technology develops, we have come to learn that corn-based ethanol and soy-based biodiesel, our "first-generation" fuels, have considerably lower greenhouse gas (GHG) reduction potential than "second-generation" fuels such as cellulosic ethanol, or even "third-generation" algae-based fuels. While biofuels can reduce GHG emissions, we must consider the full range of impacts that their production entails, including land use changes and effects on food production and prices. Truly sustainable biofuels have a role in a clean energy future as long as costs do not outweigh their benefits.

Biomass: The energy contained in plants (which absorb and store energy from the sun as they grow) can be harnessed to produce heat and electricity. Biomass energy provides vegetation-powered heat, electricity, and transportation fuel. Biomass also can be turned into transportation fuels such as ethanol.

The largest source of energy from wood is "black liquor," a waste product from the pulp, paper, and paperboard industry.

Biofuel station in Eugene, Oregon.

The second-largest source of biomass energy is waste energy, mainly created from municipal solid waste, sewage sludge, manufacturing waste, crop residues, manure, and landfill gas. Conversion of biomass wastes such as these into energy has great potential to help resolve energy and environmental problems.

Biomethane: Arguably the best and greenest of all biofuels, "super low carbon" biomethane is renewable natural gas made from organic sources that would have been released into the atmosphere if simply burned or otherwise disposed. Biomethane sources include wastewater treatment systems, landfill gas, anaerobic digesters, animal and crop waste, and most waste from agricultural and forestry operations. Besides supplementing existing natural gas supplies, biomethane provides huge GHG emissions reductions.

As the chemical compound CH_4, biomethane is no different from the fossil-fuel variety of natural gas, except that it is not a limited fossil fuel. It starts out as biogas and is "cleaned up" (impurities are removed such as carbon dioxide, siloxanes, and hydrogen sulfides) for use in compressed natural gas vehicles or any other use of natural gas.

Biomethane can displace and substitute the equivalent of 29% of all petroleum diesel transportation fuel used—almost immediately. That's about 10 billion gallons of gasoline per year! And it's ten times the amount per year projected for natural gas in the annual DOE outlook.[22]

BIOFUELS: WHAT WE CAN DO

- Policy must ensure that biofuels are not produced on productive forest, grassland, or cropland.
- Reduce subsidies to food-based biofuels (mainly corn) and increase them for fuels with a low-carbon footprint, such as waste and cellulose-derived biofuels. Biofuels made from waste biomass or from biomass grown on abandoned agricultural lands planted with perennials incur little or no carbon debt and offer immediate and sustained GHG advantages.
- Incentivize the production of biomethane from sources such as animal manure, landfills, and biomass.
- Accelerate development of cellulosic biofuel technologies and the infrastructure to harvest, transport, and process new crops.
- Provide incentives for low or no-till agriculture, the planting of cover crops, and the creation of riparian buffer zones.

- Support farmers who want to invest in sustainable fuel crops such as perennial grasses or fast-growing trees.
- Increase investment in solar, wind, and other forms of renewable energy that provide greater climate benefits than do today's biofuels.

See:

- Worldwatch Institute produced a pioneering 2007 book, *Biofuels for Transport.*
- Worldwatch Institute worked with the Sierra Club on the report, *Destination Iowa: Getting to a Sustainable Biofuels Future*, that offers recommendations, including these suggestions above.

Hydrogen

Hydrogen fuel is a promising alternative for transportation since the byproducts of its combustion are simply oxygen and water. Significant hurdles continue to stand in the way of commercializing clean and sustainable means of producing hydrogen, as well as developing the vehicle technologies required to efficiently store and use hydrogen. An extensive infrastructure investment is necessary to support its widespread use in motor vehicles.

Assessments by the Natural Resources Defense Council show that the least expensive and most developed methods of hydrogen production in use today are not necessarily environmentally sustainable. For example, one of the cheaper options currently available, producing hydrogen from coal without carbon capture and storage, will further aggravate the problem of global warming. "The most sustainable ways to produce hydrogen in the future are from wind, solar, and biomass resources, and, under certain circumstances, from fossil-fuel sources with carbon capture and storage. As a result, it will take at least two decades before hydrogen can even begin to make a significant contribution to reducing global warming pollution, improving air quality, and reducing US oil dependence."[23]

Nonetheless, initiatives to install hydrogen fueling stations are spreading in the US and beyond. Iceland installed the first one in 2003 as part of its plan to become the world's first "hydrogen society." For a list of worldwide hydrogen fueling stations (with a photo of each—pretty cool!), go to www.fuelcells.org/info/charts/h2fuelingstations.pdf.

Sweden is the global leader in cellulosic biomethane production. Sweden's goal is to *displace all natural gas use* with biomethane and also *all gasoline and diesel* with renewable fuels. Biomass sources make up 45% of Sweden's biomethane. This industry has been growing at an annual rate of around 20% over the last five years. Biomethane powers more than 8,000 transit buses, garbage trucks, and 10 different models of passenger cars in Sweden.[e]

In 2007, Spanish biofuels developers selected Kansas as the site of the first US cellulosic ethanol plant, slated to produce fuel from corn stalks, switchgrass, and other woody biomass.[f]

Ontario Power Generation's Sir Adam Beck Generating Complex.

HYDROELECTRIC
How Free Is Its Power?

The potential for free energy, the gravity-powered use of a renewable resource, the security of stored water and flood protection…The promises of hydropower have in many ways been realized, though it has taken decades to recognize the true cost of this controversial watery "freebie." Some believe that big dams rank among the last century's greatest engineering achievements, yet they could one day be widely regarded as one of our worst acts of environmental destruction. Small dams can have a large cumulative impact, destroying and/or blocking access to fish habitat.

Electricity generation via running water works well on a small scale in many parts of the world when the conditions and set-up are right. However, large-scale hydro projects have often proved disastrous in developing regions. This is not a new story, having come to light incrementally over the last fifty years. As the links between healthy environments (such as a river system) and healthy societies are more widely understood, destructive river infrastructure projects are losing favor in the Global North. Unfortunately, they are still being promoted in the Global South.

What is new is the discovery that reservoirs as well as the dam mechanism itself, in its churning of the water, are major sources of global warming pollution.[24] Dams and reservoirs release significant amounts of the greenhouse gases methane (CH_4), nitrous oxide (NO), and carbon dioxide (CO_2), according to a growing number of scientific sources. "Gases are emitted from the surface of the reservoir, at turbines and spillways, and for tens of kilometers downstream. Emissions are highest in hot climates…The 'fuel' for these emissions is the rotting of organic matter from the vegetation and soils flooded when the reservoir

is first filled…One intriguing aspect of this issue is proposed new technologies to capture tropical reservoir methane and use it to generate electricity."[25] The greenhouse gas methane is 23 times more potent than carbon dioxide.

COAL
The Dirtiest Fuel

Coal is by far the most polluting and carbon-intensive source of electricity. This industry is working hard to make us believe that "clean coal" will play a continuing part in meeting the world's energy needs, yet the promise of its expensive and unproven green technology is becoming increasingly ridden with doubt and criticism—clean coal has even been compared to a healthy cigarette. The leading clean-coal technology is called **carbon capture and sequestration (CCS)**, which aspires to "capture" and bury carbon emissions, thus keeping them out of the atmosphere (for now). For this to be an option in a warming world, the coal industry, with government help, must vastly increase investment in research and testing.

Presently coal provides about half of our electricity in the US. From the mine to the plant, coal is our dirtiest energy source. As a major contributor to global warming (CO_2) and air pollution (soot and sulphur dioxide), it is a leading cause of asthma and other respiratory and health problems; destroys mountains ("mountain-top removal" is actually the phrase for a type of coal mining); and releases toxic mercury into our communities. And because of impending carbon pricing, coal-burning plants are rapidly becoming more expensive.[26]

The coal industry spends millions on public relations and media exposure for its "green" efforts, but like Big Oil, it works simultaneously to block and delay effective federal legislation that aims to cap GHG emissions and to require utilities to include more renewable energy sources in their portfolios. How long will profits supersede climate protection as an imperative?

There is a growing trend in the US against coal-fired power plants. Since March 2006, plans for at least 25 coal-fired power plants around the country have either been rejected or significantly delayed.[27]

COAL MINING BY THE NUMBERS *[Sierra Club]*

90 million	Gallons of waste slurry produced every year while preparing coal to be burned
1,200+	Miles of streams that have been buried or polluted in Appalachia because of mountaintop removal mining
260 million	Gallons of water used for coal mining in the US every day
12,000	Miners who died from black lung disease between 1992 and 2002
55	Percent decrease in number of coal miners employed from 1985 to 2000
22	Percent increase in coal mining production from 1985 to 2005

NUCLEAR POWER
Not a Climate Solution

Because safe and healthy power sources like solar and wind exist now, we don't have to rely on risky nuclear power. As recently as July 2007 an earthquake in Japan caused leakages at a nuclear plant, raising the alarm about these severe accidents waiting to happen.[28] Yet some people tout nuclear as a potential climate solution since CO_2 emissions are relatively low.

Currently there are about 400 nuclear plants operating worldwide, 132 in the US. (Fifty-two percent of the 253 originally ordered have been built.)[29] Though no nuclear plants have been built in the US for more than 30 years, a new site permit was approved in March 2007, the first new site permit in three decades—a sign of renewed interest in nuclear.[30] Nuclear proponents say we would have to scale up to around 17,000 nuclear plants to offset enough fossil fuels to begin making a dent in climate change. See *Ten Strikes Against Nuclear Power* for reasons why this isn't possible.

"New nuclear power is so costly that shifting a dollar of spending from nuclear to efficiency protects the climate several-fold more than shifting a dollar of spending from coal to nuclear. Indeed, under plausible assumptions, spending a dollar on new nuclear power instead of on efficient use of electricity has a worse climate effect than spending that dollar on new coal power!"

—*from "Forget Nuclear" by Amory B. Lovins, Imran Sheikh, and Alex Markevich*

ENERGY CONSERVATION

Reducing the amount of energy wasted and increasing the amount of economic output that can be produced with a given amount of energy (using less to get more) is now considered the most economical way of reducing dependence on fossil fuels.[31] Energy efficiency

---

TEN STRIKES AGAINST NUCLEAR POWER

1. **Nuclear Waste** will be toxic for humans for more than 100,000 years. We can't securely store all the waste from the plants that exist now. To scale up is unthinkable.

2. **Nuclear Proliferation:** We can't develop a domestic nuclear energy program without confronting proliferation in other countries.

3. **National Security** is at risk because nuclear reactors (which are not entirely secure) are an attractive target for terrorists.

4. **Accidents**—human error or natural disasters—can wreak just as much havoc. The Chernobyl disaster forced the evacuation of nearly 400,000 people, with thousands poisoned by radiation.

5. **Cancer risk** for childhood leukemia and other forms of cancer seems to be higher in communities near nuclear plants—even when a plant has an accident-free record.

6. **Not Enough Feasible Sites** exist on Earth for new nuclear facilities, which must be near water for cooling, and safe from droughts, flooding, hurricanes, earthquakes, and other potential triggers for a nuclear accident.

7. **Not Enough Uranium:** Scientists in both the US and the UK have shown that if the current level of nuclear power were expanded to provide all the world's electricity, our uranium would be depleted in fewer than 10 years.

8. **Costs** for nuclear power increase with scale, unlike some types of energy production, e.g., solar power, which experience decreasing costs to scale.

9. **Private Sector Unwilling to Finance:** Due to all of the above, the private sector is largely taking a pass on the financial risks of nuclear power.

10. **No Time!** We have the next ten years to mount a global effort against climate change—not enough time to build enough new nuclear plants.

Reproduced, with some editing for length, courtesy of Rocky Mountain Institute.

---

simultaneously offers some of the cheapest options for reducing CO_2 emissions. This proven, common-sense approach has sometimes been denied and derided in the past: Former Vice President Dick Cheney summed up the oil industry's stance (and that of the previous administration) when he infamously said in 2001: "Conservation may be a sign of personal virtue, but it is not a sufficient basis for a sound, comprehensive energy policy."

In fact, conservation in each home as well as large-scale conservation on the part of industry and agriculture makes a huge difference in overall energy consumption and climate pollution. There are two components here: *Conservation* is saving or not using a resource in the first place. *Efficiency* is using resources, including smarter technologies, with an eye toward maximum output. Energy efficiency, for example, is about doing the same amount of work (or more, and often better) with less energy. It's not about sacrifice; it's about being smarter in how we spend our natural capital.

A recent report by the McKinsey Global Institute concluded that further improvements to US energy efficiency could offset 85% of the projected national demand for electricity by 2030, offering an excellent alternative to the relentless need to increase energy supply.[32]

According to renowned energy consultant Amory Lovins:

Increasing energy end-use efficiency—technologically providing more desired service per unit of delivered energy consumed—is generally the largest, least expensive, most benign, most quickly deployable, least visible, least understood, and most neglected way to provide energy services. The 46% drop in US energy intensity (primary energy consumption per dollar of real GDP) during 1975–2005 represented by 2005 an effective energy "source" 2.1 [times] as big as US oil consumption, 3.4 [times] net oil imports, 6 [times] domestic oil output or net oil imports from OPEC countries, and 13 [times] net imports from Persian Gulf countries.[33]

The state of California has aggressively pursued energy (as well as water) conservation for decades, with impressive results. Over the past 30 years, while per capita electricity usage in the US grew by more than 50%, California's consumption stayed flat, even while the state's economy doubled—proof that we don't need to choose between growth and sustainability.[34] (California developed the nation's first efficiency standards for appliances and buildings).

If the rest of the US followed California's lead, we could forget about new coal plants—a huge leap forward in the fight against global warming. In general, both cities and states continue to be far ahead of the US government in terms of legislation for regulation of GHG emissions.

"Are we to infer from your testimony that you still don't believe in global warming?"

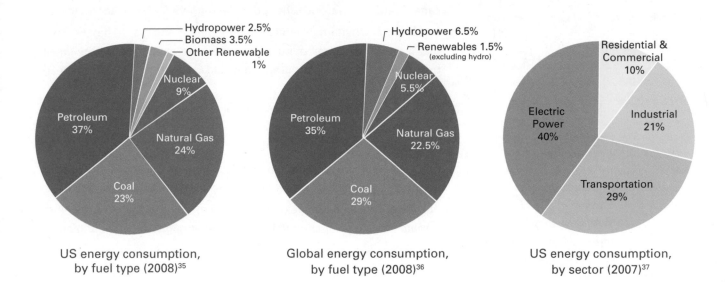

US energy consumption, by fuel type (2008)[35]

Global energy consumption, by fuel type (2008)[36]

US energy consumption, by sector (2007)[37]

> *Right now over 70 percent of the world population is convinced that something serious has to be done about the dangers facing the planet...Most of humanity wants to know how to make the change. It's one of those tipping-point times where things can change unbelievably fast...*
>
> —*Paul H. Ray and Sherry Ruth Anderson*
>
> *Transformation to me means the powerful unleashing of human potential to commit to, care about, and change for a better life. Transformation occurs when people give up their automatic way of being and commit themselves to a different future, recognizing that they can influence the flow of events and thus create new futures—individually and collectively.*
>
> —*Monica Sharma, UN Director of Leadership and Capacity Development*

WHAT WE CAN DO

- Insist on and be part of the shift to clean, renewable energy. Laws as well as individual activities must aim to rein in global warming pollution and transition to a clean energy economy. Shift to renewable and energy efficiency in all possible aspects of your life.

- In order to harness the potential of renewable energy, we need a strong Energy Efficiency Resource Standard (EERS) requiring utilities to generate 20% of their electricity from renewable resources by 2020. Such a standard would reduce global warming, create jobs, and save consumers money.

- Climate, energy, and transportation policies must complement one another and aim for similar goals.

- Urge government not to favor giant power plants over distributed solutions; nor to emphasize enlarged supply over efficient use.

- Call your local utility company and sign up for renewable energy. If they don't offer it, ask them why not.

- Make your home energy-efficient. This yields dramatic savings in heating and cooling. California building codes have resulted in an energy savings of $30 billion since 1975, more than $2,000 per household. Roll those policies out nationally, and the savings would be immense. Dept of Energy Best Practices Guidelines can be found at www.eere.energy.gov/buildings/building_america.

- Start with caulking and weather-stripping on doorways and windows. Then adjust your thermostat and start saving. Ask your utility company to do a free energy audit of your home to show you how to save even more money.

- Many homes and offices are a nightmare of passive energy use. Turn off electronics and unplug appliances when not in use.

- Replace incandescent light bulbs with compact fluorescent bulbs, which use about a quarter of the electricity and last ten times as long.

- Buy energy-efficient electronics and appliances. Look for the Energy Star label on new appliances or visit www.energystar.gov to find the most energy-efficient products.

Capitol Climate Action, Washington, DC, March 2009

Mike Krautter (www.mikekrautter.com)

Global Exchange

Part Four **A JUST SOCIETY**

A World That Works for Everyone

We are way more powerful when we turn to each other and not on each other, when we celebrate our diversity, focus on our commonality, and together tear down the mighty walls of injustice.

—Cynthia McKinney,
Green Party candidate for
US Presidency, 2008

"There are no roads to peace; peace is the road." *—Mahatma Gandhi*

"Imagine all the people, living life as one," sang John Lennon, a ballad that still brings tears of hope to many. Gandhi's metaphorical "road," the work of uplifting and uniting humanity, has countless twists and turns, multiple colors, with choices along the way, stories and strategies to share, and potential unity in our vast diversity.

This section provides but a glimpse of our collective social problems and a sample of the inspiring efforts to address social inequities and reach out to our fellow humans. On this spaceship Earth, together we face the magnitude of overpopulation, global migration due to both calamity and opportunity, and rampant human rights violations perpetrated on indigenous peoples, women, immigrants, and all the children of the world. In unity of purpose on the Earth, we look here at United Nations declarations, visionary leaders, a healthy environment, and educational opportunity for all ages—from a schoolyard garden for young mothers to the urban green jobs corps. For more background on sources of the problems (the globalized economy, for example) and solutions being implemented, see the next part, *Economics*.

The bottom line: True global security depends on equal access and opportunity for all.

"Where, after all, do universal human rights begin? In small places, close to home—so close and so small that they cannot be seen on any map of the world. Yet they are the world of the individual person, the neighborhood he lives in, the school or college he attends; the factory, farm or office where he works."

—Eleanor Roosevelt

GLOBAL CHALLENGES

Hunger

According to the Food and Agriculture Organization, as reported by the UN Millennium Campaign, "the economic crisis has resulted in 100 million more people going hungry, taking the total number of hungry people in the world to a staggering one billion." The Campaign's director adds that "since the inception of aid (overseas development assistance) almost 50 years ago, donor countries have given some $2 trillion in aid. And yet over the past year, $18 trillion has been found globally to bail out banks and other financial institutions. The amount of total aid over the past 49 years represents just 11% of the money found for financial institutions in one year."[1] Part Five, *Economics*, links resolution of global crises to fundamental changes in how wealth is managed.

"When a poor person dies of hunger, it has not happened because God did not take care of him or her. It has happened because neither you nor I wanted to give that person what he or she needed."

—*Mother Teresa*

People on the Move

Migration is a complex and shifting reality. You might be next! The 2009 UN Human Development Report, *Overcoming Barriers: Human Mobility and Development*, challenges stereotypes and broadens perceptions of migration, noting: "Migration not infrequently gets bad press. Negative stereotypes portraying migrants as 'stealing our jobs' or 'scrounging off the taxpayer' abound in sections of the media and public opinion, especially in times of recession. For others, the word 'migrant' may evoke images of people at their most vulnerable."[2] In addition to the tragically familiar fate of refugees from war and genocide, people are increasingly being uprooted by natural disasters (whether or not national borders are crossed). Environmental and resource pressures are additional drivers of displacement.[3] "Climate refugees" is a new term for those forced to relocate due to ecosystem disruption (such as increased desertification), sea-level rise, water shortages, and resulting health epidemics. All this is costly in both economic and human terms.

The quest for better economic opportunities is another factor. To quote the UN report cited above again: "For many people around the world moving away from their home town or village can be the best—sometimes the only—option open to improve their life chances. Migration can be hugely effective in improving the income, education and participation of individuals and families, and enhancing their children's future prospects. But its value is more than that: being able to decide where to live is a key element of human freedom… There is no typical profile of migrants around the world. Fruit pickers, nurses, political refugees, construction workers, academics and computer programmers are all part of the nearly 1 billion people on the move both within their own countries and overseas."[4]

Overpopulation

Human overpopulation bridges every concern related to sustainability—from food supply, health, and education to climate change and an Earth-centered economy. The good news is that our best and most effective strategies to curb population growth also achieve other sustainability goals. Actively improving the lives of people worldwide—through educating women and girls, making health care available (including family planning), and alleviating poverty—is our best insurance against the woes of overpopulation, as well as the best hedge in security matters and other universal goals.

Humans currently number about 6.8 billion, a number projected to exceed 9 billion by mid-century.[5] Consider the exponential rate of population explosion: It took all of human history until 1830 for world population to reach one billion. The second billion was achieved in 100 years, the third billion in 30 years, the fourth billion in 15 years, and the fifth billion in only 12 years.[6] This rapid population growth is exceeding the carrying capacity of our planet in terms of resource consumption and depletion, waste generation and disposal, in large part because the dominant economic model emphasizes rapid growth, wealth accumulation, consumerism, and dependence on fossil fuels.

Population growth constantly pushes the consequences of any level of individual consumption to a higher plateau, and reductions in individual consumption can always be overwhelmed by increases in population. The simple reality is that acting on both, consistently and simultaneously, is the key to long-term environmental sustainability. The sustainability benefits of level or falling human numbers are too powerful to ignore for long…

The magnitude of environmental impacts stem not just from our numbers but also from behaviors we learn from our parents and cultures. Broadly speaking, if population is the number of us, then consumption is the way each of us behaves. In this unequal world, the behavior of a dozen people in one place sometimes has more environmental impact than does that of a few hundred somewhere else.

—*Scientific American*

"The increase in the decline of Earth's biodiversity has been caused by multiple factors increased by human activities, including habitat loss, climate change, invasive species, pollution, human overpopulation, and overexploitation. Human overpopulation is the root cause for the other factors."

—E.O. Wilson, biologist, Harvard professor

Bigstockphoto.com

Art Explosion

Note also that children born in developed nations are a greater burden on the environment due to greatly increased consumption levels throughout their lifetime. That's why the population question isn't as simple as expanding numbers of people using more resources. The rate of consumption per person—which differs greatly among nations—is significant when considering national birth rates and global impacts. A recent *Scientific American* article points out: "[The] one-two punch of population growth followed by consumption growth is presently occurring in China (1.34 billion people) and India (1.2 billion). Per capita commercial energy use has been growing so rapidly in both countries…that if the trends continue unabated the typical Chinese will out-consume the typical American before 2040, with Indians surpassing Americans by 2080. Population and consumption thus feed on each other's growth to expand humans' environmental footprint exponentially over time."[7]

Stemming population growth requires education and universal adoption of sustainable lifestyle practices and policies. Progress should be measured by genuine well-being, *not* an increase in production and consumption. As people grow in understanding of the connection between natural systems and our complete interdependence, adopting sensible zero-population policies and practices will become the norm. And with reproductive freedom (not globally available yet) and an understanding of the consequences of exponentially rising population, women are individually better able to make wise decisions.[8]

Women

Without providing more rights and responsibilities for women, social justice will never be achieved and all other goals will be elusive. It is widely agreed that aid to poor countries best achieves its goal of improving economic conditions when directed toward health, education, and microfinance initiatives, especially when such programs focus upon women and girls. Benefitting the welfare of the entire community, when women hold assets, family money is more likely to be spent on nutrition, medicine, and housing, and consequently children are healthier.[9]

The obstacles to women contributing their full economic and political potential to their community—beyond their vital roles in the family—include their abuse and mistreatment in various situations, from horrific to less intense forms of cultural confinement and inconvenience. Along with lack of education for many girls and the marginalization of women, the circumstances facing millions of women and girls worldwide include mass rape, genital mutilation, sex trafficking, bride burnings, "honor killings," and more—tragically indicating that gender equality is not yet everywhere accepted as a universal human right.

"The transformation of women's roles is the last great impediment to universal progress…So-called women's issues are stability issues, security issues, equity issues."[10]

—Hillary Clinton,
US Secretary of State

Economically, socially, and geopolitically, women have tremendous contributions to make.[11] The education of women has a strong population control corollary: educating girls significantly reduces birthrates. Educated women delay child-bearing and they have fewer children. According to demographers at the International Institute for Applied Systems Analysis in Austria, "women with no schooling have an average of 4.5 children, whereas those with a few years of primary school have just three. Women who complete one or two years of secondary school have an average of 1.9 children, which leads to a decreasing population. With one or two years of college, the average childbearing rate falls to 1.7. And

when women enter the workforce, start businesses, inherit assets and otherwise interact with men on an equal footing, their desire for more than a couple of children fades even more dramatically."[12]

A report from Optimum Population Trust and the prestigious London School of Economics argues that expanding access to family planning and contraception is about five times less expensive than implementing low-carbon technology to combat climate change. The report, called *Fewer Emitters, Lower Emissions, Less Cost,* concludes that if basic family planning were available globally, we would save 34 gigatons of carbon emissions over the next 40 years.[13]

ENABLING THE GLOBAL RISE OF FEMALE EMPOWERMENT

- Women's issues should be a prominent part of foreign policy.

- Governments should make it easy for women to hold property and bank accounts. They should also make it easier for microfinance institutions to start banks so that women can save money.

- Donor countries should nudge poor countries to adjust their laws so that when a man dies, property is passed on to his widow rather than to his brothers.

- Writing that "men must raise the level of their consciousness with respect to the way in which they treat women," author Chris Maser specifies that we need to give women the choice of how many children to have and when; to value them beyond their abilities to satisfy a male's sexual urges and to bear children (especially sons); and to provide adequate counseling about birth control.[14]

EQUITABLE EARTH PRINCIPLES

The United Nations (UN) was founded in 1945 to maintain peace and security within and among nations, and to promote social progress, better living standards, and human rights around the world. Three of the most fundamental instruments developed by the UN address basic human rights for all people: they are the Universal Declaration of Human Rights (UDHR), the Millennium Development Goals, and the UN Declaration on the Rights of Indigenous Peoples. While many nations agree to the goals, it will obviously take a multitude of organizations working on many levels, and all global citizens pitching in, to turn the promises into reality. Yet they get little media attention, and many people do not know they even exist.

Universal Declaration of Human Rights

"Protecting and empowering the poor must become an urgent rallying cry to honor the spirit, the letter, and the promise of dignity for all," according to the UDHR. This document was adopted more than 60 years ago to promote equality, justice, fairness, non-discrimination, and dignity for all people across all boundaries everywhere and always.

Still, 160 million children are moderately or severely malnourished; 110 million are out of school; and at least 500,000 are left motherless each year by death in childbirth.[15] For more grim statistics like these, see the Human Rights Factsheet of the UN Cyberschoolbus (an informative website geared to youth).

The UN says that "poverty is often both a cause and a consequence of human rights violations…Destitution and exclusion are intertwined with discrimination, unequal access to opportunities, as well as social and cultural stigmatization." It is apparent that removing discriminatory practices and policies, along with providing pathways out of poverty, serves to "remove barriers to labor market participation and give women and minorities access to employment."[16]

UN MILLENNIUM DEVELOPMENT GOALS

The *MDGs*, to be achieved by 2015, are drawn from the Millennium Declaration of 2000. Adopted by 189 leaders from the north and south, MDGs explicitly recognize the interdependence among growth, poverty reduction, and sustainable development, which build on the foundations of democratic governance, the rule of law, respect for human rights, and peace and security.

1. Eradicate extreme poverty and hunger
2. Achieve universal primary education
3. Promote gender equality and empower women
4. Reduce child mortality
5. Improve maternal health
6. Combat HIV/AIDS, malaria, and other diseases
7. Ensure environmental stability
8. Develop a global partnership for development

We are not meeting the goals

"Progress towards the goals is now threatened by sluggish—or even negative—economic growth, diminished resources, fewer trade opportunities for the developing countries, and possible reductions in aid flows from donor nations," according to the UN Development Programme (UNDP) annual Human Development Report for 2009. For example, if we continue at today's pace, sub-Saharan Africa won't achieve its poverty reduction goals until 2147, the Cyberschoolbus website for youth predicts.

The UN Permanent Forum on Indigenous Issues said of the MDGs, "Indigenous and tribal peoples are lagging behind other parts of the population in the achievement of the goals in most, if not all, the countries in which they live, and indigenous and tribal women commonly face additional gender-based disadvantages and discrimination."[17] As with any process that concerns them, "including indigenous peoples in the MDG context requires a culturally sensitive approach, based on respect for and inclusion of indigenous peoples' world-views, perspectives, experiences, and concepts of development."[18]

Campaign strives to end poverty

The UN Millennium Campaign supports citizens' efforts to hold their governments accountable for achieving MDGs. Its supporters vow: "We are the first generation that can end poverty and we refuse to miss this opportunity."

See EndPoverty2015.org.

Millennium Villages show promise

Focused on sub-Saharan Africa, where 300 million people live on less than $1 a day and 500 million lack basic sanitation, Millennium Promise works in 10 countries. The Millennium Villages initiative combines community-led actions that ensure a village meets long-term needs with "simple solutions like providing high-yield seeds, fertilizers, medicines, drinking wells and materials to build school rooms and clinics…insecticide-treated bed nets, antiretroviral drugs, remote sensing, geographic information systems, and internet and mobile phone connectivity…"[19]

In West Africa, six villages with 31,000 people are clustered in the coastal area of Potou, Senegal. School meal programs, construction of schools and clinics, along with credit support and scholarships for young women, are helping to transform this remote area where only half the children attend school and 20% under the age of five are malnourished. Countering the impacts of pollution from chemical agriculture, industrial waste, and domestic refuse, a piped water network reaches most cluster residents via 119 community taps. Drip irrigation helps increase farm yields.

In southwestern Uganda, a shrub called Artemesia is processed into a drug that serves as the first line of defense against malaria, providing both a lucrative venture for many small-scale farmers and a sense of self-empowerment in the fight against malaria.[20]

Reducing poverty by supporting small business development, the UK-based organization Teach a Man to Fish helps create self-sufficient educational institutions via vocational training and entrepreneurship.

In **Kenya,** a secondary school partners with the Eco-Finders Youth Movement, raising poultry to produce eggs as well as fertilizer for horticultural plots and a fruit tree nursery. Proceeds from the sale of eggs, vegetables, and tree seedlings at the local market are reinvested in the school. In **Sudan,** the school vegetable garden helps feed the community all year around while also helping fund the school. In **Armenia,** the youth sell compost from their worm farm, supporting organic agriculture.

In the **Philippines** students of horticulture, nursery establishment, and soil and water management do work and knowledge exchange with local farmers, feed families, and reinvest their profits into scholarships.[21]

INDIGENOUS RIGHTS

The United Nations counts 370 million indigenous people in more than 70 countries with 5,000 distinct indigenous cultural identities. Although indigenous people only account for 5% of the world's population, they account for over 15% of the world's poor.[22]

The UN Declaration on the Rights of Indigenous Peoples was overwhelmingly adopted in September 2007, but significantly, not by Canada, New Zealand, and the United States. It covers protection of cultural property and identity, the right to education, employment, health, religion, language and culture; and it protects the right to own land collectively. It says, "Indigenous peoples have the right to maintain and develop their political, economic and social systems or institutions, to be secure in the enjoyment of their own means of subsistence and development, and to engage freely in all their traditional and other economic activities."[23]

"Before the day is over, an Indigenous person will be displaced or killed. Before the month is over, an Indigenous homeland will be clear-cut, strip-mined, or flooded. Before the year is over, dozens of Indigenous languages will vanish forever. Governments and powerful economic interests perpetrate this human and cultural devastation."

— Cultural Survival,
a global partner of indigenous peoples,
supporting their autonomy and welfare

Indigenous peoples and NGOs have invoked other agreements over the decades, in order to assert indigenous peoples' land rights and to insist on being consulted on projects affecting them, reports the MDG Monitor, an information-sharing project of the UNDP. Increased recognition that indigenous peoples merit special treatment based on historical pre-existence and special attachment to ancestral lands was invoked in 1989 by the International Labour Organization (ILO) Indigenous and Tribal Peoples—at the first binding international convention to address the specific rights of indigenous peoples and the legal responsibilities of governments to promote and protect their human rights.[24]

INDIGENOUS SURVIVAL

The work of keeping attention and advocacy focused on the rights of indigenous peoples is shared by many exemplary organizations around the world. For 35 years, Cultural Survival has partnered with indigenous peoples to protect their lands, languages, and cultures; educate communities about their rights; and fight against marginalization, discrimination, exploitation, and abuse—all enforcing the UN principles.

In 2006, First Peoples Worldwide established Keepers of the Earth to protect the rights of indigenous peoples, including rights related to subsistence hunting and gathering, access to sacred sites, and traditional and cultural practices—with an

"Wild rice is at the core of our being…For us, rice is a source of food and also wisdom. For the globalizers, it is just a commodity to be exploited for profit. The paradigms are at loggerheads…That philosophical, spiritual, and cultural dialogue needs to be deepened in our own communities, because it's in our hands to determine the future."

—Winona LaDuke
Native American activist, economist

overall conception of balancing biodiversity protection and sustainable economic development in indigenous territories. First Peoples' development strategy is based on culturally appropriate management and control of the ample and diverse community assets possessed by many indigenous peoples (land, natural resources, traditional knowledge, culture, etc.). In collaboration with the Calvert Group, First Peoples created the first social investing screen that protects the rights of indigenous peoples.

Creative Commons/Fod T Mike

Indigenous Support

All of us can ally with efforts to increase opportunities and living conditions for indigenous peoples, so their cultures, wisdom, and traditions are not lost.

Acknowledge Sovereignty: Vice Chairperson of Seventh Generation Fund's Board of Directors, Tonya Gonnella Frichner (Onondaga), says of sovereignty: "It's not something that's given to you—it's an expression of who you are as a nation, as a people. It's an act—not only something you think about, it's something you do. For me, sovereignty is something an Indigenous nation expresses through the act of treaty-making, because only sovereign entities can enter into treaty-making. Even though the United States takes the position that our sovereignty is now 'internal' sovereignty on a domestic level, many of our Indigenous leaders challenge this position and don't agree with it...Most important to me as an individual is that the act of sovereignty bears with it a great deal of responsibility."[25]

Seek Environmental Justice: The rights of indigenous peoples have been systematically violated by oil, gas, timber, and mining industries, creating "unconscionable destruction to traditional territories that have sustained us for time immemorial," according to the Indigenous Environmental Network. It's a pervasive and centuries-old pattern of assault on native rights as well as the Earth. But the resistance is increasingly sophisticated, as many modern First Nations' approach to economics and sovereignty reveals. Joining together strengthens the movement. For example, the Indigenous Environmental Network and the Indigenous Women's Network represent more than 200 grassroots Native communities across North America, and their partnership gives them great collective strength.

Honor the Earth works to leverage financial resources, articulate Native issues within a wide political context, and reach a non-Native public to provide support and solidarity. From their website: "Our Energy Justice Initiative is designed to strategically and actively develop community infrastructure essential to a sustainable future in Indian Country. We are addressing the issue of energy policy as a means to democratize power production and create systemic change that advances environmental and social justice...The abundance of wind and solar resources on our reservations is astounding. Tribes have the potential to produce 15% of the country's electricity with wind power, and the solar resources to power America 4.5 times over."

The Navajo Green Jobs Coalition was organized "because Navajo citizens are sick of working in dirty jobs that pose serious risks to their health, land, and water." Similarly, Diné Care is working to promote clean and sustainable living.[26]

Founded in 1989, White Earth Land Recovery Project is one of the largest reservation-based nonprofits in the US. Its multi-issue approach addresses root causes of problems faced by residents of the White Earth Reservation, including the loss of land, culture, and self-determination. Located in northern Minnesota, White Earth is the homeland to the Anishinaabeg of the Mississippi Band, also known as the Ojibwe or Chippewa. "Over the past seventeen years... we recovered more than a thousand acres of land, began restoring a traditional food system, expanded a wild rice export market, and initiated a renewable energy program," said founding director and former Green Party Vice Presidential candidate Winona LaDuke.[27]

HONORING DIVERSITY

Environmental racism refers to any environmental policy, practice, or action that negatively impacts communities, groups, or individuals based on race or ethnicity. The concept of *environmental justice* (EJ) provides a framework for communities of color to articulate the political, economic, and social assumptions underlying why environmental racism and degradation happens and how this continues to be institutionally reinforced. EJ principles prioritize public good over profit, cooperation over competition, community and collective action over individualism, and precautionary approaches over unacceptable risks.

A Need for Systemic Change

What would it take to achieve social justice and a sustainable world that works for everyone? Our present condition calls for us to claim our evolved selves and shed the skin of patriarchal attitudes, economic exploitation, dysfunctional structures, and Industrial Age mindset. All of our human institutions must be guided by the intent to give honor and future to our sacred interconnectedness.

We may be saying "yes" to the need to recycle, drive hybrid cars, and use solar and wind power, but if we are still abusing women and treating them as anything less than our sacred mothers then we can't be sustainable. "Yes" we need to eat locally, but if we are mis-educating our children and then locking them up in prisons, we are not being sustainable. "Yes" we need to buy Fair Trade, but if we are viewing human beings who happen to relocate from one place on this sacred planet to another sacred space as "illegal aliens" then we can't be sustainable. "Yes" we need to grow food organically, but we if we are denying humans full access to life experiences because of their sexual orientation, then we can't be sustainable. The sustainability movement offers us an opportunity to celebrate and embrace the fullest diversity of our humanity that mirrors the Earth's miraculous diversity.

While campaigning for President, Barack Obama said in his speech about race (March 2008), "America can change. That is the true genius of this nation…It requires all Americans to realize that your dreams do not have to come at the expense of my dreams; that investing in the health, welfare, and education of black and brown and white children will ultimately help all of America prosper."[28]

"The next American revolution will be radically different from the revolutions that have taken place in pre- or non-industrialized countries like Russia, Cuba, China, or Vietnam. As citizens of a nation that had achieved its rapid economic growth and prosperity at the expense of Native Americans, African Americans, Latinos, Asian Americans, and peoples all over the world, our priority has to be correcting the injustices and backwardness of our relationships with one another, with other countries, and with the Earth."[29]

—Grace Lee Boggs, founder, Boggs Center to Nurture Community Leadership

Climate Justice

Climate change and social justice are intertwining issues, and many people are taking notice of the consequences affecting and likely to affect poorer communities and nations disproportionately. A year before Hurricane Katrina, the book *African Americans and Climate Change: An Unequal Burden* was published by the Congressional Black Caucus Foundation. It concludes: "When it comes to US environmental conditions, African Americans are…on the frontline of the likely social, environmental and eco-

nomic upheavals resulting from climate change…are disproportionately burdened by the health effects of climate change… less responsible for climate change than other Americans…[and] will be disproportionately affected by extreme weather events, storms, hurricanes."[30] It is a fact that poor people worldwide are the most vulnerable to the coming negative consequences of climate change.

The work and mission of many organizations echo these concerns. Ella Baker Center for Human Rights (EBC), founded in 1996, has a vision for "justice in the system; opportunity in our cities, and peace on our streets." Their blog summarizes a new report on climate equity that "uncovers what researchers call a 'climate gap' or hidden pattern revealing that poor people and people of color in the United States suffer more from environmental changes than other whiter and wealthier Americans." Risk and actual occurrence of heat-related illness and death are much higher in low-income neighborhoods, and the proportion of income going to water expense is three times higher. The report also offers some climate change adaptation investment solutions that can alleviate pollution, create jobs, and lower the cost burden.[31]

Latino Communities and Immigration

Social and environmental justice issues face many Hispanic/Latino populations, especially in North America. While the US immigration system appears reasonable, and highly regulated to those not directly affected, the facts on the ground illustrate that it is badly broken and in urgent need of reform.

The National Council of La Raza (NCLR) contends that the underlying flaws of the legal immigration system must be addressed, with establishment of a fair, humane, and practical immigration system that is responsive to the needs of the economy and encourages legal behavior. NCLR—the largest national Hispanic civil rights and advocacy organization in the US—works through its network of nearly 300 affiliated community-based organizations, conducting policy analysis, and advocacy in five key areas: assets/investments, civil rights/immigration, education, employment and economic status, and health.

Environmental Service Learning Initiative (eslist.org)

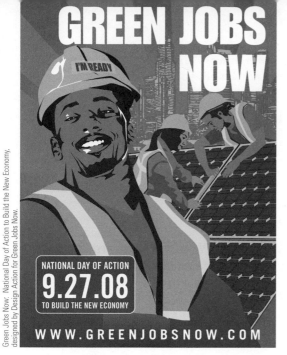

GREEN JOBS NOW

I'M READY

NATIONAL DAY OF ACTION
9.27.08
TO BUILD THE NEW ECONOMY

W W W . G R E E N J O B S N O W . C O M

Green Jobs Now: National Day of Action to Build the New Economy, designed by Design Action for Green Jobs Now.

For Latinos and other people, educating families about healthy lifestyles and increasing their access to health services can be better achieved by removing language and cultural barriers. Sisters of Color for Education hosts the oldest Promotora de Salud program in Colorado. Recently recognized by the Centers for Disease Control as a best practice for its effectiveness in Latino communities, Promotoras de Salud are well known throughout Mexico and Central America as front-line community health workers and educators. Participants access meaningful healthcare and support services through community activism, advocacy, information exchange, referrals, and art as social justice.[32]

"Census data reveal that the experience of immigration is deeply embedded in the social and political fabric. Nearly one quarter (23.4%) of the US population in 2008 consisted of either immigrants or the children of immigrants. Two out of every three Latinos (67.9%), and one out of every ten non-Latino whites (10.4%), was an immigrant or the child of an immigrant…Two in five immigrants came to this country before 1990 and therefore have deep roots in the US."[33]

Asian American Communities

From the very beginnings of American history, Asia Pacific Americans (APAs) have faced governmental and institutionalized discrimination that has prejudiced their ability to exercise the most basic rights. One of the most abusive examples was the brutal internment of approximately 120,000 Japanese Americans during World War II. It was not until 1965 that discriminatory quotas were discontinued against immigration from Asia. Since 1993, there has been a continual increase in hate crimes against APAs. Post 9/11, the level of racial profiling against South Asian Americans nationally has increased tremendously.[34]

The overall poverty rate for Asian Americans is 14% (compared to 9% for whites), based on US 2000 Census data. Hmong and Cambodian Americans have poverty rates of 60% and 40%, respectively (much higher than 27% for African Americans and Latinos). Addressing these social disparities, the Asian Law Caucus represents the legal and civil rights of Asians and Pacific Islanders.

The Asian American Justice Center promotes the human and civil rights of Asian Americans through a growing network of nearly 100 community-based organizations. Considerable health disparities persist in the Asian Pacific American community, and barriers to accessible culturally and linguistically appropriate health care is a critical goal because of the serious health trends that have emerged in this population that are out-of-step with the American population as a whole.[35]

An exemplary model for coordination among diverse groups focused on environmental health, the Asia Pacific Environmental Network and four other groups published *Building Healthy Communities from the Ground Up: Environmental Justice in California* because "Every day, communities of color across California face challenges of poverty, toxics and pollution, unsafe and unsustainable work conditions, and a lack of safe, affordable housing and basic goods and services."[36]

PATHWAYS TO AN EQUITABLE FUTURE

Restoration—from the top of the water catchments to the urban centers, and down to the rising sea—can provide sustenance to many a family and community. Reparations help fix the natural capital upon which the human social systems depend, making green jobs, energy innovations, community gardens, and farms possible as we build the Earth Community economy from the soil up.

"Whatever you love opens its secrets to you."
—George Washington Carver

Green Jobs: Repairing Ecosystems

Repairing ecosystems is labor-intensive, as tree-planters, cone pickers, wildland fire-fighters, and forest restorationists know very well. Forest worker cooperatives helped improve green-collar jobs during the timber boom of the 1970s and '80s. Like other large-scale agricultural sector labor, forestry has a history of social and ecological exploitation. Now there's a lot more focus on removing roads (before a flood does), fixing trails, reestablishing fish habitat, and thinning forests as part of a care-taking, natural resource-based economy.

The Society for Ecological Restoration (SER) and its Indigenous Peoples' Resto-

---

Community Gardens and a Pioneering Agriculturalist

George Washington Carver encouraged African Americans to create what we now call sustainable communities. He encouraged farming methods using crop rotation, cover crops, and companion planting, which we now call organic farming. Often regarded as the Peanut Wizard, Carver discovered ways to make most every item needed in the household using local farm products.

Aspiring to be the George Washington Carver of the 21st century, and modeling urban agriculture in Milwaukee and Chicago, Growing Power's Will Allen says that his group is dedicated to the idea of "growing food/fish." Sharing his methods with communities around the world, he modifies the old adage to state, "Teach people to grow fish/food and the community eats for a lifetime."

"generate more than 16 million hours of service annually." Credited with improving employment and earning gains, particularly for young African American men, Corps members show a one-third drop in arrest rates and a drop in teen pregnancies. Participating youth work on public and park lands, help with preparation and recovery from disasters, renovate housing in low income neighborhoods, and provide for after-school education programs.[39]

Inspiring Youth Engagement

Our deepest life-giving emotions, awareness, and actions need to be transmitted to the children of this generation and future generations. Adults must find ways to connect sustainability efforts in creative ways with the youth of all ages.

Art-making is a vital strategic element in social change work. The arts engage the whole person, the whole community, and the whole story, which is essential in finding our way to creating sustainable communities. Environmental education and service learning are integrated with empowerment.

Promoting the role of arts and social change, the Youth Green Corps was founded in 2007 in Lexington, Kentucky—a grassroots initiative that engages youth in local environmental, horticultural, and artistic projects that provide opportunities to be of service to their communities. In partnership with many other community groups, youth from all ages are helping to "green-ify" the community with new gardens.

Models are sprouting up all over the world. Alice Waters initiated the Edible School Yard at the Martin Luther King, Jr., Middle School in Berkeley, California. Project Sprout is an organic, student-run garden on the grounds of Monument High School in Great Barrington, Massachusetts, which supplies the school's cafeteria with fresh fruits and vegetables, helps feed the hungry in the community, and serves as a living laboratory for students.

Located on Detroit's west side in a distressed neighborhood with many empty lots and dilapidated houses, the Catherine Ferguson Academy (CFA) has 350 middle and high school students who are pregnant or are teen parents. It offers pre- and post-natal care for the students and well-baby care for the 200+ children in on-site day care. The young women at CFA have a 99%

ration Network support the integration of traditional ecological knowledge into ecosystem repair and management. SER International has members in 37 countries and 50 states, and their Global Restoration Network is a hub of information on ecosystems, toolkits on how to repair them, and links to care-takers and funders.

Green Jobs Are Local Careers

Taking the Ella Baker Center's Oakland, California-based Green-Collar Jobs Campaign to the national level, Van Jones co-founded Green For All with Majora Carter, founder of Sustainable South Bronx, in 2008. Green For All's intention is to build a green economy strong enough to raise people out of poverty, through green job creation and training, and urban energy-efficiency retrofits. Through the website, learning communities, and conference calls, members are linked to one another to find out what works, to leverage their strengths, and to build partnerships. Green For All's website includes tools and resources for removing barriers, diversifying funding, and evaluating programs.

Green For All helped ensure that green jobs provisions made it into the American Clean Energy and Security Act (June 2009). The "Pathways Out of Poverty" is one of a suite of federal grant programs, designed to fund "projects that prepare workers for careers in the energy efficiency and renewable energy sectors… [for] both green job training and research projects."[37] Groups and partnerships across the US are working to activate this vision, and communities are sharing lessons about successes and challenges.

Green For All's Clean Energy Corps program and Green Pathways Out of Poverty Community of Practice advocate building the green-collar economy "from the bottom up," offering tools for citizens working to get local governments to adopt Green Collar Jobs Taskforce and action plans. The Center for American Progress and the International Council for Local Environmental Initiatives (ICLEI) are also urging cities to sign on to the Local Government Green Jobs Pledge, whereby 500 cities around the world share models, training, software, and other resources through the international ICLEI.

Green For All collaborators include the Apollo Alliance, "a coalition of labor, business, environmental, and community leaders working to catalyze a clean energy revolution." The Innovations in Civic Participation program is focused on creating civic engagement opportunities for youth, and hosts a searchable database of organizations and initiatives around the world.

Social entrepreneur and young Latina leader Kendra Sandoval, founder of Denver-based Blue and Yellow Logic, is in business "to empower and 'green' our local economy in our historically black and brown neighborhoods" through education, training, and green jobs development. A Blue and Yellow staffer says, "It's all about diversifying the green and local-food movement. We cannot continue to let the environmental movement be separated by race. We need to remember that the green movement is not just some byproduct of rich, white culture."[38]

The Corps Network, a modern Civilian Conservation Corps, has 26,000 members ages 16 to 25 in 42 states that rate of graduation, 90% rate of graduates going on to post-secondary schools, and an 80% rate of no second pregnancy. The connection with the Earth through various farm experiences provides the young women an opportunity to dig deep into their own humanity. This is sustainability!

When we nurture all children's minds and when we keep them out of prison, we can develop sustainable communities. We need to develop educational experiences that tap into our innate abilities and allow our children to experience their divine gift of creativity. Dawna Markova's Smart Wired is dedicated to helping kids and young adults maximize their capabilities and bring out their best in all areas of life.

Manchester Craftsmen Guild, located in Pittsburgh and founded by Bill Strickland in 1968, was established to help combat the economic and social devastation experienced by the residents of his predominantly African American North Side neighborhood. Through educational experiences that utilize art and enterprise, students enhance and revitalize the economic, physical, social, and human conditions of their communities.

Based on the Guild's success, a vocational education program for adults called the Bidwell Training Center, offers multi-disciplinary courses in photography, fine arts, jazz, greenhouse production of orchids, and much more. Strickland envisions a Guild in every US center city. The resulting message is clear: When youth and adults at risk are given an environment that fosters artistic expression and high expectations, they can become part of the Cultural Creatives that Paul Ray wrote about as the driving force for the Great Turning.

"We [the youth] are not the leaders of tomorrow; we are the leaders of today!"
—Severn Cullis-Suzuki,
UN speech at the Rio Earth Summit

The Seven Foundations of a Just, Sustainable World

1. ECONOMIC FAIRNESS
A world dedicated to economic fairness would strive to meet every person's basic needs, so that no one would lack food, shelter, clothing, or meaningful work. People's strength of character and passion should determine their opportunities rather than the economic circumstances into which they were born. Everyone would benefit from economic prosperity.
- **Challenges:** Economic inequality, debt crisis and unfair trade, sweatshops.
- **Goals:** End of global poverty, fair trade in all commerce, ethical economics, regulation of multinational corporate practices.

2. COMPREHENSIVE PEACE
A world committed to comprehensive peace would shift its creative energies toward cooperating rather than competing, resolving conflict rather than escalating it, seeking justice rather than enacting revenge, and creating peace rather than preparing for war.
- **Challenges:** War and genocide, militarization, unilateralism, culture of violence.
- **Goals:** International cooperation, demilitarization and regulation of weaponry sales, nonviolent culture.

3. ECOLOGICAL SUSTAINABILITY
A world committed to ecological sustainability would create a new vision of progress that recognizes that the future of humanity depends upon our ability to live in harmony and balance with our natural world.
- **Challenges:** Resource overconsumption, pollution, global warming, overpopulation.
- **Goals:** Clean energy sources, sustainable resource use, stable population growth, global cooperation.

4. DEEP DEMOCRACY
A world built on deep democracy would empower citizens to participate in shaping their futures every day (not just on election day), provide broad access to quality information, and democratize our most powerful institutions.
- **Challenges:** Lack of democracy, money in politics, media control by corporations with vested interests.
- **Goals:** Open and honest politics, democratic media, full civic participation.

5. SOCIAL JUSTICE
A world dedicated to social justice is a place where everyone receives respect and equal access to jobs, education, and health care regardless of race, gender, ethnicity, sexual orientation, age, physical or mental abilities, or economic background.
- **Challenges:** Gender inequality, racism, heterosexism, inadequate health care, prisons based on punishment rather than rehabilitation.
- **Goals:** Equal rights for all (including rights for all living things), universal health care and education.

6. SIMPLE LIVING
A society that embraces simple living would encourage each person to find meaning and fulfillment by pursuing their true passions, fostering loving relationships, and living authentic, reflective lives rather than by seeking status and material possessions.
- **Challenges**: Advertising overload, commercialization of childhood, hyper-consumerism.
- **Goals:** Reclaimed consciousness, a culture of simplicity.

7. REVITALIZED COMMUNITY
A revitalized community would create a healthy and caring environment for people to celebrate their many shared values while embracing individual differences, and would provide support for each person's physical, emotional, and spiritual needs.
- **Challenges:** Loss of connection, lack of compassion.
- **Goals**: Revolution of caring, smart growth (cities designed to support people interacting with each other), strong local institutions.

The Seven Foundations are from The Better World Handbook.[40]

Roberta Vogel

Part Five **ECONOMICS**

WHAT COUNTS: Valuing Life

Confounded by the illusion that ours is a world of endless open frontiers with abundant resources free for the taking, we humans have created an economic system shaped by rules that… reward individualistic competition, material accumulation, and reckless consumption. We are just beginning to come to terms with the reality that we inhabit a living spaceship of finite resources and intricately balanced ecosystems…Managing economies to maximize growth … on a finite planet is the equivalent to maximizing the rate of consumption of essential resources on a spaceship. Both are actively suicidal.

—"New Rules for a SpaceshipEarth," New Economy Working Group

The necessary transition from the Industrial Revolution and growth society to a life-sustaining human presence on the planet is our current imperative, as well as our opportunity to reinvent our cultures, institutions, and ourselves accordingly. Merging all efforts to recreate our agriculture, built-environment design, exchange, and energy systems, we will be able to reconstitute the deep foundations of our beliefs and behaviors.

We can actualize new rules for "…a regenerative society [that] is a flourishing society. The revolution is not about giving up; it's about rediscovering what we most value…making quality of living central in our communities, businesses, schools, and societies. It is about reconnecting with ourselves, one another, and our fellow non-human inhabitants on Earth."[1]

New Rules could include:

■ **Surf the flux.** Live within our energy income by relying on renewable sources of energy such as solar, wind, tidal, and bio-based inputs.

■ **Zero to the landfill.** Everything, from cars and iPods to office buildings and machine tools, is 100% recyclable, remanufacturable, or compostable.

■ **We are borrowing the future from our children: we have to pay it back.** Our first responsibility is to leave a healthy global biosphere for our children, their children, and on into the future.

■ **We are only one of nature's wonders.** Just one of the countless species that all matter, we depend on each other in ways we cannot even imagine.

■ **Value the Earth's services.** They come free of charge to those who treasure them. Healthy ecosystems are precious and must be treated as such.

■ **Embrace variety and build community.** Harmony amid diversity is a feature of healthy ecosystems and societies.

■ **In the global village, there is only one boat, and a hole sinks us all.** Our mutual security and well-being depend on respect and concern for all. If any of us is insecure, then we all are.[2]

GLOBAL CRISIS = OPPORTUNITY FOR CHANGE

In *The Great Turning: From Empire to Earth Community*, economist David Korten refers to this crisis and opportunity as humanity's "defining moment of choice between moving ahead on a path to collective self-destruction or joining together in a cooperative effort to navigate a dramatic turn to a new human era."[3] The New Economy Working Group, co-chaired by Korten and John Cavanagh of the Institute for Policy Studies, affirms that "the current financial crisis has put to rest the myths that our economic institutions are sound. Financial failure is just the tip of the iceberg. Their grossly inefficient and unjust allocation of the resources necessary for human survival and well-being bears major responsibility for spreading social and environmental collapse."[4]

Korten's analysis looks squarely at economic and social justice linkages—an essential aspect of the emerging green economy that has been a long time coming: "Equalizing economic power and rooting it locally shifts power to people and community from distant financial markets, global corporations, and national governments. It serves to shift rewards from economic predators to economic producers, strengthens community, encourages individual responsibility, and allows for greater expression of individual choice and creativity."[5]

In contrast to the "Empire" money story, the "Earth Community Story" is where "mutual caring and support are the primary currency…Real wealth is created by investing in the human capital of productive people, the social capital of caring relationships, and the natural capital of healthy ecosystems…Markets have a vital role, but democratically accountable governments must secure community interests by ensuring that everyone plays by basic rules that internalize costs, maintain equity, and favor human-scale local businesses that honor community values and serve community needs."[6]

To ride the wind of current opportunities and changes we must summon the collective will and people power to "create a money system that serves people, community, and the whole of life. To do so we liberate our minds from the illusion of a cultural story that would have us believe that money is wealth and the making of money is synonymous with creating wealth."[7] In the long run, such a people-based system is the only one that can be sustainable.

On the skewed role of money, David Korten again: "Money is…a means of exchange [that] makes modern commerce possible and is one of the most beneficial of institutions… Money, a mere number of no inherent substance, utility, or worth created from nothing with an accounting entry when a bank creates a loan, shapes the boom and bust cycles of economic life. Its international flows determine the fate of nations. Individuals who have it in large supply enjoy lives of grand opulence in the midst of scarcity. Those who lack it face death by starvation in the midst of plenty."[8]

Bring On the New Economy!

To achieve the great transformation, the New Economy Working Group storyline implores that we demonstrate a new reality by supporting localization initiatives to rebuild "Main Street." This neighborly term refers broadly to economies made up of a collection of human-scale enterprises devoted to serving the needs of people and nature, fully accountable to the community. It is used to reframe the economic debate based on a vision of possibility, made popular through education and media outreach. We need to reduce aggregate consumption, and reform the way we measure economic performance by using health, equity, and well-being indicators. We need to support political action to convert the predatory Wall Street money system and war economy to a peace economy that provides direct benefit at the community level.

To bring our species into balance with Earth's life support system, we must reallocate our use of finite resources from harmful and non-beneficial to beneficial and more efficient uses. A just redistribution of wealth—both income and ownership—will help secure the health and general well-being of all. We won't be able to simply buy ourselves out of economic crises and environmental collapse.[9] More than stimulus and recovery programs, we need to restructure local, regional, and global rules and institutions. We can start with our own local municipalities.

"A crisis is an opportunity riding the dangerous wind."
—*Chinese proverb*

Top and Bottom: June Holte

Globalization

The four richest people in the world have more wealth than a billion of the poorest. The fortune of the 792 billionaires in the world increases by $300 to $400 billion annually. Global spending on armaments is an astounding $1 trillion per year. In 2004 $79 billion was spent on development projects worldwide, but $116 billion was paid in interest payments to the "donor countries."[10] Some economists consider this a form of global predatory lending.

The increasing concentration of financial power and economic growth hastens the destruction of the life-support system of the entire Earth. The evidence of systemic failure also includes livelihoods and jobs lost, displacement of indigenous peoples, and massive immigration. Most social and ecological costs (such as pollution) are still externalized; in other words, not paid for by the industry or consumer but by the public and the biosystem.

Brief History: Background on Globalization and Free Trade. In *Alternatives to Economic Globalization*, the International Forum on Globalization explains that "since World War II, the driving forces behind economic globalization have been several hundred global corporations and banks that have increasingly woven webs of production, consumption, finance, and culture across borders...These corporations have been aided by global bureaucracies that have emerged over the last half-century, with the result being a concentration of economic and political power that is increasingly unaccountable to governments, people or the planet and that undermines democracy, equity, and environmental sustainability."

The current banner-carrier of deregulation, the World Trade Organization (WTO) was set up to prevent obstacles to global commercial interests, effectively undermining working people, labor rights, environmental protection, human rights, consumer rights, social justice, local culture, and national sovereignty.

In order to assist the rebuilding of Europe after World War II, finance ministers and heads of corporations and banks convened in 1944 in a historic session in Bretton Woods, New Hampshire. They set up the centralized World Bank and International Monetary Fund (IMF). Devised to accelerate worldwide economic development and stabilize currency exchange rates, the IMF focused on bringing "underdeveloped" countries into the global economy. By 1948, the General Agreement on Tariffs and Trade (GATT) was regulating manufactured product trade quotas—later adding investment and corporate services trading. GATT folded into the WTO in 1995. Critics of the WTO point out that world trade rules continue to be set behind closed doors by corporate interests—circumventing democracy and excluding the most harshly impacted countries as well as all Non-Governmental Organizations (NGOs).

The Center for Food Safety reports that NAFTA, the WTO, and other "free trade" systems have "eliminated a nation's rights to protect its citizens and its natural resources while allowing multinational corporations uncontrolled and unrestricted access to a country's markets and resources...California's farmers and rural communities are disappearing; crops that once thrived and were profitable are now being plowed under; and ecosystems are collapsing at alarming rates." According to The Center for International Policy, Mexican small farmers are being driven off the land: "The World Bank reports that 73% of Mexico's rural population lives in poverty (a significant increase over the pre-NAFTA period), while the major US agribusiness transnationals have grown by leaps and bounds under the auspices of the free trade model."[11]

> "Whichever way forward is followed, the solution will require trust, not suspicion. Collaboration rather than confrontation in bilateral or multilateral relationships is required, as no country can deal with climate change alone in a globalized trade network...It is important to make sure trade is more ethical and more environmentally friendly and that the costs and benefits are more fairly distributed."[12]
> —Worldwatch Institute, *State of the World Report* (2008)

Trade agreements that deregulate corporations and financial markets, along with banking consolidation, are now widely seen as preparing the way for the recent financial crash. Affecting far more than trade, these instruments are about "eliminating the regulation of corporations, eliminating public services, and putting public assets up for sale to the highest bidder while holding governments accountable for enforcing intellectual property rights monopolies," as David Korten says. The "Old Economy" also privatizes the commons and reduces or eliminates taxes on the rich.

GLOBAL SOLUTIONS

Solutions lie in systemic change driven by individual actions, localized systems, organized communities of place and interest, and collaboration on a global scale, within the context of dramatic restructuring of global rules and institutions. The groundswell of new propositions and the expansion of long-standing models is awe-inspiring, springing from diverse levels of humanity and institutions.

From the halls of Columbia University, former World Bank chief economist Joseph Stiglitz, recipient of the 2001 Nobel Prize in Economics, chairs a UN Commission of Experts on Reforms of the International Monetary and Financial System. The group's preliminary report predicts that the global economic crisis is likely to hamper if not prevent poverty reduction. In already poor and developing countries, 200 million more people may be thrust into poverty, with 30 to 50 million more people unemployed globally in 2009 compared to 2007.[13] Stiglitz's UN Commission is calling for quick action and wide-ranging solutions that fill the gaps in current economic arrangements, tighten regulations, and establish a Global Competition Authority—along with better ways to handle the debt crisis for many developing countries.[14]

Numerous groups and economists are calling for action. You can too! Tell lawmakers what actions you support. We can start with:

■ Follow principles of UN agreements supporting human rights, labor standards, indigenous rights, and environmental protection.

Global Exchange

- Reform international finance institutions and rules. Reform the global governance framework.
- Institute responsible lending and expand debt cancellation.
- Reform corporate subsidy systems and institute corporate accountability.
- Redefine indicators of economic progress to include environmental and social impacts, and insist on transparency.
- Charge global transactions and consumption of resources as a source of funding.
- Raise an additional $100 billion per year for development projects.
- Reduce the need for natural resource extraction linked to conflict, war, and civil strife.[15]

The Citizens Trade Campaign promotes legislation in the US along these same lines to create "new rules for globalization that ensure economic security and the creation of quality jobs here, while offering opportunities for sustainable development in poor countries."[16]

Hazel Henderson, economist and producer of "Ethical Markets TV," advocates creating an economy aligned with true democratic access, resulting in a better world: "As world trade evolves into exchanging what works, as well as continuing to savor and trade cuisine, art, music, dance and literature, world trade can actually help our human family evolve toward higher levels of planetary awareness and Earth ethics."[17]

"Fair Trade" Certification

A market certification strategy, Fair Trade operates on principles that are monitored to ensure that trade relationships benefit local communities, workers, and the environment from which commodities originate. The price "premium" is set to cover costs *plus* investment in education, healthcare, and ecosystem restoration. Worker empowerment and collectives of small producers are essential components. NGOs promoting Fair Trade create online marketplaces, facilitate associations (World Fair Trade Organization and Fair Trade Federation), and provide education (Fair Trade Resource Network). To ensure that standards are met before products receive the Fair Trade stamp, a rigorous evaluation is performed by Transfair USA, or one of the 23 other members of the Fairtrade Labeling Organization International.

Forest products certification similarly helps protect forests from destruction. The Forest Stewardship Council (FSC) is one of the leaders of this market approach. There are multiple certification systems for wild harvesting of medicinal and aromatic plants, including, FSC, Fair Wild, and Organic Wild Crop.

When you buy crafts, clothes, cotton, coffee, tea, sugar, chocolate, honey, wine, bananas, or flowers—products grown under a Fair Trade certified label in many countries of Africa, Asia, or Latin America—you are making a difference in alleviating poverty and protecting ecosystems! Global Exchange reports a need for more demand to help ensure products become and stay within the Fair Trade realm.

Fair Trade works wonders. From a banana plantation in Ecuador to a tea producer in Kenya, to a cotton farmer in Mali, farmers are able to send their children to schools and health clinics they erected, rebuild bridges after a hurricane, and develop water, food storage, and sanitation systems. One African farmer said, "If the whole value chain was made fairer, Africa would be lifted out of poverty."[18]

Credit to the People, Global to Local

Microcredit is made available in tiny increments that make a huge difference in alleviating poverty in communities that need it the most. For example, the organization (and video) called Girl Effect illustrates the story of a young woman who borrows enough money for a cow in Bangladesh. With the cow, she feeds her family milk, sells the surplus, gets more cows, and sells more milk. She is so successful she gets on the village counsel, demonstrates that girls are valuable, and a whole new economic model—and cultural pattern—takes form. The organization Care shares the Girl Effect video in their work to create permanent social change by supporting women and children, who are known to suffer poverty disproportionately.

Grameen Microcredit—Inspiring Microfinance Institutions Around the World: Starting with the belief that credit is a human right, Grameen Bank (GB) lends money to people based on their potential, regardless of their level of material possessions. More than 90% of the borrowers are women, with repayment rates of 97%. GB is owned by the borrowers and provides customized credit in diverse countries, economies, and cultures. One study reports 68% of borrowers' families having crossed the line out of poverty. Higher education loans and scholarships help the next generation of Grameen families.

US President Barack Obama said of the 2006 Nobel Peace Prize recipient and Grameen founder, Muhammed Yunus, "He revolutionized banking to allow low-income borrowers access to credit...he has enabled citizens of the world's poorest countries to create profitable businesses, support their families, and help build sustainable communities. In doing so, he has unleashed new avenues of creativity and inspired millions worldwide to imagine their own potential." The Nobel Committee recognized microcredit as "an important liberating force in societies where women in particular have to struggle against repressive social and economic conditions."[19]

Creative Commons/Jeevs

A Bangladeshi receiving loan from Grameen bank.

Peer to Peer: Launched in 2005 to help alleviate poverty, Kiva provides a person-to-person micro-lending website, empowering individuals to lend directly to unique entrepreneurs around the world. Lenders can invest any amount between $25 and $10,000 to projects they directly choose online. While there's no financial return to investors, repayment rates are nearly 100%, a remarkable achievement. Loans are managed by Kiva's field partners, Micro-Finance Institutions (MFIs) that provide localized program support. Kiva expanded lending to entrepreneurs in the US in June 2009, through partnerships with Opportunity Fund and Accion USA.

"This is a moment in history when the average person has more power than at any time."
—*Katherine Fulton, president, Monitor Institute (community philanthropy)*

ENTERPRISE ECONOMICS

All over the world, millions of people are redefining relationships, literally reinventing the human within the community of life systems. Community work is vital in the creation of a counter-force to the old economy, providing an alternative or at least a measure of balance to individual pursuit. *It is likely the only way we can develop workable solutions.*

David Suzuki (*Time* Hero of the Environment) indicates that we have no reason to "maintain a conceit that we can manage our way out of the mess, increasingly with heroic interventions of technology...We've learned from past technologies—nuclear power, DDT, CFCs (chlorofluorocarbons)—that we don't know enough about how the world works to anticipate and minimize unexpected consequences...We have no choice but to address the challenge of bringing our cities, energy needs, agriculture, fishing fleets, mines, and so on into balance with the factors that support all life. This crisis can become an opportunity if we seize it and get on with finding solutions."[20]

The New Economy Working Group asserts that we need to "favor organization forms that lend themselves first to serving the community and treat financial return as a secondary consideration. The preferred models are small to medium-sized community-rooted cooperatives, worker owned, community owned, and various locally owned independent businesses." These structures can also "aggregate economic resources" through alliances of many forms, such that they "do not create concentrations of monopoly power or encourage absentee ownership."[21]

Nature's Design

Halting the push for so-called economic growth is the only way to conserve and maintain biodiversity because "as the economy grows, natural capital, such as air, soil, water, timber, and marine fisheries, is reallocated to human use via the marketplace, where economic efficiency rules." Nature's lessons suggest that we must "favor biophysical effectiveness over economic efficiency," and repair the ecosystems upon which life depends.[22]

Our Natural World Models What Works: Innovators in a relatively new field called *biomimicry* are looking closely at nature's designs and using its principles. Author Janine Benyus says: "Just as we are beginning to recognize all there is to learn from the natural world, our models are starting to blink out—not just a few scattered organisms, but entire ecosystems. A new survey by the National Biological Service found that one-half of all native ecosystems in the United States are degraded to the point of endangerment. That makes biomimicry more than just a new way of viewing and valuing nature. It's also a necessary race to the rescue."[23]

Biologists with the Biomimicry Guild help companies, cities, nonprofits, and agencies create products, processes, and policies using nature's time-tested patterns and strategies. The Biomimicry Institute promotes learning along a four-step biomimetic path: "quieting human cleverness, listening to life's genius, echoing what we learn, and giving thanks."

Products resulting from the application of biomimicry include a solar cell inspired by a leaf, self-cleaning surfaces, non-toxic dyes and adhesives, and passive home cooling. Night vision of a bat informed the design of a walking cane for blind people. Mercedes modeled the Bionic Car after the coral reef-dwelling boxfish—both have high strength for the low mass and are aerodynamically efficient.

Full Accounting

No-Waste Accounting: Enterprises seeking to be more sustainable analyze the steps along the *supply chain*, which starts with the natural resources used to make products and ends with waste (disposed of during manufacturing, delivery, consumption, and when the product wears out). That's the *linear model*, "cradle to grave." For a summary of the process, watch the Story of Stuff video, showing how the supply chain affects everything. Its simple sketches have educated both children and adults.

Improving "eco-effectiveness" requires *full-cycle accounting*, which ideally follows Cradle to Cradle[SM] design where the industrial processes don't generate waste or toxic pollution. With this model, "cyclical material flows...like the Earth's nutrient cycles, eliminating the concept of waste." Each part of a product is designed to be safe and effective, and to provide high quality resources for subsequent generations of products. All material inputs are conceived as nutrients, circulating safely and productively, so products are either completely recyclable in the "technosphere" or become biodegradable food for the biosphere.

Cradle to Cradle author William McDonough and German ecological chemist Michael Braungart are featured in the film *Waste = Food*, which illustrates how materials are "perpetually circulating in closed systems that create value and are inherently healthy and safe." The film tours a Swiss textile factory, a German clothing manufacturer, the Nike shoe headquarters, a US furniture manufacturer, a Ford Motor Company plant, and a government-housing project in China—showing how the "intelligent product system" has been adapted ("Cradle to Cradle Design Challenge").

Corporations Going Green: Incentives and Progress Measures

Progress toward a greener economy comes from consumers and businesses focused on sustainability, socially responsible investors, and corporate social responsibility, but many contend that the shift is too slow. Many doubt whether corporations publicly traded on a stock exchange can ever measure up to even the most basic definition of *sustainable development:* meeting "the needs of the present without compromising the ability of future generations to meet their own needs."[24]

Trends: Given the mandate to maximize profits for investors, publicly traded corporations tend not to invest in environmental and social considerations. Given this constraint, Seventh Generation, a pioneering distributor of safe and environmentally friendly household products, reverted back to private ownership after seven years of being publicly traded. Loss of control was a major factor cited in the decision to leave the market. The shareholder focus on short-term profitability, maximizing the value of stock, and showing corporate growth in order to attract investors were challenges to an ethic that did not center on profit.[25]

Even though Clif Bar's largest competitors, Power Bar and Balance Bar, are now owned by Nestlé and Kraft, owner Gary Erickson decided not to sell, in order to ensure that his progressive vision stays alive and the high organic standards are maintained.[26]

A pioneer in corporate sustainability, Ray Anderson, CEO of Interface Global, the largest commercial flooring company, has been paving the way up what he calls, "Mount Sustainability," since reading Paul Hawken's inspiring business manifesto, *The*

Make a living, not a killing.
—bumper sticker

Ecology of Commerce (1993). Ray Anderson relates his epiphany: "The biggest culprit is the industrial system with its take-make-waste system. The real telling point was that there is only one institute on Earth that is large enough, powerful enough, wealthy enough and pervasive enough to lead humankind out of this mess, but it's also the one doing the greatest damage—the institute of business."[27]

Many companies touting their good-will (advertising their green measures and publishing slick sustainability reports) are "really focused on reducing the unsustainability of a flawed economic development system that is increasingly based upon the addiction to commodified, material consumption," says John Ehrenfeld, Director of the International Society for Industrial Ecology. He calls for a radical transformation in thinking and action that acknowledges a "deep-seated systems failure."[28]

To make it feasible for corporations to internalize costs, they need a more level playing field, through government rules and incentives, or a different corporate structure. Otherwise, David Korten explains, they risk take-over or being "driven from the market by competitors that gain a market advantage by externalizing these costs, as, for example, Wal-Mart," which relies on cheap foreign supplies and ridiculously low wages.

Corporate Social Responsibility (CSR)

While some are working with corporations-from within or without—to promote CSR, others question the extent to which reform is possible: for example, Corporate Watch's 2006 report states that "CSR was, is and always will be about avoiding regulation, covering up the damage corporations cause to society and the environment, and maintaining public cooperation with the corporate-dominated system."[29] To institute sufficient change rapidly, they suggest strategies such as regulation, grassroots action and international solidarity, challenging and exposing corporations—and importantly, building viable alternatives to corporate-dominated society.

Still, companies making a lot of progress (and profit) report (and market) the results of "doing well by doing good." They reduce resource and energy consumption, attract green MBA graduates and investors,

satisfy green consumer demand, and avoid negative PR. Companies are adding hybrid and biodiesel vehicles to their operations,[30] reducing toxics used in manufacturing, conserving water, buying recycled plastics, and conserving energy. FedEx is finding more fuel-efficient airplanes and using smaller vehicles.[31] Reducing the use of the mail-order, with its heavy impacts, is a good strategy for consumers.

Companies "doing good" are said to be following the notion of Triple Bottom Line (TBL). Evaluating progress since he coined the term in 1994, John Elkington concluded that "the TBL agenda as most people would currently understand it is only the beginning." He recommends policies on taxation, technology, labor, corporate disclosure, and involving diverse stakeholders.[32] Governments can play a role beyond the regulatory realm by demanding that corporate goods, services, operations, and overall performance meet criteria set up through credible indicator systems,[33] including requiring companies to take full responsibility for (internalize) environmental and social costs.

Of the hundreds of initiatives that offer parameters for organizations seeking to embody sustainability, three prominent frameworks—the Earth Charter, the UN Global Compact, and the Global Reporting Initiative (GRI)—are voluntary, partnership-based frameworks derived from international norms (like the Universal Declaration of Human Rights) that help quantitatively measure adherence to CSR.[34] The Earth Charter is compatible with the UN Millennium Development Goals. CSR reports that follow the GRI disclose economic, social, and environmental impacts of a company based on 146 indicators ranging from water and energy use, waste and emissions, labor practices, product safety, human

"Tell me that story about the Garden of Eden again."

Vandana Shiva, author, leading proponent of sustainable agriculture (in lavender sari).

rights to community impacts. By 2008 there were more than 1,000 organizations worldwide (including 100 US companies) using GRI reporting guidelines, a 46% increase over 2007 participation.[35]

Corporate Watch reports that "the UN's Global Compact…is a set of nine principles on human rights, environmental sustainability and labour rights (now expanded to 10 with the inclusion of a principle on corruption).[36] Many NGOs, including the Corporate Responsibility (CORE) Coalition, are highly critical of the Compact as it has no monitoring or enforcement mechanism and so allows companies to appropriate the name of the United Nations to reinforce their reputations without requiring them to change any aspect of their activities."[37]

Investing in CSR: Ceres is a US-based network of investors and environmental and public interest groups that works with companies and investors to integrate sustainability into capital markets. Their analysis concluded that while many companies "are making progress, their actions to date are only the beginning of what is needed."[38] Among their recommendations, companies should tie compensation packages to climate performance measures.

Socially Responsible Investing (SRI) is not new. In the mid 1700s, Quakers were not allowed to have slaves, and many religious groups promoted worker health during the Industrial Revolution. Modern SRI expanded with the Civil Rights Movement

and rapidly grew in the 1980s.

A growing number of investors, pension funds, agencies, and collectives pay close attention to where their money goes. A leading source of information about SRI for the US, Green America (formed as Coop America in 1982) offers guidance, links to resources, and community investing opportunities. Green America's Green Business Network features more than 4000 carefully screened small to medium-size business members.

The Investors' Circle (IC) Foundation has many partners as well, and since 1992, IC has supported more than 200 companies with $130 million, investing in energy, health, education, and media, as well as community development and minority- or women-led enterprises. They call it *patient capital*, and a study they commissioned showed that the "buy-and-hold" strategy could yield 5-14% returns. The IC set up a new nonprofit in 2008 named after Woody Tasch's book *Inquiries into the Nature of Slow Money: Investing as if Food, Farms and Fertility Mattered*. Following on the "slow food" movement, the Slow Money Alliance aims to relocalize money and jobs, thereby countering the corporate culture's tendency toward speed, quantity, and growth. Slow Money advocates promote the expansion of Community Supported Agriculture (CSAs), as well as new structures like B Corporations, investment cooperatives, and social enterprises that combine nonprofit and for-profit goals.[39]

"The individual is forcing the change. People are shopping around, not only for the right job but for the right atmosphere. They now regard the old rules of business as dishonest, boring, and outdated. This new generation is saying, 'I want a society and a job that values me more than the gross national product. I want work that engages the heart as well as the mind and the body, that fosters friendship and that nourishes the Earth. I want to work for a company that contributes to the community.'"

—Anita Roddick, founder, The Body Shop

Greenwashing: Citizens and environmental groups who are paying attention to the corporate marketing messages warn of greenwashing and, lately, "local" washing. The US-based CorpWatch defines greenwash as "the phenomena of socially and environmentally destructive corporations, attempting to preserve and expand their markets or power by posing as friends of the environment."[41]

While there can be truth to the positive spin, the average TV-watcher is probably unaware of negative company news. For example, Chevron underwrites public TV that carries ads touting the oil giant's investments in green energy and innovation. At the same time, the international campaign seeking justice in Ecuador, Chevron-Toxico, launched by Amazon Watch, urges consumers, shareholders, and the public to take action, support the people and communities of the rainforest, and pressure Chevron to clean up. "Over three decades of oil drilling in the Ecuadorian Amazon, Chevron dumped more than 18 billion gallons of toxic wastewater into the rainforest, leaving local people suffering a wave of cancers, miscarriages and birth defects."[42] An award-winning independent documentary by Joe Berlinger, *Crude*, tells this story.

Greenpeace hosts an information, news, and action website about greenwashing that explains how consumers suspecting misleading advertising can contact the US Federal Trade Commission (FTC). Meanwhile, "Green Guides" for the "Use of Environmental Marketing Claims" are being revised by the FTC, as they evaluate terms such as "eco-friendly," "sustainable," and "carbon neutral."[43]

To help consumers evaluate marketing claims, hold businesses accountable, and stimulate the market demand for sustainable business practices, EnviroMedia Social Marketing and the University of Oregon set up a Greenwashing Index online. Users post and rate ads.

Climate Washing: The most blatant examples of this new PR trick are seen among corporations claiming to support GHG emissions reductions, while at the same time paying lobbyists and trade associations to defeat such policies and legislation. Friends of the Earth International (FOEI), known for tackling corporate greenwash, will announce "Worst Climate Lobby Awards" at "COP15" in order to highlight how corporate lobbying is delaying effective action.[44] The Corner House asserts that both financial markets and new climate markets (carbon credits trading, for example) "involve regressive redistribution and the destruction of crucial knowledge; are vulnerable to bubbles and crashes; erode notions of transparency and conflict of interest; and call into question the assumption that each and every market can be successfully regulated simply by virtue of being a market."[45]

Local Washing: Food corporations are gaining notoriety for "local washing" (Hellmans, Unilever, Frito Lay, Foster Farms), while a giant bank, HSBC, inaptly calls itself "the world's local bank." Even Wal-Mart, Winn-Dixie, and Starbucks are getting in on the local act.[46] As a result, some true localization efforts are more specific with their claims: "locally-owned and *independent* businesses." Vermont has strict rules about claims made, and other places could follow their lead using the model that Vermont has pioneered.

Researchers with the Institute for Local Self-Reliance report that communities with buy-local campaigns are faring better financially right now, and that "In city after city, independent businesses are organizing and creating the beginnings of what could become a powerful counterweight to the big-business lobbies that have long dominated public policy. Local business alliances have formed in more than 130 cities or states and together count some 30,000 businesses as members."[47] To advance localization campaigns, communities can get support from the American Independent Business Alliance and the Business Alliance for Local Living Economies (BALLE).

LOCAL SOLUTIONS
The Earth Community Economy

"The communities with the best prospect to weather the mounting forces of a perfect economic storm will be those that act now to rebuild local supply chains, reverse the trend toward conversion of farm and forest lands, concentrate population in compact communities that bring home, work, and recreation in easy reach by foot, bicycle, and public transportation, support local, low input, family farms, and seek to become substantially self-reliant in food and energy."

—David Korten,
The World We Want

Cooperation is key to building the local economy, which requires restoring caring relationships and finding common values. Sustainability advocate Chris Maser writes: "To protect the sustainability of a resident's community within a landscape, the community's requirements must be met before other considerations are taken into account; if this does not happen, no other endeavor will be sustainable…The choice of how and why we alter the Earth is ours, the adults of today. The consequence we bequeath to every child of today and beyond. How shall we choose—to protect the commons as the unconditional gift of Nature that is everyone's birthright or

---

Yes, banking *can* serve the public interest!

Government-owned banks, an option that has existed for decades, serve the public interest and are doing relatively well in the current crisis. Public banking does not suffer from the private banks' flaw, "because interest is not drawn out of the system but is returned to the public coffers. Public banking is thus mathematically sound and sustainable."

Advocating that California's governor use a public bank model to address that state's budget crisis, economist Ellen Brown explains the benefits: "Money in a *government-owned* bank could give us…all the credit-generating advantages of private banks, without the baggage cluttering up the books of the Wall Street giants." A state could deposit its vast revenues in its own bank and proceed to fan them into 8 to 10 times their face value in loans…[and] control the loan terms. The state could lend at ½% interest to itself and to municipal governments, rolling the loans over as needed until the revenues had been generated to pay them off.

Since 1919, North Dakota's revenues have been deposited in the state-owned Bank of North Dakota, enabling that state to supply low-interest loans to students, farmers, and others. It's one state not feeling the pinch of the credit crisis. Canada's Alberta Treasury Branches, initiated during the Great Depression, has been self-funded since 1938. India's banking system is 80% government-owned and is credited with keeping the country's financial industry robust at a time when the private international banks are suffering their worst crisis since the 1930s. China's state-owned bank invested in local government and state-owned enterprises "to create a real fiscal stimulus that put workers to work and got money circulating again in the economy" when external markets declined drastically.[40]

continue to fight over how we are going to carve it up for personal gain and so despoil it unto everlasting?"[48]

Bioregional solutions include learning from and applying traditions (ecological knowledge, permaculture, organic farming, appropriate technology, low-impact design, seed swaps, and other "back to the land" strategies), reclaiming community support "commons," and rebuilding the resiliency we need to adapt to change. Prevalent among rural strategies we find a restoration-based economy in natural resource sectors, such as sustainable forestry, fishing, and agriculture—including enterprises involved in urban-to-rural market linkages.

Localization is helping to restore an efficient balance between local production and global imports, and reduces local economic vulnerability. Redefining Progress (a policy think tank that created the Genuine Progress Indicator) finds that a focus on local also minimizes the negative social and environmental externalities of inefficient trade and concentrated absentee ownership in Wall Street financial institutions. Localization enhances equity and stewardship as well, when people come together to take care of one another and their environment.

Smart Revolution

Spending money in your neighborhood creates the local multiplier effect—measured in jobs, income, tax revenues, and wealth. Local businesses are essential to healthy tourism, participation in politics, charities, and social activities.[49] Michael Shuman (author of *The Small-Mart Revolution: How Local Businesses Are Beating the Global Competition* and *Going Local: Creating Self-Reliant Communities in a Global Age*) helps communities plug "leakage" of money out of the local system.

Dollars leave the community unnecessarily when imported products and services could be sourced locally. Other than new electronic devices, appliances, cars, and fossil fuel, there are few things that even a rural community could not supply its residents—provided the local independent businesses exist and are supported. The more money that circulates in an area, the more income, wealth, and jobs it generates (as opposed to being sent to some corporate headquarters). A dollar spent at a local restaurant has 25% more impact than in a chain, 60% for a re-

tail shop, and 90% for services.[50]

The Small-Mart Revolution Checklist offers 96 suggestions—ones that can save money include "honor junk," use local currency and barter systems, and rent more. Their "daily mantra" for policymakers: "Remove all public support, including anything that requires city staff time and energy, from nonlocal business and refocus it instead, laser-like, on local business."

Local Empowerment

You can help ensure public interest is served, citizens are valued, and basic human rights are met. Among "31 Ways to Jump Start the Local Economy," *YES!* magazine suggests that you:

- **Help folks cope in the crisis** and act together to create the new economy: start a **Common Security Club** in your faith community or neighborhood.
- **Reach out** to groups that are organizing people on the frontlines of the crisis, like Jobs with Justice and Right to the City.
- **Keep your energy dollars circulating locally.** Launch a clean energy cooperative to install wind turbines or solar roofs, and to weatherize homes and businesses.
- **Declare an end to corporate personhood** in your community.

Communities demanding to decide for themselves what industry and outside corporations can or cannot do have passed ordinances that ban destructive practices. For example, three communities in Maine have done it. With the help of the Community Environmental Legal Defense Fund, the entire town of Barnstead, New Hampshire, passed an ordinance in 2006. To keep out-of-state sludge dumping and corporate feedlots from taking over small farmland, more than 100 communities in Pennsylvania have passed ordinances to protect themselves where regulations did not.[51]

Community-Friendly Enterprises

The Small-Mart blog offers information on legal structures for stimulating investment in local businesses and entrepreneurs, including micro-lending and cooperatives.[52] Besides finance, food, and energy sectors, local economic development can focus on recycled and reclaimed products, entertain-

ment, and healthy lifestyle and services.

Social enterprises focus on public benefit and community service—where the financial return is a means for meeting the community needs rather than private profit. The Social Enterprise Alliance of Midlothian in Scotland includes business-like enterprise, cooperatives, and credit unions, as well as traditional nonprofits, in their definition of social enterprise.

Associations of small businesses and entrepreneurs are more resilient than individual competitors. For example, farms can cooperate in community-supported agriculture programs (CSA) offering a wider variety of products to their customers under one umbrella—adding value to the benefits of individual farm CSAs. Limited liability partnerships are a newer model than consumer, producer and worker cooperatives, are fairly flexible, and can combine aspects of cooperatives with other goals.

"Good society" advantages of innovative locally-owned enterprises, according to the National Center for Economic and Security Alternatives, include their emphasis on democratic values, accountability, and local control of assets, and capital that stays around. This group tracks many emerging forms of community-rooted, asset-building institutions and enterprises such as community development financial institutions (CDFIs), municipal and nonprofit enterprise, urban land trusts, and local currency and barter systems.

Community-Wealth.Org hosts a directory of community-building resources, covering many types of financial institutions and municipal initiatives, socially responsible investing, partnerships, transportation-oriented development, and more. For example, a 2006 survey found nonprofit community development corporations (CDCs) to be responsible for developing more than 86,000 affordable housing units and 8.75 million square feet of commercial and industrial space a year.[53] CDCs now number around 4,600 in the US, growing from a handful in the late 1960s, and there are approximately 11,000 worker-owned firms (ESOPs).[54]

There's no shortage of creative ideas and opportunities, particularly when groups join forces to use tried and true principles with the new wave of expanded technology applications. For example, David Korten suggests that the Consumer Cooperatives Management Association "think about an alliance between the cooperatives movement and the green jobs movement."[55]

COOPERATIVES
Membership-Based Banking and Business

One member, one vote. —A co-op principle

Cooperatives subscribe to seven principles: voluntary and open membership; democratic member control; member economic participation; autonomy and independence; education, training and information; cooperation among cooperatives; and concern for community. The three main types of cooperatives are consumer cooperatives (including credit unions and food coops), producer cooperatives (such as agricultural producers), and employee-owned.

Credit unions, local member-owned and democratically governed, invest in their members and communities while offering standard banking services. In a recent innovation, credit unions in South Carolina, Texas, and Alberta and British Columbia offer Living Young and Free services, information, and a social network for members (or anyone) 25 years or younger, so they can discover that "banking doesn't have to suck."[56]

The World Council of Credit Unions, with 177 million individual members served by 49,000 credit unions in 96 countries, is among a growing number of institutions that have revolutionized micro-enterprise finance to improve incomes in the developing countries. To raise awareness about the challenges that women face daily in accessing financial and other resources, the Council's Global Women's Leadership Initiative works in partnership with the Canadian Co-operative Association that was started in 1909.

The International Cooperative Alliance (ICA), with 223 member organizations from 87 countries, representing 800 million people who participate in the cooperative movement, reports that even in the financial sector, locally controlled, fiscally conservative credit unions and cooperative banks are faring well. The rate of new co-op formation of all varieties is rising.[57]

In rural Mississippi, Winston County Self Help Cooperative brings small farmers and landowners together to overcome adversities. When they started in 1985, "small family farmers were under siege due to unfavorable financial conditions and USDA's lack of interest in serving black farmers, [who] needed an outlet to earn more income from products..."

Small farmers and landowners sell and buy in bulk, and adopted a mantra of "Saving Rural America" to emphasize the stewardship of their natural resources. Key partners include the Federation of Southern Cooperatives and Heifer International, supporting long-range planning and farm diversification. University Extension and cost-share incentives from the Natural Resource Conservation Service also help.

INNOVATIVE COMMUNITY DEVELOPMENT BANKS

"Communities cannot achieve economic prosperity if entrepreneurial activities and residents' health are compromised by toxins in the land, air and water, or if natural resources are consumed in an unsustainable way."

—*ShoreBank Corporation*

To create economic equity and a healthy environment, one of the oldest Community Development Banks, ShoreBank, headquartered in Chicago, invests proceeds from their traditional banking services to support borrowers who "convert deteriorated apartment buildings into income-producing properties, expand their small businesses, and upgrade their homes and property" in Chicago, Detroit, and Cleveland.[58]

By lending to "local companies that use energy efficiently, reduce waste and pollution, and conserve natural resources," ShoreBank Pacific fulfills its goal of "creating a conservation economy in the rainforest of the Pacific Northwest."[59] Their nonprofit subsidiary, ShoreBank Enterprise Cascadia (SBEC), covering enterprises that don't qualify for bank loans, invests money and expertise in sustainable farming, toxic cleanup, green building, child care, substance abuse, and affordable housing. SBEC

Left: Woodshanti, Middle: Rainbow Grocery, Right: Scott Braley, Courtesy of Inkworks Press

The Network of Bay Area Worker Cooperatives is a grassroots organization dedicated to building workplace democracy in the San Francisco Bay Area and beyond. Members include Woodshanti (left), Rainbow Grocery (middle), and Inkworks Press (right).

bigstockphoto.com

helps protect habitats by supporting value-added production that enables harvesters to afford coastal projection.

Lakota Funds

Modeled after the Grameen Bank microcredit structure (see "Global Solutions"), Lakota Funds serves the Oglala Lakota Oyate (People) on the Pine Ridge Indian Reservation (South Dakota) with business loans, technical assistance, leveraged funding from outside sources, and facilitation for groups of borrowers. This first Native American Community Development Financial Institution helps to break the cycle of poverty. When Lakota Funds started there were only two Native American-owned businesses on the reservation. Eighty-five percent of borrowers had never had a checking or saving account; seventy-five percent had never had a loan; and ninety-five percent had no business experience. Today there are over 328 licensed businesses.

Small Is Beautiful

One of the earliest "ecological economy" voices, E. F. Schumacher wrote the classic *Small Is Beautiful: Economics As If People Mattered* (1973). He knew that nature can only handle so much pollution, and the focus on rapid output of consumer products through advancing technology based on non-renewable fossil fuel was destructive and unsustainable.

Developed by The E.F. Schumacher Society, the Self-Help Association for a Regional Economy (SHARE) is a nonprofit membership organization that partners with a local bank to offer microcredit loans at manageable interest rates to businesses that are often considered "high risk" by traditional lenders. The bank makes the loans and han-

dles the accounting, but the lending decisions, based on a unique set of social, ecological, and financial criteria established by SHARE, are made by the community of depositors, thus increasing their sense of responsibility.

A multi-program organization, the Society uses Community Land Trusts to foster "common land ownership…[that] remove[s] land from the speculative market." The Society also developed a local currency called BerkShares as a "tool for community empowerment, enabling merchants and consumers to plant the seeds for an alternative economic future for their communities."

EARTH ECONOMY TIPS

■ Consume wisely:
  • Pay cash and shop at local independent stores; buy locally made/grown items
  • Join a cooperative and shop there; support worker-owned companies.
  • Favor companies in the *National Green Pages*, and get tips from Green America.
  • Ask for Fair Trade, FSC, and other third-party-accredited certified products.
■ Support or start a local BALLE affiliate network.
■ Support local currency, timeshares, barter, and other local economic innovations.
■ Use a local community development bank or credit union.
■ See greenwash? Report it to the FTC and post on the Greenwashing Index at the University of Oregon.
■ Invest well:
  • Become a micro-lending investor.
  • See the Microcredit Primer of microcredit resources and links from kbyutv.org.
  • See Green America's *Investing in Communities* guide.
  • Find a mutual fund through the Social Investment Forum's directory.
■ Get longer lists of tips from:
  • *Global to Local: What You Can Do*—www.IFG.org.
  • *YES!* Magazine.
  • *Better World Handbook*.
  • The Small-Mart Revolution.
  • Sierra Club's *Green Life* tips.
  • Earth Day tips: Earth911.com.
  • National Geographic's *Green Guide*.

Part Six **COMMUNITY**

LIVING WELL TOGETHER: Growing and Nurturing Strong Communities

A too highly developed individualism can lead to a debilitating sense of isolation so that you can be lonely and lost in a crowd… *Ubuntu* speaks to the essence of being human. The solitary individual is, in our understanding, a contradiction in terms.

—Archbishop Desmond Tutu

"You need other people in order to be. You need other beings in order to be…you also need sunshine, river, air, trees, birds, elephants, and so on. So it is impossible to be by yourself, alone. You have to 'inter-be' with everyone and everything else."

—*Thich Nhat Hanh, Buddhist monk and peace activist*

Every community can be part of the worldwide sustainability movement! What is emerging in Lexington, Kentucky, exemplifies what is possible and what is, in fact, emerging in communities everywhere. With the multitudes of environmental initiatives, urban gardening programs, and other sustainability projects that have emerged in recent years, the challenge is how to coordinate, how to connect the fragmented dots, how to surrender our disconnected efforts to the magic of synergistic and integrated systems. Sustainlex.org, formed in 2005, is guided by four principles: environmental stewardship (the foundation), economic prosperity, community empowerment/involvement, and social equity. These provide the framework for bringing together previously disparate elements of what Paul Hawken calls "the movement that doesn't yet know itself as a movement." The network includes education, government, business, faith, and community-based efforts. Integrating these initiatives has been enhanced by the creation of the Bluegrass Partnership for a Green Community.

"Never doubt that a small group of thoughtful, committed people can change the world. Indeed, it is the only thing that ever has."

—*Margaret Mead, cultural anthropologist*

Bringing the Wisdom of the Community Together

Social process may be conceived either as the opposing battle of desires with the victory of one over the other, or as the *confronting and integrating of desires*. The former means non-freedom for both sides, the defeated bound to the victor, the victor bound to the false situation thus created—both bound. The latter means a freeing for both sides and increased total power or increased capacity in the world" (Mary Parker Follett).

How do we begin to come together and create the future based on this emerging "ancient future" wisdom of interconnectedness and sufficiency? How do we organize ourselves *in* and *as* community around issues of sustainability? How do we do so in a fair and inclusive way? There are dozens of initiatives for working together toward a sustainable future, in community: *coming together in unity*. Explore tools for embodying community from the perspective of the oneness—tools of co-creation, co-intelligence, building united vision, and healing through communication.

Foundational to growing successful community-based initiatives are skills for *integrating voices and desires/needs:* communicating clearly, sharing power, collaboration, and honoring diversity of culture, background and skill. Tom Atlee's *The Tao of Democracy* provides an overview of many excellent tools, exercises, frameworks, and resources for all of these areas. Non-Violent Communication is a simple, profound method that provides a needs-based way of transforming what is possible through communication. Another practice for building human connections is Relational Presence. A consensus-based process for self-organizing groups is Sociocracy (aka "Dynamic Governance"). Other group process approaches worth investigating include Open Space Technology, and Dynamic Facilitation.

How do we link groups of people who want to make changes toward sustainable living? It's really as simple as starting a series of conversations, as exemplified in the initiatives highlighted here. Many effective models are emerging for rapidly diffusing the knowledge, skills, tools, and support needed for broad-scale, systematic community change. Each uses some version of the time-honored format of self-organizing circles of 8-12 people who meet regularly, linked together to build momentum and broader impacts. Over 200,000 people have participated in the eight Northwest Earth Institute discussion courses, whose orientation is education. Empowerment Institute offers five distinct empowerment-based, team-oriented programs for creating sustainable lifestyles and communities. Be the Change Circles offer study-action-support groups with a variety of curricula, as well as periodic symposia and quarterly gatherings. This is a great way to stay engaged and continue to educate yourself on the issues, so that you can be an effective agent of change.

For those wanting to clarify just what their own unique role is in the Great Turning, What's Your Tree? offers circle-courses to support participants in finding and acting on their purpose, passion, and personal power, within a growing network of others likewise engaged. The Center for Partnership Studies offers tools to create a Partnership Community, a group of people committed to facilitating the emerging shift to a Partnership society, and the Real Wealth Community Project, training dozens of leaders to engage their various communities in lively discussions about creating an economic system that values people who do the work of caring for others and a sustainable planet.

Founded in the UK, Transition Towns[1] are a system for communities to organize in response to peak oil and climate change, through a structured process, resulting in a community-defined, community-implemented 15- to 20-year "Energy Descent Action Plan." Links to resources, toolkits and a growing network of 227 Transition communities in 15 countries are available. One Transition group in Washington started simply with "Potlucks With a Purpose," and has grown to over 300, with a *LETS* (Local Exchange Trading System) of over 160, along with The Whidbey Community Exchange, and Whidbey Island Food Asset Mapping Project. They offer a "Re-Skilling Digest" of many practical self-reliance classes, workshops, and tours.

---

12 Steps to Becoming a Transition Town (TT)

1. **Steer the Transition.** You need a core group of people to "drive the project forward during the initial stages."

2. **Raise Awareness.** Teach and learn about Peak Oil and Climate Change from experts; screen key movies; get media attention.

3. **Lay the Foundations.** Network, build alliances and honor the existing groups.

4. **Stage a Great Unleashing Event.** Launch the TT Initiative into the broader community.

5. **Form Working Groups.** Invite the "collective genius of the community" to focus on specifics: food, waste, energy, youth, transport, water, economics, education, and local government.

6. **Use Open Space.** Transition Network folks find Open Space Technology effective for running meetings.

7. **Be Visible.** Actions attract people. Plant trees. Do something beyond the planning talk.

8. **Share Skills.** Relocalization includes learning skills in gardening, repairing, insulating, etc.

9. **Build a Bridge to Local Government.** Explore planning coordination.

10. **Honor the Elders.** Learn from the past and develop connections.

11. **Let It Go Where It Wants to Go**…Be flexible. Inventive solutions will emerge from a focus on "building community resilience and reducing the carbon footprint."

12. **Create an Energy Descent Plan.** Form working groups for key aspects of planning and management, and create integrated action plan.

—Adapted from the *Transition Initiatives Primer*

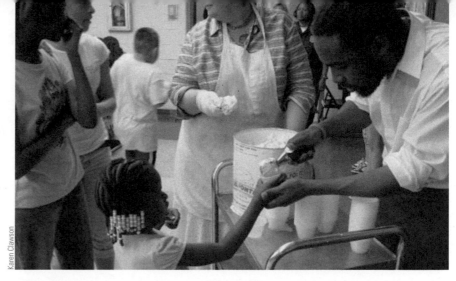

GROWING COMMUNITIES

Land Use and Local Government

"When we see the land as community to which we belong, we may begin to use it with love and respect."

—Aldo Leopold,
author, **A Sand County Almanac**

Re-visioning how we relate to and utilize the land is foundational to creating a sustainable future. From there, we must learn how to work with local and state government to influence land-use policies and practices.

The Institute for Sustainable Communities (ISC) is an example of resources available for learning to successfully work with local government. They helped the people of Moss Point, Mississippi, recover from the devastation of Hurricane Katrina, working with city officials to create a neighborhood advisory committee, making sure neighborhoods were represented in the city-rebuilding planning processes.

For planning building and development that meets sustainability criteria, check out The Urban Land Institute and the Project for Public Spaces (PPS). Smart Communities offers support and success stories for both renovating existing structures and building new ones. Partners for Livable Communities has an "Aging in Place" initiative, developed to help US communities become places that are good to grow up and grow old in.

Whether you are a landowner interested in protecting property from future development, or a citizen wanting to mobilize your community in support of protecting undeveloped land, Land Trust Alliance can direct you to opportunities in your locale. An example of success in such action is western North Carolina's Blue Ridge Forever initiative, where thirteen organizations joined to protect 50,000 acres of land and water through agreements and acquisitions.

Many communities are implementing sustainable economic alternatives, such as Time Banks, and Local Exchange Trading Systems (LETS). Concepts such as "cooperative cooking" and "supper swapping" can be explored on GreenAmericaToday.org.[2] Green America recommends creating a neighborhood Home Repair Team, where members contribute time and talent to each others' home projects. The Business Alliance for Local Living Economies (BALLE) is building a vast international network of communities, bringing together small business leaders, investors, entrepreneurs, development professionals, government officials, social innovators, and community leaders to build local living economies. Their Living Economy Principles are an excellent roadmap for sustainable communities.

"A person's heart away from nature becomes hard…lack of respect for growing living things soon leads to lack of respect for humans, too."

—Lakota proverb

Sometimes community planning is undertaken to start from the ground up, as in Arcosanti, in the high desert of Arizona, "built to embody a fusion of architecture with ecology." **Intentional Community** is an inclusive term for eco-villages, co-housing, residential land trusts, communes, urban housing cooperatives, and other planned communities where people live together with a common vision. The mission of *Communities* magazine is "creating and enhancing community in the workplace, in nonprofit or activist organizations, and in neighborhoods."

Three Model Communities

Sirius, *Shutesbury, Massachusetts*. Modeled after Scotland's Findhorn community, Sirius was established in 1978 on ninety acres, and is home for 30 community members. Seminars and certifications in permaculture and green building are offered regularly. Governance is by consensus. Buildings utilize passive solar construction, non-toxic materials, composting toilets, and solar and wind electricity. Vegetable oil powers vehicles. Gardening is organic both on the grounds and in the greenhouse, and meals are shared. What little food they do not grow is purchased in bulk, and all scraps are composted. "Ecology comes from a deep inner sense of the sacredness of life. We want people to have a deep experience so they will alter their life patterns."[3]

Hammarby Sjöstad, *Stockholm, Sweden*. This former industrial brownfield was developed to be an environmental role model. Author Bill McKibben writes that in this community residents "live half again as lightly as the average Swede, who is already among the most ecologically minded citizens of the developed world…the level calculated to be sustainable for all the world's six billion humans."[4] Garbage is almost eliminated, with combustibles burned to produce heat and electricity and food remains composted. Wastewater has multiple lives: the sewage treatment plant separates liquids and sludge; sludge produces biogas to fuel kitchen stoves and buses, as well as fertilizer for farms. Treated wastewater goes into radiators, heating apartments. As the water cools, it is used to cool office computer rooms and grocery store coolers.[5] The City Project Manager says that "75% of Hammarby's sustainability is integrated into buildings and infrastructure—the remaining 25% is up to the residents themselves." The "Hammarby Model" has been exported to Russia, England, and China.[6]

Los Angeles Ecovillage (LAEV). *Los Angeles, California*. Some 500 people live in this two-block working-class neighborhood near downtown LA. After the 1992 civil unrest in Los Angeles several people began to transform their own troubled neighborhood. The first three years (1993–1996) were about building trust and a sense of safety, planting trees and small gardens, and acquiring property. The first purchase was a 40-unit apartment building, with a community revolving loan fund. Substantial renovations were done, mostly by training residents, and utilizing the best sustainable and recycled materials available. One unit is used as a "common house" for gatherings, and another is for bicycle parking. Residents without cars get a $25 rent discount.

They were among the first LA apartments to set up an extensive recycling program, influencing neighbors to recycle as well. To further "re-use," residents put items no longer needed on a "free table." A self-help bicycle repair shop called "The Bicycle Kitchen" started in the kitchen of one of the apartment units. "The Food Lobby," an organic food-buying coop, minimizes waste through bulk produce and grocery purchases. Composting is part of everyday life in LA Ecovillage, and the neighborhood now showcases several water-harvesting permaculture gardens. A variety of small business start-ups provide livelihood for several neighbors, including fair-trade coffee, vegan chocolates, and custom bike building companies.

Food and Meals

The ultimate in eating locally is to grow it yourself! Even apartment dwellers can participate. To start, join, or help defend a community garden, The American Community Gardening Association offers practical advice. Food Not Lawns offers educational, organizational, and hands-on services to support transitioning from lawns to home grown food.

Local Food: How to Make It Happen in Your Community, by Tamzin Pinkerton, is the first in a series of how-to books, based on wisdom gained by Transition Towns from around the world. Larger-scale community efforts to make quality food available across the social spectrum include Food Not Bombs, an all-volunteer organization where local groups recover food that

would otherwise be thrown out and make free, fresh, hot vegan and vegetarian meals served outside in public spaces. "Farm Fresh Choice," a program of Berkeley, California's Ecology Center, supports healthy local agriculture as well as the health of poorer citizens nearby. Fresh, organic fruit and veggies are purchased wholesale from growers at Berkeley Farmers Market, then sold at wholesale to residents at markets set up near schools and childcare centers.

Re-imagining Sustainable Culture

Community-based arts and cultural organizations supported by the Ford Foundation are revitalizing neighborhoods by partnering with traditional community development groups to build common vision, create tolerance and respect, and boost economic prospects in rapidly changing underserved neighborhoods. A key goal of the Shifting Sands Initiative of Culture Shapes Community is to accumulate best practices that highlight a new role for arts and culture groups in community development, through programs supporting social integration across race and class, upward economic mobility, neighborhood identity, and civic engagement.

Beginning and Ending: Home birth, midwives, and dulas have long been an option for healthy childbirth. TheMatrona. com has been "promoting quantum midwifery and undisturbed birth in the global village since 2001." And while good cooperative childcare models are easily found, far fewer cooperative elder care models exist. Green burial is also gaining recognition as a final testimony to the impact we can have on the environment. Kim Zorn's Green Casket Company offers beautiful, 100% biodegradable pine coffins, and Carol Motley's Bury Me Naturally even offers 100% recycled cardboard coffins!

Taking Care: Based on the psychology of interdependence, Gentle Teaching International trains caregivers and companions of those who have inherent vulnerabilities, such as extreme poverty, homelessness, mental disability or illness, focusing on being kind, nurturing and loving.

Waste Not, Want Not: Among our most overlooked natural resources are the skills honed by our elders, especially those who lived through the Great Depression.

Since the economic downturn of 2008, an increasing number of individuals and families are returning to the practices and perspective of an older generation, who conserved in every respect, cultivating ingenuity, resourcefulness, and commitment to community. Sharing labor, food, child and elder care, along with enjoyment of simple (often free) pleasures, supports the well-being of individuals and families, but also builds a strong sense of community.

YOUTH-LED ACTIVISM

"You are brilliant and the Earth is hiring."
—*Paul Hawken, to the graduating class of 2009, University of Portland*

From the coal fields of Appalachia to liquid gas terminals in California, young people are reclaiming their communities and the planet. Ivan Stiefel and Erica Fernandez became just two of many young *Eco-Heroes* by following the path of their hearts. Young people who similarly feel the call to right an injustice or stand up for something they love will find venues across the globe where they can collaborate, jam, query, network, and gain skills to work the media, and organize powerfully. The *Resource* section in this book lists a number of them.

Ivan Stiefel: No Clean Coal in Appalachia

Observing a persistent, convulsive cough of a loved one who came from West Virginia coal country led Ivan Stiefel to create an alternative to beaches and beer for college spring break destinations: Mountain Justice Spring Break (MJSB). Students met with people in coal communities, held workshops on mountaintop removal mining, coal slurry injection, the toxic coal cycle, the connection between poverty, and the destruction of the local environment. Students learned media outreach, campus and community

organizing, and building bridges with communities of faith.

MJSB 2007 focused on securing a new, safe school for Marshfork Elementary, sited next to a coal silo, a coal processing plant, a leaking coal slurry impoundment, and mountaintop removal mines. The Mines appeal board released a decision for a second coal silo to be built next to the school. Students and community members conducted a sit-in at the Governor's office; the occupation ended with 13 being arrested, including Ivan, but no commitment from the Governor to build a new school.

In 2008 students blocked American Municipal Power from building a fifth coal-fired power plant in an area with some of the highest cancer rates in the country. In Wise County, Virginia, one of the most heavily strip-mined counties in the country, students joined residents in pressuring the Virginia Dept of Environmental Quality to deny Dominion Power the permit for a coal-fired plant—and they ultimately won! Ivan's efforts contributed to decisions by the US EPA to delay action on 79 mountaintop coal mining projects (EPA Takes on the Coal Industry 2009), and to halt the Clean Water Act permit for the nation's largest proposed mountaintop removal coal mining site in West Virginia.

Erica Fernandez: Triumph over LNG

Erica came from a conservative Mexican family where girls were taught not to speak up, but at 16, she was the most riveting speaker at the California State Lands Commission hearing on the BHP Billiton Liquid Natural Gas (LNG) project.

LNG is primarily methane, chilled to minus 260 degrees. Methane is 23 times more potent as a greenhouse gas than carbon dioxide. Three-foot-wide pipelines carrying LNG through residential communities are at risk of rupture and explosion from corrosion, metal fatigue, manufacturing defects, leakage, human error, earthquakes, and terrorist sabotage. Accidents have occurred worldwide from Cleveland to Algeria.

Shortly after moving to California at age 12, Erica volunteered at beach cleanups, and joined with adults working to delay the LNG project. To get low-income Latinos active, in whose neighborhood the pipeline would go, Erica posted flyers and spoke everywhere, galvanizing thousands, demonstrating what one person can do.

The result of Erica's three years of work? Agencies and the Governor nixed the multinational corporation's project in May 2007. Erica is currently collaborating with Mexican students and concerned adults on 350.org.

GREEN BUILDING
A Green Village Begins with Green Homes

Imagine being outside in winter with holes in your pockets and rips in your garments, money and body heat leaking out with each passing moment. Our buildings squander precious resources in much the same way. Enhancing energy efficiency is a big step in greening our homes.

We spend 90% of our lives inside buildings.[7] They are akin to a body, as a coordinated system[8] which protects and keeps us warm. The future will see *smart buildings* responding so seamlessly to our sweat, our shivers, our need for hot water and other shelter-related details, that we will view our present-day programmable thermostats as we now do our phonographs.[9] But right now we need those thermostats, along with every other technology available, from ancient (plugging the leak and facing the sun), to modern (solar panels and *whole-house switches*[10]), to combinations of both (geothermal applications with vast swaths of urban green roof "prairies"). We also need *major* investment—public and private—in commercial building retrofits.

Green building is a phrase with wings so wide it covers everything from the practical (adding insulation), to the visionary (the Cellophane house[11]), to building entirely new communities from scratch (Greensburg, and Eco City).[12]

"Green, or sustainable, building refers to a set of new construction practices that consider energy and resource use; environmental and site impact; product and building durability; and the impact of the built environment on occupant health and safety." Considered "through every step of the design and construction process," a home's negative impact on people and planet is reduced.[13]

"Retrofitting existing houses to achieve a two- to three-fold reduction in energy use is necessary if we are to achieve the emissions reductions scientists say are required for avoiding catastrophic climate change."

—*BuildingGreen, publishers of* **Environmental Building News**

SEVEN STEPS TO A SUSTAINABLE BUILDING

1. **Siting** and **orientation** are the greatest gifts for a high-performance building.[18]

2. **Energy Efficiency.** Good insulation, low-energy lighting and appliances. **Water.** Hardy landscaping, low-flow devices, and awareness of water usage.

3. **Natural Light, Heating, and Cooling.** Windows and skylights provide daytime light, while thermal mass, overhangs, and ventilation help you stay comfortable. Once installed, it's free energy.

4. **Indoor Environmental Quality.** Balance a tight building envelope against need for fresh air; avoid products that outgas,[19] such as some paint and particle board.

5 **Recycled and Renewable Materials.**

6. **Solar and Wind.**

7. **Regenerative/Adaptive** uses technologies that positively respond to the greater environment.

Creative Commons/Green For All

Taking Stock

Energy audits are available at low cost in almost every state. Save up to 40% on your power bill by simply sealing leaks and insulating ducts and furnaces.[20] Identify problems, prioritize, then retrofit. A retrofit can be as low-cost as adding some insulation, as significant as adding a geothermal system. Your climate, site, budget, DIY skills, and green builder availability will drive your process.

Most areas of the country have local experts (profit and nonprofit) who are eager to advise. The US Green Building Council serves as a clearinghouse for technologies old and new, and points toward experts and forums on retrofits and new construction, whether you want simple tips on weatherization, solar hot water, or a cutting-edge heating/cooling system. Its global counterpart, the World Green Building Council, has chapters from Croatia to Brazil. California's Flex Your Power website has step-by-step instructions on affordable ways to retrofit your house, with do-it-yourself videos hot-linked. The EPA's sustainability website and Treehugger have additional resources for home energy efficiency.

The US Department of Energy Weatherization Assistance Program has been helping low-income families for 30 years. The program got a major boost in 2009 with

$5 billion issued to state programs.[21] At the other end of the financial spectrum, sample some of the incredible homes on Planet Green TV's "Ultimate Green Homes" or in a copy of *Dwell* magazine, for fun.

"Architects and designers can save money up front...by incorporating good *thermal bypass mitigation* techniques right from the beginning," says green designer Armando Cobo. *Thermal bypass* is conditioned air seeping out of your dwelling, which kicks on your HVAC and ratchets up fossil-fuel use and GHGs. Net-zero status—no greenhouse gas emissions and off-the-grid power—is most attainable when built into the design itself.

Leading-edge green prefabs, such as Warren Buffet's Clayton Homes, are

---

Between 2000 and 2005, electricity bills have gone up approximately 20%, fuel oil, 50%; and natural gas, more than 60%. Energy costs are expected to continue to rise, so the investments in both energy efficiency and conservation have increasingly shorter payback periods.[26]

---

becoming more available as affordability is addressed in design.[22] A 1500-square-foot modern jewel-box prefab that you'll cherish won't cost more than a 2500-square-foot McMansion with rooms you'll heat and cool but never use. From affordable to high-end luxury, well-designed smaller buildings feel and function better than cavernous spaces.[23]

The Rocky Mountain Institute states the obvious: "**Efficiency first, and then renewables**. Do everything you can to cut power usage and then supply what's still needed with renewable energy sources."

There are several rating systems in use for green buildings: Energy Star/Green Star, LEED (Leadership in Energy and Environmental Design), and BREEAM (the UK's Building Research Establishment Environmental Assessment Method).[24] LEED's thorough checklist of green building components is often linked to US tax incentives,[25] and LEED certification raises property values and is increasingly coveted by residential and commercial real estate investors.

Greener Housing for All

All over the country municipalities, nonprofits, and incentive-driven private companies are building green affordable housing. Tassafaronga is an award-winning 7-acre community in Oakland, California, full of affordable green dwellings and community spaces. Phase 2 will include a former pasta factory being green renovated for people living with AIDS.[27]

New Orleans, devastated by Hurricane Katrina, has become an experiment in green building. Habitat for Humanity, Global Green, Home Depot, and Brad Pitt's Make It Right Foundation are working diligently to build the town back green, with an emphasis on affordable housing.[28] Holy Cross village, in the Lower 9th Ward, has become a workshop for green building as it constructs homes and trains local builders.[29]

Federally, Housing and Urban Development (HUD)[30] is spending $500 million in recovery act grants to add affordable rental housing and to green existing public housing. Internationally, Architecture for Humanity is addressing innovative sustainable disaster housing and longer-term solutions.[31] As Australian UN ambassador Hugh Jackman commented: "You can't separate the issues of climate change and poverty. They are inextricably linked." He points out that greenhouse gas emissions from developed nations have brought on many of the grave problems that developing countries face, creating a profound ethical obligation. On World Habitat Day (in October), we are asked to "reflect on the state of human settlements and the basic right to adequate shelter for all."[32]

Commercial building retrofit costs are off the charts when compared to residential. In his cautionary screed, "Losing Money Through the Walls," Arthur Schlender says, "We're a motivated company with [a track record that] puts us at the forefront of the sustainability movement. And yet we're having trouble fixing just one of our buildings. We [need] a comprehensive national program to finance this work...cobbled together through government, nonprofit, and foundation. [The] vast majority of building owners, no matter how well-intentioned, will sit on their hands. We need a program that literally pays for a portion of these retrofits, donating cash so that the return on investment becomes acceptable, or at least so the price of the fix isn't prohibitive. This program has to happen soon; almost instantly. Scientists are telling us we have a decade to replace the inefficient infrastructure that is hobbling our climate. They are speaking, in part, about our buildings—about the building you're sitting in right now."[33]

Passive Survivability? When the power and water go out, how long would you be able to stay alive in the house or apartment you live in? The question points to **passive survivability,** a concept introduced in *Environmental Business News* in 1995. Tom Whipple of the *Falls Church News-Press* reminds us that "the temperature, moisture, and even the oxygen content of the air we breathe are all kept at acceptable levels by—you guessed it—energy. Take away the energy and, under some circumstances, a cave, tent, or even sitting under a big tree might be preferable to being indoors."[34]

"Cooling-load avoidance strategies, shades on the southwestern windows of the Langston High School & Community Center in Arlington, Virginia, help maintain livable thermal conditions in a building even when the power goes out."[35] As we retrofit existing buildings and build new,

this feature should be required in standard design for our schools, hospitals, and homes, and should take a place on the LEED list.

Greener schools save precious dollars. Sustainably built pre-fab classrooms by Toby Long, of Clever Homes, are now part of the New High School Project.[36] These can be retrofitted as residences, with 300 square feet of glazing, clerestory windows (a band of windows at the top of a high wall), radiant flooring, recycled wallboard, and non-formaldehyde insulation. Even though pricey, initially, they pay for themselves over time in re-use potential and energy savings.

The passive solar system of North Carolina's Durant Middle School saves $50,000 a year in energy costs.[37] Nevada plans to replicate a green school prototype across the state, using *integrated design* to reduce energy consumption by 50% and construction costs by 20%.[38] An addition to the Da Vinci Arts Middle School in Portland, Oregon, uses skylights and a diffuser to avoid using electric lights during the day.[39]

Greening Government Buildings

The Big House: A LEED platinum White House? As a protected historic building there are limitations, but they're working on it. Smart switches, low-emitting finishes, window films, green cleaners, and recycled equipment are all in the works.[40]

The other "Big House": In Washington State, prisons are saving millions in energy costs via retrofits. Might they spend the savings on rehabilitation and training for sustainable jobs? In 2009, a federal prison in Butner, North Carolina, became the first to achieve LEED certification. Besides saving money, architect Ken Ricci says green design is a "plus for a population that's confined 24 hours a day. Environment cues behavior." Incarcerated individuals are more likely to re-enter the world less damaged and angry if they have been treated humanely in sustainable environments, making the world a safer place for all. Removing freedom is punishment enough. Let in the daylight, reduce the noise, create gardens and green jobs.[41] Reducing the number of people locked up for petty crimes must take place simultaneously at the policy level. Fewer prisons = less energy needed, and a huge leap in our collective ethics and humanity.[42]

GREENING CITIES

The *New Yorker*'s David Owen dubs NYC "the greenest community in America" for reasons including its density, shared walls (easier to heat), and high use of public transportation.[43] If GHG emissions can be stemmed using green roofs, efficient buildings, and commercial retrofits (like the $500 million retrofit planned for the iconic Empire State Building[44]), our densest city can maximize its strengths. Policy initiatives under Mayor Bloomberg's tenure have stimulated public and private green investment.[45] Cities across the country like Portland, Chicago, Austin, Seattle, San Francisco, and urban centers in more traditionally conservative states like Texas and North Carolina are all seeing green.[46]

In Washington, DC, GreenHOME aims to make our nation's capital a model for sustainable development and has moved from small-scale demos to actively marketing larger developments.[47] Seattle's 120-acre "High Point is the first large-scale development in the country to feature low-impact, sustainable design in a dense urban setting. It is a model for healthy home development that benefits the environment and promotes healthy living."[48] Sustainable Jersey, Sustainable Seattle, and Sustainable South Bronx sites may serve as a source of ideas, inspiration and incentives for entire municipalities to go green.

Greening Greensburg, Kansas: After the largest tornado in the state's history completely leveled Greensburg, Kansas, its green rebirth is being documented step by step, with a goal of having more LEED buildings per square foot than anywhere on Earth. View Greensburg, the TV show, on Planet Green (a Discovery channel).[49]

Greening roofs: Every city has hundreds of acres of flat, black-tar roofs, creating a *heat-island effect.* Simply painting them white or with solar-reflective paint could go a long way (www.ultimatecoatings.net). "White roofs can cut a building's energy use by 20%," says California Energy Commissioner, Art Rosenfeld. "The potential energy savings in the US is in excess of $1 billion annually. And by conserving electricity we are emitting less CO_2 from power plants."[50] Even better, create a green roof. They reduce storm water runoff, last 50+ years (20 years for black tar), increase the value of any nearby property with a view, and have a long-term fiscal payoff. The view of Chicago City Hall's 12th floor "prairie" is coveted. Green rooftops immediately reduce the carbon footprint, reduce heat generation, and are up to 60% cooler. Green walls, or vertical plantings, are starting to take root across America, reducing cooling costs and adding value.[51]

Water and Sewage

Stewardship of our natural resources is the sine qua non of sustainable living. The conscientious community must establish its development practices, including water harvesting, conservation, and management of solid waste and greywater. The Greywater Guerrillas are educators, designers, builders, and artists who've made their mission

Why dinosaurs really became extinct

to educate and empower those interested in building sustainable water culture and infrastructure. Ecological sanitation, i.e., the composting toilet,[52] has made impressive improvements to health and cleanliness in rural regions, and the day is near when those same methods can be implemented in urban environments. Large-scale ecological sanitation can be integrated into any urban environment.

Greening wastewater: Innovative wastewater treatment technology is becoming state of the art. The *Solid Immobilized Bio-Filter* (SIBF) system, for example, eliminates some drawbacks of conventional treatment plants, costs less to start up and operate, and can save 90% of ongoing energy costs. Reusable treated water is used for groundwater recharge, and creates on- and off-site gardening irrigation opportunities.[53] At home, new Energy Star toilets offer useful flush options. Specialized composting toilets, though expensive, are the solution for some. If a retrofit, replace the potty. If building new, consider a greywater recycling toilet/sink. (Japan has been using these combo potties for years.)[54]

"Single stream" recycling helps cities divert up to 70 percent of their waste from the landfill by allowing households to put all their recyclables in the same bin. The ultimate goal is Zero waste.[55] Sustainable Communities Network provides profiles of innovative projects across the US.

Policy and decision-makers: Elected officials need to know we want the fiscal ›port needed to retrofit our vast inven- y of commercial buildings. "Most major

projects will not be driven by cost savings, but instead will be initiated to meet broader policy and business objectives, such as lower carbon footprints, higher employee productivity, and higher property values."[56] The US Department of Energy plans to advance the development and market adoption of net-zero commercial buildings by 2025. The American Reinvestment and Recovery Act of 2009 provided $25 billion for weatherization and energy-efficiency upgrades for commercial and government buildings.[57]

Transportation
Rethinking How We Get Around

Transportation is the way we move goods and people from one place to another. Most Americans today make the best of a rather dysfunctional transportation system, given the totality of pan-social-strata and ecological needs. Heavily reliant upon individual automobile ownership (a system perpetuated by the flawed tenet that owning a car is equivalent to personal freedom), and struggling to refurbish aging infrastructure, a heavily indebted US now faces a multiplicity of transportation-oriented crises.

Scientists tell us that we have a 10-year window before catastrophic climate change becomes inevitable and irreversible.[59] We need to re-think our transportation systems, attitudes and behaviors—now!

Motor vehicles are major sources of carbon dioxide, carbon monoxide, suspended particles, nitrogen oxides, and volatile organic compounds (VOCs), contributing mightily to ground-level ozone and smog.[60] Ozone and suspended particles induce and exacerbate respiratory ailments, a cost disproportionately borne by communities of color and lower income.

Back to the Hood

As US communities sprawled over decades past, today's transportation quagmires were largely unforeseen. Yet substantially modifying this live/work arrangement is essential. Changes at both the personal and policy level become critical at this juncture, as communities cast a keen eye on eco-sensitive development, and wise land-use planning. Individuals and families need to find ways to stem dependence on private automobiles, keep commutes short and/or work from home. Taxes at the pump can become revenue streams for public transportation systems—buses, light rail, cycling paths, walkable downtowns, and the like. For intercity travel, the future belongs to high-speed trains.

Taking public transit, ridesharing, biking, or walking may mean it will take us a little longer. What's more important, small inconveniences and a few extra minutes per day to reach our destination, or exacerbated global warming bringing irreversible change for this and all future generations? There are many benefits to a lifestyle shift, including keeping more money local, spending less of our lives on gridlocked highways, saving the Earth, and much more yet to be realized.

Sustainable Transportation Planning Recommendations: "Smart growth" includes linking the transit system to a network of walkable/bikeable streets, mixed-use retail, residential areas which include affordable housing, and workplaces, according to the Center for Transit-Oriented Development. It provides improved quality of life and reduced household transportation expenses. Any region benefits with stable mixed-income neighborhoods that reduce environmental impacts and provide alternatives to traffic congestion.

Transportation for All: A new United for a Fair Economy[61] report finds that transportation is the second biggest expense for American households, after housing, according to the Surface Transportation Policy Project. Evacuation planning focuses on traffic management for those with cars and for institutionalized people, not on non-institutionalized people without vehicles. New Orleans had only one-quarter the number of buses needed to evacuate car-less residents during the Hurricane Katrina disaster. In the case of a mandatory evacuation order, 33% of Latinos, 27% of African Americans, and 23% of whites say that lack of transportation would be an obstacle preventing them from evacuating, according to the US National Center for Disaster Preparedness.

Idling Gets You Nowhere

Idling damages our vehicle, our health, and our environment. It creates soot deposits and water vapor which mixes with sulphur oxide to become sulphuric acid in the crankcase. Just 10 seconds of idling uses more fuel than restarting the engine—idling burns almost one gallon of gas per hour.[62] Engines emit three times the amount of exhaust gases when idling than when pulling the vehicle. The most effective way to warm up a car in cold weather is to drive at a moderate speed.[63] US drivers waste 2 billion gallons of fuel each year idling.[64] For European drivers, idling is viewed as irresponsible and politically incorrect behavior.[65]

WHAT YOU CAN DO

■ Be aware of when your car will be idling and turn off the engine, then restart rather than idle.

■ Drive less! Start going car-free just one day a week. You'll be surprised at all the benefits.

■ Start an anti-idling policy in your town.

Redesigning Urban Transport: What Works

Around the globe city planners and citizen activists are finding that a blend of rail, bus, bicycle lanes, and pedestrian pathways offers the best set of options to provide mobility, cost effectiveness, and a healthy and pleasing environment.

Optimally, rail provides the hub with bus lines intersecting. Bogotá's highly successful bus rapid transit system, Trans-Milenio, uses special express lanes to move people quickly through the city. This is being replicated in other countries.[66] Japan's legendary bullet trains have carried billions over the past 40 years without a single casualty. Europe has 4,745 miles of high-speed trains. Carbon dioxide emissions from high-speed trains are a third those of cars and a quarter those of airplanes. If the grid were powered by green electricity, emissions from trains would be zero. A train averaging 170 miles per hour could travel North America coast to coast in 15 hours, even with stops in major cities along the way.[67]

Cities such as London, Singapore, Stockholm, and Milan are reducing traffic congestion and air pollution by charging cars to enter the city. In 2003, London began charging $10 per car entering the city center between 7 am and 6:30 pm—this immediately reduced vehicles, and within a year, bus ridership increased 38%,

ICE (Intercity Express) trains are fast, safe, reliable, comfortable and low emission.

Claus Wawrzinek

traffic delays decreased 30%. In July 2005, the fee was raised to $16. Overall, traffic has declined 36% and bicycle usage has increased 50%.[68]

According to Earth Policy News, Paris Mayor Bertrand Delanoe, elected in 2001, faced some of Europe's worst traffic congestion and air pollution. He decided that traffic would have to be cut 40% by 2020. The first step was investing in better transit for outlying regions. Next express lanes for buses and bicycles were created on thoroughfares, decreasing lanes for cars. The third step was establishing a city bicycle rental program that by the end of 2007 had 20,600 bikes at 1,450 docking stations. Accessed by credit card at inexpensive daily, monthly, or annual rates, the bicycles are immensely popular. Paris is well on its way to its 2020 goal.[69]

In Copenhagen, each day 500,000 people bicycle commute to work or school. The Danish are now investing $47 million in building "bicycle superhighways" extending far into the suburbs. Elements include smooth, even surfaces free of leaves, ice, and snow with sufficient width for passing, "service stations" with air and tools along the routes, and "Green Wave" sections with timed stoplights (cycle 12 miles per hour and you hit green lights all the way).[70]

The US lags far behind in diversifying transit options. The National Complete Streets Coalition lobbies for streets that are also friendly to pedestrians and bicycles, so far establishing "complete street" policies in 14 states and 40 metropolitan areas.[71]

Greener Trucking: Since it will be with us for a while longer, trucking needs to be cleaned up. Heavy-duty, long-haul truck smokestacks emit 6% of the United States' carbon dioxide each year. Doubling the efficiency of trucks from 6.5 miles per gallon to 12.3 mpg could save 3.8 billion gallons of diesel annually. According to the Rocky Mountain Institute, this could be done with readily available technology, including auxiliary power units, more efficient wide-base tires, and improved aerodynamic mechanisms such as trailer side skirts.[72] And no idling!

Hybrids and Electric Vehicles: The Best for Now

The Obama administration has mandated an increase in passenger vehicle fuel economy to a fleet average of 35.5 mpg by 2016. Each gallon of gasoline emits an amazing 24 to 28 pounds of carbon dioxide.[73] Until more sustainable transportation systems are created, alternative vehicles are essential to slow global warming and to serve as a bridge: necessary but not sufficient. While ample information on hybrid and hydrogen fuel-cell vehicles is readily available in the mainstream press, for depth of understanding look to The Union of Concerned Scientists' website comparing hybrid vehicles (www.hybridcenter.org). Small Neighborhood Electric Vehicles (NEVs) are gaining in popularity for off-road use in airports, college campuses, retirement communities, and other areas.[74] Looking for the most efficient car to buy? Check out the American Council for an Energy Efficient Economy's Green Book (www.greenercars.com).

Cleaner cars should come from cleaner plants. Toyota is focusing on building model manufacturing facilities. Their Tsutsumi plant has reduced carbon dioxide emissions by 50% compared to 1990 levels. Its Thailand plant is solar-operated, recycles wastewater, and has contributed no waste to landfill since the beginning of operation in 2007.[75]

Commercial car companies aren't on their own to come up with new technologies. They can get a little help from our friends, the Union of Concerned Scientists and the Rocky Mountain Institute.

An extensive body of technology and fuels already exists to enable cleaner and affordable vehicles to be manufactured today. That such vehicles are not on the road was the impetus for Union of Concerned Scientists engineers to create the Vanguard—a safe, fuel-efficient minivan that meets California's (and 14 other states') global warming emission standards by using existing technologies and fuels. "Many cars and trucks on the road today already use at least one of the climate-friendly components used in the Vanguard, but none come close to matching the potential benefits of the full Vanguard package."[76]

Hypercar Equals Hypercool: The Rocky Mountain Institute (RMI) has designed a prototype Hypercar whose synergy of ultra-light composite materials, low-drag design, hybrid-electric drive, and efficient accessories achieve a 3- to 5-fold improvement in fuel economy along with equal or better performance, safety, amenities, and affordability. RMI has placed the Hypercar in the public domain so that any car company can utilize the technologies they have developed. Their for-profit venture, Fiberforge, continues to research advanced-composite structures to further lower costs.[77]

A Word About Biofuels: Production of biofuels (ethanol and biodiesel) is growing worldwide, but this much-touted technology is loaded with problems. 1) Net energy gain is minimal. 2) Its demand is causing too much conversion of native forests in Southeast Asia and Indonesia to palm oil plantations. 3) Its demand is causing increased mono-cropping of corn, often genetically modified, to the exclusion of diversity of local food crops

Cityhop New Zealand's plug-in car share service

Author and global activist, Vandana Shiva, sheds light on the increasing demand for biofuel production this way: When global commodities double in price due to biodiesel demand, those in the industrial world may cheer for reduced energy costs and lowered GHGs, but the other half of the world which depends on these crops for basic sustenance, those who previously only ate two meals a day, suddenly can only afford to eat one meal a day! Many countries have experienced food riots due to these international energy dynamics.[78]

Counting on biofuels to keep piloting a massive fleet of combustion engine-driven private vehicles is an attempt to hang on to obsolete paradigms. Nonetheless, mandates for blending biofuels into vehicle fuels have been enacted in a number of states, provinces, and nations. Most mandates require blending 10–15% ethanol with gasoline, or blending 2–5% biodiesel with diesel fuel. Fuel tax exemptions and/or production subsidies have become important biofuels policies in more than a dozen countries, which increases their production. See *Part Three, Energy*, for more on biofuels.

Ridesharing

Ridesharing is gaining momentum in companies and on campuses. In 1973, Ecology & Environment, Inc. (E&E) created a Web-based alternative transportation program for its 20-plus offices around the country. GreenRide (www.greenride.com) now coordinates ridesharing, rail, and bicycle routes across the United States, Canada, and Europe. It has saved 31 million miles of driving and prevented 13,000 tons of carbon dioxide emissions.

The University of Florida in Gainesville—the nation's fifth-largest campus—was the first American university to implement the program. They initially experimented with their 17,000 employees, then extended it to their 46,000 students. GreenRide matches not only student class schedules, but also weekend and vacation destinations. The service includes an online calculator that determines how much money and pollution is saved. GreenRide usage saved the university $1 million—the amount a new parking structure would have cost—demonstrating clearly that making sustainable choices can be both good for the planet and financially prudent.[79]

WHAT YOU CAN DO

Sierra Club's Green Transportation initiative promotes actions everyone can take to reduce their carbon footprint.[80] The good news is that you can take *many* small steps on a daily basis to do your part in the fight against global warming:

- DRIVE LESS!

- If you're in the market for a new car, buy the most fuel-efficient vehicle that meets your needs. Better fuel economy = a better environment.

- Check tire pressure frequently and keep tires fully inflated; this can improve your fuel economy up to 10%. Also keep your car tuned up.

- Use a GPS—using a navigational device can reduce miles traveled up to 16%.

- Sell your car and join a car sharing company instead. See www.carsharing.net.

- Find out your car's optimal speed for fuel economy and set your cruise control.

- Choose an efficient route for your errand-running and combine errands to avoid multiple short trips. If you plan to make multiple stops at a shopping center, park your car in the middle and walk to your individual destinations. Cars emit more pollution in the first mile than the next 10 miles!

- Roughly 44% of car trips taken are fewer than 2 miles. Burn calories instead of gasoline—walk or ride a bike. Commit to taking public transit, walking, or riding a bicycle at least one day a week.

- Telecommute a number of days per week.

- Carpool with co-workers. If a daily carpool won't work, try one or two days per week.

- If you have two cars and are taking a trip, choose the more fuel-efficient car.

- If you're driving a standard, save gasoline by downshifting instead of braking in neutral.

- Don't drive with windows down at high speeds—it creates drag and reduces your fuel economy.

- lActively support public transporation in your community! Increased use and demand for public transportation can improve the level of service.

- After the headlines, the second most widely read part of the newspaper is the Letters to the Editor. Write, write, write. Raise awareness on some aspect of the transportation issue; perhaps include a short vignette from your life.

- Express yourself to your legislators! Keep a page in your schedule book where you write the names, phones, emails, and addresses of state and national officials and your local Board of Supervisors. It takes only a couple of minutes to register your views.

- Contact your federal legislators to allocate more funds for public transit than for highway construction.

- Express your support for raising taxes on gasoline as a stimulus to get people into alternative modes of transportation.

- Advocate and work for meeting the needs of all strata of society, addressing issues of income, age, and disability disparity.

- If your public transit system excludes bikes from rush hour, write or call and ask them to accommodate bicycles. This is when the most automobile trips and pollution could be saved!

- The Surface Transportation Policy Project promotes "location-efficient incentives," targeted subsidies to employers that locate in transit-accessible places, and sprawl-prevention measures so that people who cannot afford (or choose not to own) a car can still access jobs.[81]

THE EARTH CHARTER

The Earth Charter is one of the most unique documents in human history, created through a series of consensus-based dialogues, with thousands of people participating from all over the world, over the course of more than a decade. Now endorsed by more than 4,500 organizations and governments, it inspires shared responsibility "to bring forth a sustainable global society founded on respect for nature, universal human rights, economic justice, and a culture of peace."

The Earth Charter Initiative promotes living by example, with the help of The Action Guidelines, which suggest that people focus on root causes of problems and be resourceful.

Earth Charter

Principles

I. RESPECT AND CARE FOR THE COMMUNITY OF LIFE
1. Respect Earth and life in all its diversity.
2. Care for the community of life with understanding, compassion, and love.
3. Build democratic societies that are just, participatory, sustainable, and peaceful.
4. Secure Earth's bounty and beauty for present and future generations.

II. ECOLOGICAL INTEGRITY
5. Protect and restore the integrity of Earth's ecological systems, with special concern for biological diversity and the natural processes that sustain life.
6. Prevent harm as the best method of environmental protection and, when knowledge is limited, apply a precautionary approach.
7. Adopt patterns of production, consumption, and reproduction that safeguard Earth's regenerative capacities, human rights, and community well-being.
8. Advance the study of ecological sustainability and promote the open exchange and wide application of the knowledge acquired.

III. SOCIAL AND ECONOMIC JUSTICE
9. Eradicate poverty as an ethical, social, and environmental imperative.
10. Uphold the right of all, without discrimination, to a natural and social environment supportive of human dignity, bodily health, and spiritual well-being, with special attention to the rights of indigenous peoples and minorities.
11. Ensure that economic activities and institutions at all levels promote human development in an equitable and sustainable manner.
12. Affirm gender equality and equity as prerequisites to sustainable development and ensure universal access to education, health care, and economic opportunity.

IV. DEMOCRACY, NONVIOLENCE, AND PEACE
13. Strengthen democratic institutions at all levels, and provide transparency and accountability in governance, inclusive participation in decision-making, and access to justice.
14. Integrate into formal education and lifelong learning the knowledge, values, and skills needed for a sustainable way of life.
15. Treat all living beings with respect and consideration.
16. Promote a culture of tolerance, nonviolence, and peace.

"Let ours be a time remembered for the awakening of a new reverence for life, the firm resolve to achieve sustainability, the quickening of the struggle for justice and peace, and the joyful celebration of life."

—*Earth Charter conclusion*

Jim Enby

Part Seven GETTING PERSONAL

OUR CHOICES MATTER: Creating a Sustainable Future with Our Daily Actions

The time of the lone wolf is over.

Gather yourselves!

Banish the word "struggle"

from your attitude

and your vocabulary.

All that we do now

must be done in a

sacred manner and

in celebration.

We are the ones

we've been waiting for.

—The Elders
Oraibi, Arizona, Hopi Nation

FOOD

We Are What We Eat

Few personal choices and acts bring us closer to the core of sustainability than locally sourcing our own nutritious food supply. This topic is wide-ranging in both scope and implication, from personal health and well-being to the planetary consequences of large-scale agriculture. How we feed ourselves is linked to all planetary sustainability issues: pollution, population, transportation, energy, social justice, economics, animal welfare, the risks of genetically modified organisms, and more.

Mass-production techniques developed over the last 50+ years are highly polluting, energy-intensive, delocalized, and hazardous in many ways — from toxic inputs (pesticides, herbicides, fungicides, and synthetic fertilizers) and fossil-fueled global shipping, to a loss of biodiversity resulting from vast monocultures. Processed foods are far less nutritious than fresh foods. Consumption of "dead" food in plastic packages adds another aspect of disconnection between human life and the life-generating Earth. (*And* we're eating the breakdown products of that plastic.) Industrial agriculture degrades the very soil it depends upon for nourishment. We need to move away from this model toward biologically informed approaches that keep yields high while reducing environmental harm.

With each dollar spent on food and drink, we vote for the system that produces what we buy, whether it benefits our body and the planet or wreaks havoc on both. So, by learning about what we eat, we can learn to "vote" consciously for a life-nourishing food system. Over the past few decades, books such as *Diet for a Small Planet* (Frances Moore Lappé),

Diet for a New America (John Robbins), *Fast Food Nation* (Eric Schlosser), *The Omnivore's Dilemma* and *In Defense of Food* (Michael Pollan), to name only a few, have raised awareness about the personal and planetary impact of each food choice we make.

Yes, a little short-term convenience will be sacrificed when you eat consciously. But once you realize the true cost, cheap food no longer seems inexpensive, and the investment in organics and your body becomes less an indulgence and more a form of personal and planetary health insurance.

A World of Food and a World of Want

Every day, almost 16,000 children die from hunger-related causes—one child every five seconds. An estimated 963 million people worldwide are hungry, and more are chronically malnourished.[1]

It has long been said that global food production is sufficient to meet the current needs of all people; getting it distributed is the problem. With human population growing exponentially and effective food strategies not yet in place, world hunger, malnourishment, and starvation are sure to be exacerbated. The number of the world's hungry is projected to reach 1.2 billion by 2025.[2]

The Food Sovereignty movement champions the rights of people, communities, and countries to define their own agricultural and other land-use policies in ways that are appropriate to their unique circumstances (see Food Sovereignty sidebar). It stresses the universal right to sufficient, healthy food, and rejects the idea that food is another commodity to be exploited. It's a proactive step for a better world and local security, and against purely profit-seeking entities with little or no stake in an area or community's long-term quality of life.

What's the Trouble with my Packaged Food?

On the average, US produce is shipped 1500 miles[3]—more if you add produce imported from other countries and continents. Nutritional value decreases with every day of transport and storage. Fossil fuels used in fertilizers, fertilizer production, and food transport contribute to global warming and pollution. The luxury of our purchase of internationally produced food is only possible due to artificially low energy prices that externalize the environmental cost of a wasteful food system. Clearly the less transportation used to bring food to market, the better for the Earth—and the less packaging, the less waste.

Modern industrial agriculture is polluting and unsustainable, and has a highly detrimental environmental impact. In addition to more obvious effects of toxic inputs and byproducts, "about 60% of our country's land area is devoted either to crops or to livestock grazing, often greatly diminishing its ability to support natural wildlife. [Food is] second perhaps only to transportation as a source of environmental problems."[4]

Factory farming has become a public health issue, as it's a leading cause of the development of antibiotic-resistant strains of bacteria.[5] Animal waste, pesticides, and fertilizers contain nitrates, which contaminate surface and ground waters and have been linked to various ailments and birth defects. Being a vegetarian is a major act of conservation.

And let's not forget nutrition. In contrast to industrial food, organic produce can contain at least twice the nutritional mineral content of regular supermarket produce by weight and far less dangerous pesticide and heavy-metal residue. One must definitely eat organic foods or better (such as homegrown or wild foods) in order to get enough quality minerals in the diet.[6]

Thinking It Through

It's time to fundamentally reevaluate our food systems in light of energy efficiency and environmental impact. Encourage your elected officials to act in support of this change. Cheap energy and agricultural subsidies facilitate a type of agribusiness-oriented mass food system that weakens communities and family farms, creates mountains of solid waste, and funnels wealth into the hands of fewer and fewer people and corporations. The overhaul of agriculture and food policy at the federal level can complement health care reform by encouraging better nutrition to prevent disease, and be part of the effort to combat climate change as well.

THE SIX PRINCIPLES OF FOOD SOVEREIGNTY

1. Food for People: All individuals, peoples, and communities have the right to sufficient, healthy, and culturally appropriate food. Food is not just another commodity for international agribusiness.

2. Food Providers: All are valued who cultivate, grow, harvest, and process food. Policies, actions, and programs that undervalue them, threaten their livelihoods, and eliminate them are rejected.

3. Localized Food Systems: Food providers and consumers resist governance structures, agreements, and practices that depend on and promote unsustainable and inequitable international trade and give power to remote and unaccountable corporations.

4. Local Decisions: Food sovereignty seeks territory, land, grazing, water, seeds, livestock, and fish populations for local food providers. These resources ought to be used and shared in socially and environmentally sustainable ways that conserve diversity. Privatization of natural resources through laws, commercial contracts, and intellectual property rights regimes is rejected.

5. Knowledge and Skill-Building: Build on the skills and local knowledge of food providers and their local organizations, and reject technologies that undermine, threaten, or contaminate them, e.g., genetic engineering.

6. Working with Nature: Use the contributions of nature in diverse, low external-input, agro-ecological production and harvesting methods that maximize the contribution of ecosystems and improve resilience and adaptation, especially in the face of climate change. Rejected are methods that harm beneficial ecosystem functions and/or depend on energy-intensive monocultures and livestock factories, destructive fishing practices, and other damaging production methods.

Instead of massive subsidies—such as the $7.5 billion paid to farmers in 2008 for growing grains and soybeans, resulting in an abundance of corn and soy that provide cheap feed for livestock and inexpensive food ingredients like high-fructose corn syrup[7]—farm policy and federal dollars should encourage planting more diverse crops, reward conservation efforts, and promote local food networks, not industrial agriculture.

Human culture historically has revolved around agriculture. Management, use, and conservation of useful flora, including wild food plants, are important features of non-industrial agricultural societies.[8] Until relatively recently, organic agriculture had been the only form of agriculture practiced on the planet, but the last century saw technology override traditional methods of food production in favor of petroleum-based fertilizers and genetic modification. It is crucial that science incorporate traditional knowledge, put farming back in balance with the Earth, and reverse the trend in small farmland losses.

WHAT YOU CAN DO

Go Organic

Would you deliberately dump poison on your food? Would you purposely spray farm workers with toxic chemicals? Would you intentionally eradicate butterflies, or kill millions of birds annually? When we buy conventionally grown food, we are contributing to all of these. Foods carrying the "organic" label too pricey? Try buying organic a portion of the time, and reach for natural, unprocessed food for the rest. Eat lower on the food chain. Buy locally grown products. Join an organic foods coop. Slow Food USA and Organic Consumers both offer a wide range of topics on organic food.

Greenhouse Gases per US Food Sector[a]	
Red Meat	30%
Dairy Products	18%
Cereals/Carbs	11%
Fruit/Vegetables	11%
Chicken/Fish/Eggs	10%
Other	9%
Beverages	6%
Oils/Sweets/Condiments	5%

Buy Local

Local food is fresher and tastes better. It aligns us with the seasons, and a sense of place. Farmers' markets are a good option for buying locally grown food, as are Community Supported Agriculture farms (CSAs). Typically, CSA members or "subscribers" pledge in advance to cover the anticipated costs of the farm operation. In return, they receive shares in the farm's harvests, often on a weekly basis. To find your local farmers' market, CSA, or food coop, go to the Local Harvest website: www.localharvest.org.

Seek Out Fair Trade Products

For commodities such as spices, coffee, chocolate, and bananas, make an effort to find "fair trade" products. This will help ensure that our taste for the exotic reduces harm on the world's farmers and the planet. For more information, check out Fair Trade Federation, www.fairtradefederation.org, or Global Exchange, www.globalexchange.org.

Eat Less Meat

How do our food choices affect the climate? Animal agriculture is directly or partially responsible for many of the world's most serious environmental problems, including global warming, deforestation, air and water pollution and species extinction. The United Nations Food and Agriculture Organization's (FAO) recently released 400-page scientific study called "Livestock's Long Shadow" reveals that animal agriculture causes more greenhouse gas emissions than all of the world's transportation combined.[9] Two senior

A community farmers' market in Portugal

DEFINING SUSTAINABLE AGRICULTURE

Organic agriculture is farming without synthetic chemicals. A pioneer of the organic movement, Lady Eve Balfour, provides a useful description: The criteria for a sustainable agriculture can be summed up in one word—permanence—which means adopting techniques that maintain soil fertility indefinitely, that utilize, as far as possible, only renewable resources; that do not grossly pollute the environment; and that foster biological activity within the soil and throughout the cycles of all the involved food chains.

Living sustainably means, in writer Derrick Jensen's elegantly simple definition, that whatever we do, we can do indefinitely.

advisors to the World Bank on climate issues published a major new study in the Nov/Dec 2009 issue of *Worldwatch* demonstrating that livestock actually contributes up to 51% of global GHGs.[10] Over half the total amount of fresh water consumed in the US goes to irrigate land growing feed for livestock and to water them.[11]

Switching just two meals a week to a plant-based diet is ecologically better than buying all locally sourced food, according to a study in the journal *Environmental Science and Technology*.[12] The American Dietetic Association, the leading nutrition authority in the United States, affirms that "appropriately planned vegetarian diets are healthful, nutritionally adequate, and provide health benefits in the prevention and treatment of certain diseases."[13] The farming of animals also causes great suffering. *Reducing or eliminating the consumption of animals and animal products is one of the most effective ways any individual can heal the environment, help animals, and live a longer, healthier life.*

PERMACULTURE

When we mimic the wisdom of nature's systems and turn our homes, landscapes, and communities into productive, resilient ecosystems, we not only rebuild self-reliance, we address enormous problems such as climate crisis, topsoil loss, drought, and the collapse of fish, bee, and songbird populations.

Permaculture is about having a planet-wide circle of concern while focusing on our areas of influence. Yes, we need systemic change, and the most accessible whole system is our self, our home, our garden, and our relationships. By re-skilling and reclaiming our power through meeting basic needs, we reconnect and renew ancient cycles of sowing, harvesting, and processing food together—composting, grafting, catching the rain, using greywater.

Every ounce of the needs we meet locally with our hearts, hands, and neighborly relations grows our power and connection. It grows the fertility of an emerging culture of stewardship, celebration, and resilience— a regenerative culture that treasures every drop of water, scrap of carbon, and act of living by assembling communities that catch, store, and sustain more life nutrient then they use. This is what Sharif Abdullah calls becoming "menders" rather than "takers."

Being the Change in Your Own Yard

Where to start is where you are, with whom and what inspires you. Observe, interact, and ask: "How do we grow a regenerative culture, a permanent culture of care?" This is the fundamental question of *permaculture*, an ethics- and principles-centered system for sustainable living and land use. Adopting the permaculture model for living is an empowering response to our environmental and social crises, centered in three ethical principles: earth care, people care, and setting limits to consumption to ensure fair share. Grounded in self-sufficiency, permaculture is being applied from urban yards to intentional communities, and from 40,000-person Kosovo refugee camps to the Jordan desert.

Istock Photo/Amanda Rohde

Instead of a resource-hungry lawn, why not a patch of strawberries, a veggie garden edged by chives and culinary herbs? How about a fedge—a food hedge made with berries, artichokes, or dwarf fruit trees? Rather than reading about collapsing critter populations, why not create gardens full of plants that feed beneficial insects and birds while providing pest control? Need privacy? Try a living fence of apples, citrus, pineapple, guavas, or olives. Care for some edible air conditioning and cheaper bills? Plant deciduous fruit trees and vines that shade the summer sun, but let winter light in.

Is Seafood a Good Choice?

Oceans are becoming dangerously depleted due to commercial fishing operations, which, in addition to their intended catch, haul in and throw away enormous amounts of sea life as "bycatch." Fish farming operations are often toxic and unsustainable. For example, native Pacific Northwest salmon's endangered species status is further impacted by the parasites resulting from commercial salmon farming.

Helene York, foundation director for the Bon Appetit Management Company, a food service group that provides 80 million meals a year based on a low-carbon diet, recommends clams, mussels, and oysters, which require "practically zero" energy to farm. Other good choices are herbivorous fish, like tilapia and catfish; and species low on the food chain, such as mackerel, herring, and sardines.

The Monterey Bay Aquarium supports responsible seafood choices and has excellent literature on this.[b]

Vertical gardening beautifies habitat while supplying food. Grapes, hops, runner beans, and kiwi are just a few multi-beneficial vining plants. Container gardening reclaims unused space. Try dropping the one-crop-per-spot paradigm and grow a food forest of purposeful plants from canopy to root zone, using trees, shrubs, herbs, roots, and vines. Rather than throw food scraps and yard waste away and buy fertilizers, try composting to enrich soil life, retain water, and produce strong, healthy plants.

Explore, experiment, and just keep on planting. Together we are growing community self-reliance rooted in ecological resilience. We are nourishing our land as we transform waste into fertility. It's the smell, touch, and taste of the world being born, and it's right out your door. As Fritjof Capra writes, nature sustains the web of life by creating and nurturing communities. Life is about relationships, and ecosystems are communities.[14]

HOME SWEET NONTOXIC HOME
Creating a Haven in a Hazardous World

You may have an uneasy suspicion about how toxic and polluted our environment is—it's worse than you thought. Each year, astonishingly, 5,000 new chemicals enter the marketplace.[15] The only requirement for approval is for the company to send the Environmental Protection Agency (EPA) the structure of the chemical. Most have never been tested for their effects on human and animal health, much less tested in the combinations that occur in the real world, which can increase their potency and toxicity 10 to 20 times.[16]

Newborns today begin life with almost 300 chemicals in their bodies.[17] Likely lifetime health risks are cancers, allergies, asthma, skin disorders, and hormonal disruption. According to the EPA, 40% of US rivers, lakes, and coastal waters are so contaminated that they are unfit for humans to fish in, swim in, or drink.[18] It is expected that 1 in 3 of us will have cancer in our lifetime.[19] Cancer's major contributor is exposure to the 85,000 chemicals in use today, more than 90% of which have never been tested for effects on human health.[20]

Question: Who is #1 in Environmental Leadership in the World?

US chemical lobbyists claim that removing hazardous chemicals would have dire economic consequences. Yet European goods now live up to strict toxin-free codes, having endured no such economic catastrophe. In *Exposed: The Toxic Chemistry of Everyday Products and What's at Stake for American Power*, award-winning investigative journalist Mark Schapiro reveals how US companies have reconfigured products without toxic chemicals for the European market while continuing to manufacture the same products in the United States *with* toxins.

Answer: the EU. The European Union has adopted the precautionary principle to safeguard its 450 million citizens. This principle assumes possible health and/or environmental risks instead of waiting for them to arise. Companies must be able to demonstrate that a product is safe. Every three months a scientific committee convenes to assess substances, posting on the EU web site a growing inventory of several hundred ingredients that are considered potentially harmful. It is time that we demand that the precautionary principle be the standard in the US, as it is in Europe.

The cosmetics industry is a flagrant example of a double standard. In 2005 the EU Cosmetics Directive banned the use of chemicals determined to be carcinogens, mutagens, or reproductive toxins. Proctor & Gamble redesigned their products for Europe but fought potential US regulations for two years, until conceding in 2007 to make all cosmetics to EU standards. But a great many US firms still use toxic ingredients and hormone disrupters. The Campaign for Safe Cosmetics encourages companies to sign their Compact for Safe Cosmetics, a pledge to replace hazardous chemicals with safe alternatives within three years of signing.

Flame Retardants: From Furniture to Children's Pajamas

One of the disruptive and unhealthy chemicals that we regularly come in contact with through our skin is flame retardants made from PBDEs (polybrominated diphenyl ethers), which are found to be doubling in human tissue every three to five years. These carcinogenic substances can cause birth defects and hormone disruption (thyroid, estrogen, testosterone), as well as irreversible learning and behavioral effects, including hyperactivity.[21]

Since the Consumer Product Safety Commission mandates that non-cotton fabrics for children's pajamas must pass a fire retardancy test after 50 washings, PBDEs are widely utilized.[22] So, if you don't want toxic chemicals next to your baby's skin, buy snug-fitting cotton shirts and pants instead of pajamas for sleepwear.

Avoid contact with PBDEs by purchasing furniture without foam, and covered by naturally fire-resistant fabrics, such as cotton or wool. The *National Green Pages*, published yearly by Green America, lists companies offering nearly every product and service needed for a healthy life. Another annual compilation of natural home products is published by *Natural Home* magazine.

Everyday Green Practices

While many organizations and websites offer suggestions, the Environmental Working Group has particularly succinct Guide Sheets for citizens to make informed choices. Some highlights from EWG:

Choose better body-care products. "Gentle" or "natural" or "nontoxic" have no legal definition or guidelines. Read the ingredients. Avoid triclosan, BHA, fragrance, and oxybenzone.

Pick plastics carefully. Avoid clear, hard plastic bottles marked with a "7" or "PC" and toys marked with a "3" or "PVC." Give your baby a frozen washcloth instead of vinyl teethers.

Filter your tap water. Use a reverse osmosis system or carbon filter pitcher. Don't drink bottled water.

Cook with cast iron or stainless steel only. Nonstick can emit toxic fumes and leach into your food.

Use a HEPA-filter vacuum. Kids spend a lot of time on the floor, and household dust can contain contaminants like lead and fire retardants.

Get your iodine. Use iodized salt. Iodine buffers against chemicals like perchlorate, which can disrupt your thyroid system and affect brain development.

Do not heat plastics in a microwave. This causes chemicals to leach from plastic into food and beverages.

Avoid anything plastic for infants and young children.

House cleaning: The Berkeley Ecology Center offers a Fact Sheet of Alternative Cleaning Recipes. You'll notice that nontoxic alternatives are less expensive. *Basic nontoxic ingredients:* Baking soda, vegetable-based liquid soaps, white vinegar, borax, cornmeal, citrus-based cleaners, lemons, toothpaste, salt, hydrogen peroxide.

All-Purpose Cleaner

1 quart warm water
1 teaspoon liquid soap
1 teaspoon borax
1/4 cup undiluted white vinegar

Mix ingredients and store in a spray bottle. Use for cleaning countertops, floors, walls, carpets, and upholstery.

Rethink Landscaping

In water-stressed areas like California and the US Southwest, artificially green lawns have become an unaffordable luxury on practically every level. Many locales are already formulating water restrictions, new pricing structures, and laws to limit water use for what has come to be seen as irresponsible landscaping. The new "green" for landscaping is back to a native ecosystem! Save water, labor, and fertilizers, and pesticides by choosing landscaping plants adapted to your area. Drought-tolerant plants are ideal—*xeriscaping* is using plants that require very little water. Consider replacing turf grass with native plants, shrubs, and trees that generally grow well without a lot of watering, and contribute to biodiversity not chemical pollution.

Another option for sustainable landscaping is found in the Food Not Lawns movement: "Besides global inequity and agricultural chemical dependence, some elements of this culture include the erosion and loss of our topsoil at the rate of 38 tons per acre per year and the pollution and salinification of whole watersheds by fertilizers and industrial waste, leading to the desertification of once fertile land and mass species extinction. This is also facilitated by the 2,500,000 tons of pesticides used every year. We are losing diversity both in nature and in our agricultural systems, as represented by a 75% decrease in crop diversity in the last hundred years."[23]

Humans have disrupted an enormous amount of natural habitat, causing a resulting decline in wildlife. "Habitat gardening," which includes the use of native plants in landscaping, helps offset this damage by providing natural food and shelter for birds, butterflies, and other creatures. The National Wildlife Federation offers information on backyard habitat gardening.

Utilize Greywater

A good portion of household wastewater, called "greywater," can be reused in landscaping. Recycling greywater helps to conserve water, lower water bills, reduce the load on sewer systems, and maintain eco-wise landscapes. Greywater may contain detergents with nitrogen or phosphorus, which are plant nutrients, resulting in more vigorous vegetation. However, you'll want to research ways to minimize sodium and chloride, which can be harmful to some sensitive species. Energy is also saved, thereby lowering your carbon footprint. Greywater systems are site-specific. Start your online research with Greywater Guerillas.

June Holte

THE ECOLOGICAL FOOTPRINT
Squaring humanity's demand with nature's supply

Just like any company, nature has a budget—it can only produce so many resources and absorb so much waste every year. The problem is, our demand for nature's services is exceeding what it can provide.

Using a resource accounting tool called the Ecological Footprint, we can measure the land area it takes to produce the resources a population consumes and absorb its CO_2 emissions. Ecological Footprint accounting enables us to compare human demand against biocapacity—what nature can supply—in the same way that financial accounting tracks expenditures against income. And the current ledgers are sobering.

According to Global Footprint Network, a research institution that calculates the Ecological Footprint for humanity and 150 nations, globally, we demand the resources it would take 1.4 planets to renewably produce. Put another way, it takes about 16 months for nature to produce the biological resources humanity demands in one year.

We maintain this ecological overspending by liquidating the planet's natural resources. For example, we can cut trees faster than they re-grow, and catch fish at a rate faster than they repopulate. While this can be done for a short while, this ultimately leads to the depletion of resources on which our livelihoods, and very lives, depend.

While globally we are demanding the resources of 1.4 planets, some countries demand much more and some much less. In the US, the average person's Ecological Footprint is 23 global acres, the equivalent of 17 football fields.

At the other end of the spectrum are countries like Haiti, Afghanistan and Malawi with Ecological Footprints of less than 1.3 global acres per capita—in most cases, too small to provide for the basic needs for food, housing and sanitation.

Although high-income nations tend to be clustered at the high end of the Footprint scale, nations with similar living standards—as measured by UN statistics on longevity, income, literacy rate, child mor-

tality and other factors—can have very different levels of resource consumption. The average resident of the European Union, for example, has a Footprint half that of the average American (although still well above what is replicable worldwide.)

Why is this the case? The answer lies partially in the way our societies are structured. Consider Italy, which has a per capita Footprint of 12 acres.

Most people live in compact cities, where they can walk to work, school and shopping, or use extensive bus and train systems. Public transportation is easily accessible, and is often more convenient and cheaper than driving. People get much of their food from local markets and food producers, and eat less packaged and frozen food. Also, by living in more compact cities with less housing surface per person, the houses consume less energy for cooling and heating.

In the US, some of the Ecological Footprint is related to individual choices we make that affect our resource consumption, such as whether to walk, drive or ride the bus, whether we live in a multi-unit dwelling or detached home, how much stuff we buy, how much meat we consume and how much of our diet is unprocessed and local. Much of our footprint is determined by our daily choices and is completely within our control.

Much of our Ecological Footprint, however, is the result of infrastructure decisions made by business leaders and policymakers, in some cases decades ago: decisions such as investing in highways rather than public transportation, and suburban growth over concentrated, urban development. For that reason, one of the most important individual actions we can do is hold our business and government leaders accountable to make decisions that will help balance our budget with nature, not further aggravate the debt.

You can determine your personal ecological footprint and what actions you can take to reduce it at www.footprintnetwork.org/calculator.

The Way Forward

While the realities we face are indeed troubling, there are key opportunities to reverse current trends. On a community level, creating resource-efficient cities and infrastructure, fostering best-practice green technology and innovation, and making resource limits central to decision-making at all levels of leadership can begin to turn the tide. Human ingenuity has transformed the way we use nature. We must now put that talent toward another transformation: creating a society that provides prosperity and opportunity within the bounds of what the planet can provide.

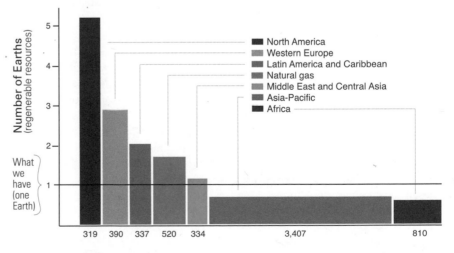

This chart shows both total footprint per capita and total population by region. The volume (both vertical and horizontal) represents the total footprint (Global Footprint Network, 2006).

Creative Commons/Always Breaking

THE CONSUMPTION CONUNDRUM

Let's tell this one with an economy of words: we in the West buy and throw away way too many things. Our appetite for everything from sports cars to swordfish is driving climate change, extinction, and an inequitable economic system. The widespread American assumption that consumption and growth is a healthy, sustainable model is myopic and fallacious, not to mention a root cause of environmental degradation.

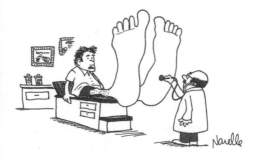

"It started when I bought the Hummer"

Collapse or change of this economic model is 100% predictable. We simply cannot go on living this way. As a writer mused in *Grist* magazine, "Bitter climate truths are fundamentally bitter cultural truths… Our version of life on Earth has come to an end."[24]

Rapidly growing energy and critical resources consumption is consistently breaking records[25] on this planet. The Earth's global ecosystem, upon which life depends, is being stretched to the limit by climbing consumption patterns. While environmental, social, and other challenges are being addressed in innovative ways, a requisite change in consumption patterns lags. High-consumption nations must find wisdom and pleasure in simplicity, as opposed to acquisition; in the inner as opposed to the outer; the ethereal as opposed the material. Embracing this truth may be the only way the real work can begin.

Consumer Spending Can't Save Us

Commercialism and retail therapy won't save our economy, or our ecosystem. As economist and "New Dreamer" Juliet Schor tells us, "The current decline in spending is an effect of the recession, not the cause."[26] The standard remedy of getting consumers or the government to spend more (to "grow" our way out of recession) can no longer work because the planet is telling us, loud and clear, than it can't cope with business as usual. Whatever government and consumers spend on needs to reflect that reality.

Schor advises more sharing: job sharing, property and income re-distributing, and sharing of access and know-how. "This time the economic pain needs to be assuaged by deeper structural changes that re-introduce fairness into our system. That's not just moral, it's also good economic sense."[27]

Opportunities for future spending include purchases that enhance and regenerate the Earth and its inhabitants, businesses that are truly sustainable, support of nonprofit groups doing important work, and other aspects of the green economy. But what is also necessary is moving toward voluntary simplicity—in other words, consuming only what is needed—and restructuring the economy for shared distribution of the fruits of our economy.

Consumption patterns are a function of lifestyle choices and political, economic, and sociocultural structures. A child born today in an industrialized country will pollute and consume more over his or her lifetime than 30 to 50 children born in developing countries.[28] With judicious use of our purchasing power, we can shift these institutions and habits toward sustainability. The Center for a New American Dream offers a wide variety of tools for re-conceiving our cultural patterns of consumption and choosing sustainable practices.

A Culture of Simplicity

Voluntary simplicity is a movement based on a new vision of progress: our ability to live in balance, deriving a sense of fulfillment from relationships and authentic living. The focus is on developing talents and passions rather than status and materialism, placing high value on social issues and creation of a better society. As we move beyond a cultural obsession with trying to achieve happiness through material possessions, we become more and more unwilling to sacrifice quality of life, equality of opportunity, and even our health for meaning and status based on accumulation.

Many people are working longer hours than ever and beginning to ask themselves: "Am I working to live or living to work?" To pull back from this competitive, consumption-oriented lifestyle, try joining a Simplicity Circle.

Participants learn to look at the consumption-based patterns of their lives and develop action-plans to help them

> ### WHAT'S THE STORY WITH "THE STORY OF STUFF"?
>
> An Internet sensation, "The Story of Stuff" is a concise look at our production and consumption patterns, and the global economy we are enmeshed in. The corresponding website lists NGOs working on the issues of extraction, production, distribution, consumption, and disposal. Check it out! www.storyofstuff.com.

consume less, work less, slow down, and devote more time to their passions. Group members choose to simplify their lives by streamlining daily habits, cutting consumption, carrying less debt, changing careers and/or spending more time with friends and family. An international listing of in-person Circles, as well as online Simplicity Study Groups, is available on the Simple Living Network website, www.simpleliving.net.

WHAT YOU CAN DO

Practical ways to lower your consumption and spare the Earth

- Power down! This includes shutting down your computer at work and at home. Also, wash your clothes in cold water. About 90% of the energy used for washing clothes is for heating the water. Unplug (the TV and internet) and plug in (the community).
- Consume less, waste less. Don't drink bottled water. Bring a reusable bag wherever you go (not just the grocery store). Excess bags add to the landfill and you don't need them.
- Ditch the processed food, the energy it takes to produce it, and its tons of packaging.
- Make your own cleaning products (see "Home Sweet Nontoxic Home").
- Pass up the fast food joint.
- Skip the franchised coffee conglomerate and brew your own. Skip the store-bought cereal and make your own granola instead.
- Become a vegetarian
- Grow some of your own food. This way you don't have to buy it and it's about as local as it gets.
- Consider the "embodied energy" of every article you use and consume, meaning its cost to be made, stored, and carried to where you are. Get clarity on your wants vs. your needs.
- Park your car and walk, and when necessary MARCH!
- Change your lightbulbs…and then, change your paradigm.
- Recycle your trash.
- Talk to everyone about these issues.
- Buy green, buy fair, buy local, buy used, and most importantly, buy less—voluntary simplicity is the new cool.

SPIRITUALITY
A Personal Compass for Today's World

"In a real sense all life is inter-related. All persons are caught in an inescapable network of mutuality, tied in a single garment of destiny. Whatever affects one directly, affects all indirectly. I can never be what I ought to be until you are what you ought to be, and you can never be what you ought to be until I am what I ought to be."

—*Martin Luther King, Jr.*

The times in which we live are perhaps more challenging than many of us are willing to admit. Increasingly people are becoming aware of the scope, scale, and urgency of our global crisis, aware of financial instability, terrorism, climate change, the destruction of our natural world, and widespread social injustice. It's natural that we would feel anxiety or despair, trying to cope with what looks like chaos, sensing our limits and our vulnerabilities.

It's when things get most difficult that we begin to ask existential questions: Is life an ordered system where good triumphs and justice prevails, or a mere flip of a coin, roll of the dice, survival of the fittest? Not having answers, either intuitively or by faith, could certainly be considered a crisis of spirit.

To be positively engaged in today's world, it helps to feel connected, worthy, and happy to be alive, and to know we are not powerless. To know we are actively making a contribution to the world, be it in our family, community, or civil society, gives us a sense of hope and energy.

When Going Within Means Going Away: In the face of profound and frightening change, people tend to contract spiritually and emotionally to stave off fear, anger, loneliness, and grief. But this causes us to lose our connection with other human beings and with our natural world. It causes us to lose spiritual perspective, and our capacity for empowering visions and creative solutions. We begin to look outside ourselves for fulfillment. We see this played out in addictions, rising school violence, suicides, and depression. All are states of disconnection, isolation, and the feeling that we do not belong to each other.

Make a Space for What's Good in the World: These days we are living in a sea of loneliness and separation. Many of us are acting out our anger and fear because we have not embraced our grief. We avoid feeling the painful issues and by doing so inevitably cause more of the pain. Yet, underneath all that, intuitively each of us knows that life will survive. Our global crisis is not a reason to go unconscious and disconnect, to spiritually cop out. Within

Connie Barlow

"The best way to tell whether we are moving in the direction of greater wellbeing is by listening to our inner messages of comfort or distress. Our highest evolutionary path is the one that generates the least resistance and the most joy."

—*David Simon, M.D.*

the nature of the sacred and spirit, of all life, is the inherent ability to awaken toward life, toward harmony. If we look at Earth's history, this is what has happened repeatedly.

There is tremendous pressure to evolve, to awaken, just to be able to cope. To survive we must *consciously* choose to evolve, and to change our beliefs and behaviors. The world is going through a crisis, but crisis births transformation. To be spiritually fulfilled requires transformation. As Gandhi said, "If we want to remake the world, we must remake ourselves."

So what does being spiritually fulfilled mean? While spiritual leaders may have somewhat different answers to what spiritual fulfillment means, all agree that to survive as a species, compassion and inner peace are crucial. We are solitary creatures

and what we yearn for most is connection—to ourselves, to each other, and to our world. To achieve these qualities on a deep level, we must commit to our own inner development. We must look closely at our feelings

of loneliness, anger, and grief, embrace the feelings and transform that energy into strength, passion, and commitment; into a knowing that every life does matter and makes a difference.

Steps to Change from the Inside Out

Asking powerful questions provide access wisdom. Here are a few to ask:

■ What are you spending and being spent for?

■ What commands and receives your best time, your best energy?

■ To what or whom are you committed in life? In death?

■ With whom or what group do you share your most sacred and private hopes for your life, and for the lives of those you love?

■ What are your most compelling goals and purposes in your life? (from *Stages of Life* by James Fowler.)

The answers will help you move in the direction of your own transformation and spiritual fulfillment. Like all things, though, we don't do this alone. Spiritual fulfillment is a two-fold path, the inner path of our own personal journey, and the outer path of compassion and caring for others.

"The environmental crisis is an outward manifestation of a crisis of mind and spirit. There could be no greater misconception of its meaning than to believe it to be concerned only with endangered wildlife, human-made ugliness, and pollution. These are part of it, but, more importantly, the crisis is concerned with the kind of creatures we are and what we must become in order to survive."

—*Lynton K. Caldwell, author, professor*

THREE FACETS OF "THE GREAT TURNING"

"Reminded that 'fear is excitement that has forgotten to breathe,' we can see distress as opportunity, the seedbed of the future. Then, as countless men and women are doing in this time of Great Turning, we join hands in learning how the world self-heals." —Joanna Macy

Joanna Macy coined The Great Turning, as "the transition from an industrial growth society to a life-sustaining society," with "three simultaneous and mutually reinforcing dimensions":

- Holding Actions: the front-line, direct actions to stop or limit the immediate damage, as well as all political, legal, and legislative work;

- Systems Change: solutions that address structural causes of the crises and offer alternative models;

- Shift in Consciousness: a profound shift in our perception of reality, our values, our attitudes, our goals.

As we engage "the essential adventure of our time," Macy cautions that there is no guarantee that we will make this transition in time for the survival of civilization or even of complex life systems. It is in the not knowing how the future will turn out that we will find our passion, which will inform and sustain us in striving to bring forth the Great Turning.

RESOURCE DIRECTORY

"What kind of world do we want? This is a fundamental question that most of us are asking. Does it make sense to participate in the existing world order? We want a world where life is preserved, and the quality of life is enriched for everybody, not only for the privileged...I want to make this world good. Not better. But to make it good! Why not? It is possible. Look around...all this knowledge, energy, talent, and technology. Let's get off our fannies, roll up our sleeves and get to work passionately in creating an almost perfect world."

—Isabelle Allende, TED talk, *A Tale of Passion*

Welcome to the vast array of organizations we invite you to sample for deeper research, links to videos, toolkits, etc. Organized by relationship to *SourceBook* chapters, the organizations listed represent a sample of the amazing work going on (the majority are based in the US). Within each chapter, they are listed alphabetically. Many of the groups are cross-cutting, working on a range of issues and offering many programs. Visit www.swcoalition.org to submit your suggestions, and to access the searchable version of the *SourceBook*.

ENVIRONMENT

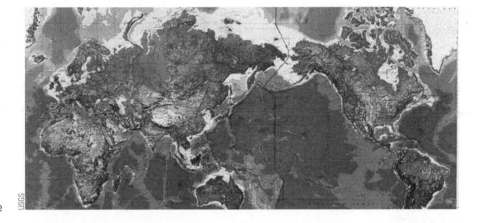

1Sky
Washington, DC; Communicating a positive vision for coherent climate challenge policies. www.1sky.org

Acterra
Palo Alto, CA; Protecting environment with restoration, education, environmental leadership. www.acterra.org

Algalita Marine Research Foundation
California-based nonprofit, independent marine research, education organization. www.algalita.org

Amazon Watch
San Francisco, CA; Defends the environment, rights of indigenous peoples of the Amazon basin. www.amazonwatch.org

American College and University Presidents Climate Commitment
Higher education to achieve climate neutrality. www.presidentsclimatecommitment.org

Apollo Alliance
Coalition catalyzing clear-energy revolution in America. www.apolloalliance.org

Association for the Advancement of Sustainability in Higher Education
Information on campus sustainability, discussion forums. initiatives and consortiums. www.aashe.org

Barataria Terrebonne National Estuary
Educational website, includes restoring America's coastal heartland of Louisiana. www.btnep.org

Bay Institute
Novato, CA; Model scientific research, education, advocacy to protect and restore the bay, delta and estuary ecosystems. www.bay.org

Biomethane.com
All about biomethane—links to related info, products and uses. www.biomethane.com

Black Mesa Water Coalition
Funding green businesses and community projects for the Navajo Nation. www.blackmesawatercoalition.org

Blue Green Alliance
Steelworkers and Sierra Club spur dialogue on climate, clean energy, toxics, fair trade. www.bluegreenalliance.org

Blue Planet Project
Justice for water as a public trust, part of the commons. www.blueplanetproject.net

Bluewater Network
San Francisco, CA; Stops environmental damage from vehicles, vessels, reducing dependence on fossil fuels. www.bluewaternetwork.org

California Academy of Sciences
San Francisco, CA; Explore, explain, protect our world: the Aquarium, Natural History Museum, Planetarium, & Rainforest. www.calacademy.org

Campus in Power
Comprehensive organizing and funding guide for student organizers working for sustainability on their campus. www.campusinpower.org

Center for Biological Diversity
Working through science, law, media for all species on the brink of extinction. www.biologicaldiversity.org

Claus Wawrzinek

Center for Environment, Health and Justice
Falls Church, VA; Fights toxic dumps, works with victims of contamination. www.chej.org

Climate Education Initiative
Durham, NH; Online learning community using Curriculum, Operations, Research and Engagement. www.sustainableunh.unh.edu

College Sustainability Report Card
In-depth profiles of hundreds of colleges in US and Canada. www.greenreportcard.org

Conservation International
Empowering societies to care for nature and the well-being of humanity. www.conservation.org

Earthday Network
Washington, DC; Explore annual Earth Day festivals everywhere. www.earthday.org

Earth Justice
Public interest nonprofit law firm dedicated to a healthy environment.www.earthjustice.org

East Bay Municipal Utilities District
Comprehensive consumer site for information, conservancy and education on community water supply. www.EBMUD.com

Ecology Action
Santa Cruz, CA; Education and programs on environmental awareness, change, and sustainable economy. www.ecoact.org

Energy Action Coalition
US and Canada; Youth coalition for clean energy. www.energyactioncoalition.org

EnviroLink Network
Up-to-date news and links to thousands of orgs. www.envirolink.org

Environmental Action
Boston, MA; Protects the environment from special-interest polluters and their allies in govt. www.environmental-action.org

Environmental Research Foundation
Supports grassroots activists working on toxics and social justice issues. www.rachel.org

Environmental News Service
Independent daily international wire service of the environment. www.ens-newswire.com

Environmental Service Learning Initiative
Youth empowered service learning in San Francisco high school classrooms
www.eslisf.org/

Food and Water Watch
Consumer rights org challenges corp control, abuse of food, protects water resources.
www.foodandwaterwatch.org

Friends of the Earth
Washington, DC; Focusing on clean energy, global warming, toxin protection, smarter transportation. www.foe.org

Global Footprint Network
Oakland, CA; Make informed choices based on human impact on the planet.
www.footprintnetwork.org

Green Belt Alliance
San Francisco, CA; Protecting the green belt while improving the livability of cities and towns. www.greenbelt.org

Greenpeace USA
San Francisco, CA; Ordinary people working to save the planet. www.greenpeace.org/usa

Greywater Guerillas
Educating, empowering to build sustainable water culture, infrastructure.
www.greywaterguerrillas.com

Harvest H2O
Advancing sustainable water management practices. www.harvesth2o.com

Health Care Without Harm
Promotes ecologically sound alternatives to health care practices that pollute the environment. www.noharm.org

Indigenous Environmental Network
Bemidji, MN; Links grassroots and tribal governments protecting the sacredness of water. www.ienearth.org

International Rivers
Works to halt destructive river projects worldwide, and to support equitable sustenance. www.internationalrivers.org

International Scientific Congress on Climate Change
Providing a synthesis of existing and emerging scientific knowledge to make sound decisions. www.globalwarmingisreal.com

ItsGettingHotinHere.org
Media project featuring student leaders, to stop global warming. www.itsgettinghotinhere.org

Jane Goodall Institute
Arlington, VA; Empowers people to make a difference for all living things.
www.janegoodall.org

Living Planet Index
Measures trends in the Earth's biological diversity; from World Wildlife Fund International. www.panda.org

Marine Mammal Center
Sausalito, CA; Appreciation of marine mammals through rescue and treatment, scientific inquiry, education and communication. www.tmmc.org

Millennium Ecosystem Assessment
Washington, DC; Assessing the consequences of ecosystem change for human well-being.
www.maweb.org

National Audubon Society
New York, NY; To conserve and restore natural ecosystems and bird diversity.
www.audubon.org

National Geographic
Multi-media producer exploring, educating and conserving the natural world around us.
www.nationalgeographic.com

National Park Conservancy Association
Washington, DC; Safeguarding America's scenic beauty, wildlife, historical treasures.
www.npca.org

Natural Resources Defense Council
New York, NY; Safeguarding Earth's natural systems on which all life depends.
www.nrdc.org

Nature Conservancy
Washington, DC; Protecting ecologically important land and water worldwide for people and nature. www.nature.org

NatureBridge
San Francisco, CA; Residential, nonprofit environmental, field science educator partnered with the National Park Service. www.yni.org

NoNukes.org
Global library, links to info about nuclear power, weapons, contamination, citizen action.
www.nonukes.org

Ocean Arks International
Falmouth, MA; Global leader in the field of ecological water purification. www.oceanarks.org

Ocean Futures Society
Exploring our global ocean, inspiring responsible action through membership and education. www.oceanfutures.org

Oceanic Society
Protecting endangered wildlife and marine habitats worldwide. www.oceanicsociety.org

Orion Grassroots Network
Great Barrington, MA; Resources for sustaining and funding nonprofits. www.oriononline.org

Planet Walk
Pt. Reyes, CA; Raises environmental consciousness and earth stewardship, emphasis on experiential learning. www.planetwalk.org

Portland State University
Resources, tools, technical assistance for clean energy on campus. www.nwgreencampus.org

PowerShift09.org
Young people demand bold action on climate and energy. www.powershift09.org

Project Kaisei
Studying the North Pacific Gyre plastic debris. www.projectkaisei.org

Public Citizen
Ralph Nader-founded consumer protection and government accountability. www.citizen.org

Public Interest Research Groups (PIRGs)
Hundreds of grassroots groups disseminating info on justice, environment. www.pirgs.org

Rails to Trails Conservancy
Washington, DC; Nationwide network of trails along former rail lines. www.railtrails.org

Rainforest Action Network
San Francisco, CA; Transforming the global marketplace via education, organizing, non-violent direct action. www.ran.org

Rocky Mountain Institute
Providing R&D, funding, resources that create pollution-free power. www.rmi.org

Sarvodaya
Sri Lanka; Transformation of human consciousness through spiritual, moral and cultural awakening. www.sarvodaya.org

Save San Francisco Bay
Oakland, CA; Working to protect and restore watersheds. www.savesfbay.org

Sierra Club
San Francisco, CA; Environmental action and green shopping. www.sierraclub.org

Species Alliance
Emeryville, CA; Raise public awareness, education and policy advocacy on mass extinction. www.speciesalliance.org

StopGlobalWarming.org
Demanding a freeze and reduction of CO2 emissions. www.stopglobalwarming.org

StopWaste.org
San Leandro, CA; Environmentally sound solid waste management and resource conservation program. www.stopwaste.org

Student Conservation Association
Charlestown, NH; Engaging youth in hands-on service. www.thesca.org

Suzuki Foundation
Canada; Finds ways for society to live in balance with the natural world. www.davidsuzuki.org

Trust for Public Land
San Francisco, CA; Conserving land in 50 states for public enjoyment. www.tpl.org

United Nations Environmental Program
Providing leadership and partnership in caring for the environment. www.unep.org

United Nations Geo Report
Overview and reports on state of environment and policy. www.unep.org/geo/geo3

Water Resources Research Center, University of Arizona
AZ; Promotes understanding of critical state and regional water management and policy issues. ag.arizona.edu

Water for All Campaign
Protecting essential resources by transforming public consciousness. www.wateractivist.org

Water Institute
Information and resources for local watershed activism. www.oaec.org

Water Quality Association
Representing all levels of water treatment use and industry. www.wqa.org

Water.org
To raise awareness and funds for safe, adequate water. www.water.org

WaterSense
Washington, DC; Sponsored by EPA, seeks to protect the future of US water supply. www.epa.gov/watersense/basic/index.htm

Water Use It Wisely
100 ways to conserve water; reports, videos, links to water conservation products. www.wateruseitwisely.com

Wilderness Society
Washington, DC; To protect wilderness and inspire Americans to care for the wild places. www.wilderness.org

Wind Energy Institute
To educate consumers about wind power and other renewable energy. www.windenergyinstitute.com

World Resources Institute
Washington, DC; Many resources moving society to live in ways to protect the environment and capacity. www.wri.org

World Wildlife Fund
US, Canada, Switzerland; Working to preserve the diversity and abundance of life on Earth. www.worldwildlife.org

Worldwatch Institute
Accessible, fact-based analysis of critical global issues. www.worldwatch.org

Zero Waste Alliance
Promotes practices that lead to the reduction and elimination of waste and toxics. www.zerowaste.org

ENERGY

American Council on Renewable Energy (ACORE)
Bringing all forms of renewable energy into the mainstream. www.acore.org

Build It Green
Berkeley, CA; Energy- and resource-efficient building practices. www.builditgreen.org

California Cars Initiative
Palo Alto, CA; Promoting efficient, non-poluting automotive public policy and technologies. www.calcars.org

Kelly Slocum

Creative Commons/Think Panama

Capitol Climate Action
Activists uniting to stop global warming.
www.capitolclimateaction.org

EcoGeek
Technology news, tips, and blogs on energy, policy, green food, and alternatives to cars.
www.ecogeek.org

Energy Efficiency Resource Standard
Advancing energy efficiency as a means to economic prosperity. www.aceee.org

Green Building Councils
Woodbridge, ON, Canada; Helping the construction industry reduce GHG emissions from the built environment. www.worldgbc.org

Home Energy
News on energy-efficient, durable, comfortable, and green homes. www.homeenergy.org

McKinsey Global Institute
Original research on critical economic issues facing businesses and governments.
www.mckinsey.com

National Renewable Energy Laboratory
Washington, DC; Basic onformation about renewable energy for consumers, homeowners and businesses. www.nrel.gov

Native Energy
Charlotte, VT; Offering Native Americans certified RECs and CO_2 offsets that help build new renewable energy projects.
www.nativeenergy.com

Natural Resources Defense Council
Environmental action group; 1.2 million+ members strong. www.nrdc.org

US Department of Energy Efficiency and Renewables
Washington, DC; US govt. gateway to energy efficiency info. www.eere.energy.gov

Veggie Van Organization
Green curriculum includes www.thefuelfilm.com.
www.veggievan.org

A JUST SOCIETY

Aboriginal Mapping Network
Information-sharing on indigenous land claims, treaty negotiations and development.
www.nativemaps.org

Alternative Information and Development Centre
South Africa; Works in Africa for economic justice and social transformation.
www.aidc.org.za

Amazon Alliance
Defending rights, territories, environment of Amazon basin peoples. www.amazonalliance.org

Amnesty International
London, UK; Preventing human rights abuse and demanding justice. www.amnesty.org

Anti-Privatization Forum
South Africa; Unites workers against privatization, promotes living-wage jobs.
www.apf.org.za

Applied Research Center
Racial justice research, policy, media, activism.
www.arc.org

Asian American Justice Center
Advancing the human and civil rights, with a growing network of nearly 100 community-based organizations. www.advancingequality.org

Asian Law Caucus
Promoting legal and civil rights of Asians and Pacific Islanders. www.asianlawcaucus.org

Asian Pacific Environmental Network
Empowers grassroots social and environmental justice. www.apen4if.org

Bidwell Training Center
Pittsburgh, PA; Occupational / adult vocational education. www.bidwell-training.org

Blue and Yellow Logic
Social enterprise of young leaders that cultivates economic, social and racial diversity.
www.blueandyellowlogic.com

Boggs Center to Nurture Community Leadership
Multi-cultural community activism encouraging strategies for rebuilding our cities.
www.boggscenter.org

California Indian Basketweavers Association
Preserving tradition and access to healthy gathering areas. www.ciba.org

Centre for Justice and Reconciliation
Clearinghouse for restorative justice, repairing harm caused by criminal behaviour by bringing parties to meet cooperatively.
www.restorativejustice.org

The Center for Media Democracy
Promotes media transparency and informed debate, engaging the public in collaborative, fair and accurate reporting. www.prwatch.org

Color of Change
Strengthening black America's political voice.
www.colorofchange.org

ColorLines Direct
Oakland, CA; News on race, politics focused on structural solutions to advance racial justice.
www.colorlines.com

Confederation of Indigenous Nationalities of Ecuador
Ecuador; Guaranteeing indigenous peoples' political voice; defending rights, livelihood.
www.conaie.org

Congress of Racial Equality (CORE)
Activists expose racism and achieve civil rights.
www.core-online.org

Congressional Black Caucus Foundation
Policy research and education to improve socioeconomic circumstances of underserved communities. www.cbcfinc.org

Cultural Creatives
Uniting 50 million adults in the US who share worldview, values and lifestyle.
culturalcreatives.org

Cultural Survival
Cambridge, MA; Promotes the rights, voices, and visions of indigenous peoples.
www.culturalsurvival.org

Delancey Street Foundation
San Francisco, CA; Residential mentoring beyond crime.
www.delanceystreetfoundation.org

EarthJustice
Oakland, CA; Non-profit, public interest law firm. www.earthjustice.org

Edible School Yard
Berkeley, CA; Urban garden, nutrition and science lab. www.edibleschoolyard.org

Ella Baker Center for Human Rights
Oakland, CA; Four cutting-edge campaigns offer alternatives to violence and incarceration. www.ellabakercenter.org

Engage Network
Creating self-replicating groups that take care of people while changing the world. www.engagenet.org

Environmental Justice Resource Center at Clark Atlanta University
Atlanta, GA; Clearinghouse for environmental justice. www.ejrc.cau.edu

Environmental Working Group
Washington, DC; Protecting public health; pushing for national policy change. www.ewg.org

Equality Now
Works to end violence and discrimination against women and girls around the world, including female genital mutilation. www.equalitynow.org

Fairness and Accuracy in Reporting
Well-documented criticism of media bias, censorship. www.fair.org/index.php

Federation of Southern Cooperatives
Saving black-owned land across the South. www.federationsoutherncoop.com

First Peoples Worldwide
Led by Indigenous Peoples, dedicated to Indigenous economic determination. www.firstpeoplesworldwide.org

Free Press
Reform media, transform democracy. www.freepress.net

Genesys Works
Houston, TX; Designed to arm students with the knowledge they need to provide value to corporations. www.genesysworks.org

Global Restoration Network
Ecosystem restoration resource hub. www.globalrestorationnetwork.org

Green For All
Working to build an inclusive green economy to lift people out of poverty. www.greenforall.org

Growing Power
Milwaukee, WI; Building equitable, ecologically sound, sustainable food systems, one community at a time. www.growingpower.org

Harlem Children's Zone
Harlem, NY; Replicable holistic system of education, social-service and community-building. www.hcz.org

Healthcare Without Harm
Arlington, VA; Working to transform the health care sector worldwide. www.hcwh.org

Heifer International
Little Rock, AR; Helping to end hunger and poverty through providing livestock as source of food and self-reliance. www.heifer.org

Highlander Research and Education Center
New Market, TN; Grassroots education for sicial justice in Appalachia and the South. www.highlandercenter.org

Honor the Earth
Native-led support for grassroots efforts; forging change in Indian country. www.honorearth.org

Howard Gardner, Harvard University
Cambridge, MA; Harvard cognition and education professor's site about multiple intelligences. www.howardgardner.com

Human Development Reports
Making the case for a new vision with research, statistics and analysis. www.hdr.undp.org

Human Rights Watch
New York, NY; Defending human rights, seeking justice globally. www.hrw.org

Hunger Project
New York, NY; Ending poverty by mobilizing self reliance and empowering women. www.thp.org

ICLEI Local Governments for Sustainability
Helping local governments go green. www.icleiusa.org

Immigration Policy Center
Accurate information about the effects of immigration on the US economy and society. www.immigrationpolicy.org

Indigenous Environmental Network
Empowering Indigenous Nations, demanding environmental justice and maintaining traditions. www.ienearth.org

Indigenous Women's Network
Training and publications link women globally. www.indigenouswomen.org

Innovations in Civic Participation
Links to organizations worldwide on civic engagement policies and programs. www.icicp.org

International Labour Organization (ILO) Indigenous and Tribal Peoples
Promoting social justice and internationally recognized human, labor rights. www.ilo.org/indigenous/lang--en/index.htm

Intertribal Council on Utility Policy (Intertribal COUP)
Policy and education for tribal governments, colleges and orgs. www.intertribal.org

The Jellybean Conspiracy
Kansas City, MO; High school drama template, explores inclusivity and compassionate relationships. www.jellybeanconspiracy.org

Just Think
Innovative youth media education programs and curricula. www.justthink.org

League of United Latin American Council
Serving Hispanics with a full range of community-based programs; operating 700 councils across the US. www.lulac.org

Manchester Craftsmen Guild
Pittsburgh, PA; Youth arts and vocational education. www.manchesterguild.org

Millennium Development Goals
Tracking the progress toward a sustainable and just world for all. www.un.org/millenniumgoals

National Conference for Community and Justice
Chapters around the US; fights racism, promotes understanding and respect. In New York: www.nccjny.org

National Council of La Raza
Largest Latino civil rights and advocacy in the US. www.nclr.org

Art Explosion

National Network for Immigrant and Refugee Rights
Educates and advises on immigrant and refugee issues. www.nnirr.org

Natural Resource Conservation Service
Cost share and technical assistance for landowners. www.nrcs.usda.gov

Navdanya International
Delhi, India; Promoting peace, seed-saving, fair trade, and more. www.navdanya.org

ONE
Committed to the fight against extreme poverty and preventable disease in Africa. www.one.org

Oxfam International
UK; Long-term solutions to poverty, hunger, and social injustice around the world. www.oxfam.org

Pew Hispanic Center
Pew Global Attitudes Project; research, news, and trends about Hispanics and Latinos. www.hispanicpewresearch.org

Population Connection
Education and action toward population stabilization. www.populationconnection.org

Population Institute
Washington, DC; Seeks to voluntarily reduce excessive population growth through universal access to family planning information, education, and services. www.populationinstitute.com

Population Reference Bureau
Washington, DC; Empowering information to advance the well-being of current and future generations. www.prb.org

Raffi
Canada; Promoting "child honoring," sustainable communities; offers children's songs by Raffi. www.raffinews.com

REACH Center
Respecting Ethnic and Cultural Heritage curriculum for schools. www.reachctr.org

Research Foundation for Science, Technology, and Ecology
India; Protecting rights to livelihood and environment threatened by centralized monoculture. www.vshiva.net

Richard Louv
Getting kids back to nature. http://richardlouv.com

Rockwood Leadership Program
Berkeley, CA; Promotes social change through training progressive nonprofits. www.rockwoodfund.org

Roots of Peace
San Rafael, CA; Removing land mines in exchange for vines. www.rootsofpeace.org

Ruckus Society
Oakland, CA; Training for peace, social and environmental justice. www.ruckus.org

Seventh Generation Fund for Indian Development
Upholding the sovereignty of Native peoples, with grassroots support. www.7genfund.org

Smiles Change Lives
Kansas City, MO; Helps low-income children receive braces. www.smileschangelives.org

Sisters of Color for Education
Colorado-based health education and advocacy program for Latino communities. www.sistersofcolor.org

Society for Ecological Restoration
Tucson, AZ; SER and the Indigenous People's Restoration Network integrate tradition and western science. www.ser.org

Southern Poverty Law Center
Montgomery, AL; Civil rights/anti-hate group law center, promotes tolerance. www.splcenter.org

Survival International
UK; Working for tribal peoples' rights through education, advocacy and campaigns. www.survival-international.org

Sustainable South Bronx
Dedicated to environmental justice solutions informed by community needs. www.ssbx.org

Terra Madre
Italy; Slow food communities network. www.terramadre.info

UN Millennium Campaign to End Poverty 2015
New York, NY; Supports UN Millennium Development Goals. www.endpoverty2015.org/

US Labor Education in the Americas Project
Supports economic justice and rights for workers in Latin America. www.usleap.org

United for a Fair Economy
Boston, MA; Popular economics education bridging the equity divide; great library, training tools. www.faireconomy.org

United Nations Association
New York, NY; UNA-USA encourages responsible US leadership in the United Nations. www.unausa.org

United Nations Development Programme
New York, NY; The UN's global development network. www.undp.org

United Students Against Sweatshops
Washington, DC; Students organizing for sweatshop-free labor conditions and workers' rights. www.studentsagainstsweatshops.org

Universal Living Wage
Austin, TX; To ensure that every American is working and paid a Fair Living Wage. www.universallivingwage.org

Via Campesina
Honduras; Coordinates small- and middle-scale producers, agricultural workers, rural women, and indigenous communities. www.viacampesina.org

Washington Peace Center
Washington, DC; Anti-racist peace, justice and social change advocates. www.washingtonpeacecenter.org

White Earth Land Recovery Project
Native Harvest catalog, alternative energy projects, preserving cultural heritage. www.nativeharvest.com

The White House Project
Advancing women's leadership across sectors. www.thewhitehouseproject.org

Winston County Self Help Cooperative
Jackson, MS; Saving rural America with youth gardens, keeping land in black ownership. www.wcshc.com

Witness for Peace
Washington, DC; Committed to nonviolence, led by faith and conscience. www.witnessforpeace.org

Women for Women International
Washington, DC; Addresses the unique needs of women in conflict and post-conflict environments. www.womenforwomen.org

Women's Learning Partnership
Working on rights, development, and leadership. www.learningpartnership.org

World Vision International
Monrovia, CA; Christian relief to overcome poverty. www.wvi.org/wvi/wviweb.nsf

Youth GreenCorps
Lexington, KY; Sustainable Communities Network partnership for youth in horticulture and art. www.sustainlex.org/ygc.html

ECONOMICS

50 Years is Enough
Coalition to reform international financial institutions, including debt cancellation. www.50years.org

Accion International
Boston, MA; Poverty alleviation through micro loans, training, financial services. www.accion.org

Action, Research and Education Network of Aotearoa (ARENA)
Aotearoa, NZ; New Zealand network resisting corporate globalization and promoting alternatives. www.arena.org.nz

Ad Busters
Global network of culture jammers and creatives working to change the way information flows, and the way meaning is produced in our society. www.adbusters.org

Alliance for Responsible Trade
US network promoting equitable trade and development. www.art-us.org

American Booksellers Association
Tarrytown, NY; National independent booksellers. www.bookweb.org

American Independent Business Alliance (AMIBA)
Bozeman, MT; Representing community-based independent businesses. www.amiba.net

American Pictures
Denmark; A multi-media presentation on racism, oppression, and the underclass. www.american-pictures.com

Appalachian Sustainable Development
Cooperative networks and marketing for sustainable forestry/products and agriculture. www.asdevelop.org

Association for the Taxation of Financial Transactions for the Aid of Citizens (ATTAC)
France; Advocating the Tobin tax, and democratic control of global financial markets/institutions. www.attac.org

Australian Fair Trade and Investment Network
Community and union education and debate on trade and investment policy. www.aftinet.org.au

B Corp
Web network of new B corporations solving social and environmental problems. www.bcorporation.net

Bank Information Center
Fosters socially just development and policies. www.bicusa.org

Bank of North Dakota
State run bank promoting citizens, agriculture, commerce and industry. www.banknd.nd.gov

Bay Area Green Business Program
CA; Gov agencies and utilities help local businesses conserve resources, prevent pollution, minimize waste. www.greenbiz.ca.gov

Bay Localize
Oakland, CA; Catalyzing regional self-reliant economy for Bay Area. www.baylocalize.org

Better Business Bureau
Check out a business, charity or file a complaint. www.bbb.org

Better World Club
Portland, OR; USA's only environmentally friendly auto club. www.betterworldclub.com

Biomimicry Guild
Helena, MT; Helps designers, engineers, architects, and businesses learn from and emulate natural models.www.biomimicryguild.com

Biomimicry Institute
Missoula, MT; Education, training, resources, case studies. www.biomimicryinstitute.org

Business Alliance for Local Living Economies
San Francisco, CA; Conferences, training, and tools for localization of wealth. www.livingeconomies.org

Business for Innovative Climate and Energy Policy (BICEP)
Boston, MA; Supporting comprehensive energy and climate legislation. www.ceres.org

Calvert Foundation
Bethesda, MD; Investment network helping communities globally. www.calvertfoundation.org

Bigstockphoto.com

Canadian Co-operative Association
Canada; Represents coop and credit union members in Canada and 40 countries. www.coopscanada.coop

Center for American Progress
Progressive think tank improving the lives of Americans. www.americanprogress.org

Center for Community Self-Help
Durham, NC; Credit union, real estate developer, policy advocate, investment link. www.self-help.org

Center for Parnership Studies
Pacific Grove, CA; Promotes realization of human capacities for consciousness, caring, and creativity. www.partnershipway.org

Center for Popular Economics
Amherst, MA; Economics training for community organizers, activists and social change initiators. www.populareconomics.org

Center for Responsible Lending
Durham, NC; Tools, resources and action tips about money and credit. www.responsiblelending.org

Center for State Innovation
Helping states implement innovative, progressive policies. www.stateinnovation.org

Center for Sustainable Economy
Santa Fe, NM; Policy and analysis by experts in economics, law and biology. www.sustainable-economy.org

Center of Concern
Catholic research, educational org promoting just, sustainable international finance, trade systems. www.coc.org

Center for the Advancement of Steady State Economy
Arlington, VA; Promotes the steady state economy as a desirable alternative to economic growth. www.steadystate.org

CERES
Investors, environmental, public interest groups working w/ corps to address climate change. www.ceres.org

ChevronToxico
Justice campaign in Ecuador to hold Big Oil accountable for contamination.
www.chevrontoxico.com

Chilean Alliance for Just and Responsible Trade
Chile; Coalition of environmental, labor, and others supporting economic integration.
www.comerciojusto.cl

Citizens Trade Campaign
National coalition opposing NAFTA; promoting just trade legislation in US.
www.citizenstrade.org

COP15 United Nations Climate Change Conference
2009 UN conference in Copenhagen; with climate facts, blogs, news, and more.
http://en.cop15.dk

ClimateBiz
Business resource for climate management: news, analysis, reports, policy links, and more.
www.climatebiz.com

Common Frontiers
Canada; Examining the effects of economic integration in the Americas.
www.commonfrontiers.ca

Common Security Club
Network to prepare for economic change.
www.commonsecurityclub.org

Community Environmental Legal Defense Fund
Chambersburg, PA; Legal services for building sustainable communities and ending corporate governance. www.celdf.org

Community Investing Center
Washington, DC; Online investing in microenterprise, women, communities around the world. www.communityinvest.org

Community Investment NetworkSM
Online credit, funding, assistance, and capital tools. www.communityinvestmentnetwork.org

Community-Wealth.org
MD; Wealth building information, tools and links. www.community-wealth.org

Consumer Cooperative Management Association
Working together to achieve social, economic well-being thru orgs we own and control.
www.cdsus

CooperationWorks!
Ames, IA; Created to grow the cooperative model across the United States.
www.cooperationworks.coop

Corner House
Supporting democratic, community movements for environmental, social justice in the UK.
www.thecornerhouse.org.uk

Corporate Responsibility (CORE) Coalition
UK; Alliance promoting respect for rights of workers, local communities and the environment. www.corporate-responsibility.org

Corporate Watch
Exposing corporations' detrimental effects on society, the environment.
www.corporatewatch.org

CorpWatch
Corporate greenwash watchdog.
www.corpwatch.org

Cost of War
Running calculator of the costs of war.
www.costofwar.com

Council of Canadians
Canada; Citizens' watchdog org promoting economic justice, environmental preservation.
www.canadians.org

Cradle to CradleSM **Design**
Charlottesville, VA; Certifies environmentally-intelligent design. www.c2ccertified.com

E.F. Schumacher Society
Great Barrington, MA; Building local economies: microcredit, land trusts, local currency, training, publications. www.smallisbeautiful.org

Economic Policy Institute
Broadening public debate strategies to achieve prosperous and fair economy. www.epinet.or

Environmental Defense Fund
Nonpartisan environmental advocacy group.
www.edf.org

Ethical Markets
Television, website, promoting a green economy. www.ethicalmarkets.com

Fair Trade Federation
Washington, DC; Global association of wholesalers, retailers, producers in N.A.
www.fairtradefederation.org

Fair Trade Resource Network
Education on fair trade.
www.fairtraderesource.org

Fairtrade Labeling Organization International
Maintains standards for certification and labeling. www.fairtrade.net

Forest Stewardship Council
Germany; Supporting environmentally-appropriate management of forests via certification program. www.fsc.org

Foundation for International Community Assistance
Washington, DC; Provides financial services to lowest-income entrepreneurs.
www.villagebanking.org

Foundation for Sustainable Development
San Francisco, CA; Throughout Asia, Africa, Latin America: supporting sustainable solutions.
www.fsdinternational.org

Girl Effect
Video showing the benefits of valuing girls.
www.girleffect.org

Global Business Network
San Francisco, CA; Helping orgs adapt and grow effectively in the face of mounting uncertainty.
www.gbn.com

Global Compact
Promoting accountability to human rights, labour, environment, anti-corruption principles.
www.unglobalcompact.org

Global Environmental Management Initiative (GEMI)
Washington, DC; Guidebook on forging corporate-nonprofit partnerships.
www.gemi.org

Global Exchange
San Francisco, CA; Offering tours, a fair trade store, and resources supporting human rights.
www.globalexchange.org

Global Giving
Washington, DC; Thriving online marketplace of goods and ideas. www.globalgiving.com

Global Greengrants Fund
Boulder, CO; Financial support for grassroots groups in developing countries.
www.greengrants.org

Global Marshall Plan Initiative
Promoting an eco-social market economy globally. www.globalmarshallplan.org

Global Policy Forum
New York, NY; Monitors UN policy, informs citizen action for peace and justice.
www.globalpolicy.org

Art Explosion

Goods from the Woods
Licking, MO; Demonstrating certified organic wild crop harvesting. www.wildcrops.com

Grameen Bank
Bangladesh; Providing micro credit to the poor in rural Bangladesh. www.grameen-info.org

Grassroots.org
Bethesda, MD; Serving nonprofits with free information, internet services, legal consulting. www.grassroots.org

Grassroots Leadership
Charlotte, NC; Training and resource center to end social and economic oppression, and achieve justice and equity. www.grassrootsleadership.org

Great Old Broads
Durango, CO; Unites voices and activism of elders to preserve and protect wilderness and wild lands. www.greatoldbroads.org

Great Turning
Changing the defining stories of the prevailing culture. www.thegreatturning.net

Green America
Washington, DC; Providing economic solutions via National Green Pages, resources, Green Festivals and more. www.greenamericatoday.org

Greenpeace Greenwashing
Washington, DC; Corporate watchdog, accountability advocate, exposing deceptive environmental and social claims and ads. www.stopgreenwash.org

Institute for Community Economics
Community Land Trust model of building, rehabilitation of urban, rural housing. www.iceclt.org

Institute for Local Self-Reliance
Supports local enterprise, principles of governance. www.ilsr.org; www.newrules.org

Institute for Policy Studies
Washington, DC; Policy and research for social and environmental justice. www.ips-dc.org

Interfaith Center on Corporate Responsibility
Puts pressure on companies to be socially and environmentally responsible. www.iccr.org

International Co-operative Alliance
Costa Rica; Uniting, representing and serving co-operatives worldwide. www.ica.coop

International Fair Trade Association (IFAT)
UK; Promoting organizations for greater justice in world trade. www.ifat.org

International Forum on Globalization
San Francisco, CA; Stimulating new thinking, activity in response to economic globalization. www.ifg.org

International Society for Ecology and Culture
UK; Promotes locally-based alternatives to global consumerism. www.isec.org.uk

International Sustainability Conference
Basel, Switzerland; Social scientists working toward sustainable development. www.isc2008.ch

Investors' Circle Foundation
"Patient capital for a sustainable future" from venture capitalists. www.investorscircle.net

Jobs with Justice
Washington, DC; Protects workers' rights and standards of living. www.jwj.org

John Perkins
Former "Economic Hit Man" promotes ecology, sustainability. www.johnperkins.org

Jubilee
Joining hands against debt and global poverty. www.jubileeusa.org

Kiva
San Francisco, CA; Web-based microlending to alleviate poverty around the world. www.kiva.org

Lakota Funds
ND; Growing businesses on Pine Ridge Indian Reservation by microlending and coaching. www.lakotafunds.org

McDonough Braungart Design Chemistry
Charlottesville, VA; Trasnforming the design of products, processes and services to an eco-friendly environment. www.mbdc.com

Mexican Action Network on Free Trade
Mexico; Labor, environmental, human rights groups promoting alternative to free trade. www.rmalc.org.mx

Movimento Dos Trabalhadores Rurais Sem Terra (Landless Workers Movement; MST)
Brazil; Land reform in Brazil helps reduce poverty, increase literacy. www.mstbrazil.org

National Center for Employee Ownership
Oakland, CA; Clearinghouse for all things related to employee ownership. www.nceo.org

National Community Reinvestment Coalition
Association of groups supporting affordable housing, job development. www.fairlending.com

National Housing Trust
Preserving affordable homes across the US. www.nhtinc.org

Natural Capitalism Solutions
Eldorado Springs, CO; Providing leaders with tools and strategies for companies, communities and countries. www.natcapsolutions.org

Natural Capitalism, Inc.
Eldorado Springs, CO; Sustainability tools for increasing profits and efficiency. www.natcapinc.com

Natural Logic
Berkeley, CA; Assessment to recover lost profit in waste. www.natlog.com

Natural Step
Sweden; Creating a fundamenal paradigm shift to true sustainable development. www.naturalstep.org; in the US: www.naturalstepusa.org

New Economics Foundation
UK; Challenging mainstream thinking on economic, environmental, social issues. www.jubilee2000uk.org

New Economy Working Group
Virtual think tank reframing the economic policy debate. www.neweconomyworkinggroup.org

Northwest Earth Institute
Portland, OR; Workbook articles by leaders in many fields, for use by dicussion groups. www.nwei.org

Oakland Institute
Oakland, CA; Policy think tank focusing on food issues. www.oaklandinstitute.org

Opportunity Fund
Lending working capital to working people. www.opportunityfund.org

People-Centered Development Forum
Global network of activists resisting corporate globalization. www.pcdf.org

Rainforest Alliance
Protects ecosystems, people and wildlife. www.rainforest-alliance.org

Right to the City
National alliance working for urban justice. www.righttothecity.org

ShoreBank
Chicago, IL; Community Development Bank. www.shorebankcorp.com

ShoreBank Enterprise Cascadia
Ilwaco, WA; Loans and support for green businesses and social entrepreneurs. www.sbpac.com

Slow Money Alliance
Brookline, MA; Building new financial means to invest in local food systems. www.slowmoneyalliance.org

Small-Mart
Takoma Park, MD; Ideas and tools for building healthy local economies. www.smallmart.org

Social Enterprise Alliance of Midlothian
Scotland; Resources for local benefit. www.seamidlothian.co.uk

Social Equity Group
Berkeley, CA; Specializing in socially responsible investment. www.socialequity.com

Social Investment Forum
Washington, DC and San Francisco, CA; Responsible investing and financial services directory. www.socialinvest.org

Soul of Money Institute
San Francisco, CA; Transform your relationship with money and life. www.soulofmoney.org

SourceWatch
Wiki site of organizations and issues shaping the public agenda. www.sourcewatch.org

Southwest Network for Environmental and Economic Justice
Albuquerque, NM; Grassroots lilinqual groups developing regional strategies on injustices and policies. www.sneej.org

State of the World Forum
San Francisco, CA; Guiding humanity to an increasingly global and interdependent civilization. www.worldforum.org

SustainLane
San Francisco, CA; Directory for green everything. www.sustainlane.org

Teach a Man to Fish
UK; Supports schools, education and vocational training to achieve self-sufficiency. www.teachamantofish.org.uk

Third World Network
Malaysia; Southern perspectives on economic, social, and environmental issues. www.twnside.org.sg

Transfair USA
Certifies Fair Trade products; links to Fair Trades sites. www.transfairusa.org

Transnational Institute
The Netherlands; Network of activist-scholars providing critical analyses of global problems. www.tni.org

UN-HABITAT
Promotes a better urban future. www.unhabitat.org

Urban Institute
Nonpartisan economic and social policy research. www.urban.org

US Federal Trade Commission
Link to legal filing about greenwashing. www.ftc.gov/opa/reporter/greengds.shtm

World Council of Credit Unions
Advocates for credit unions; information and serivces about finance. www.woccu.org

World Fair Trade Organization
Online marketplace and association support. www.wfto.com

WorldChanging
Seattle, WA; Journalists for sustainability. www.worldchanging.org

COMMUNITIES

Action Without Borders
Connecting people w/resources to help build a free and dignified world. www.idealist.org

American Center for Energy Efficient Economy
Researchers advancing energy efficiency. www.aceee.org

American College for Advancement in Medicine
Physicians combine conventional and alternative medicine; offer training, referrals. www.acam.org

Frank Taylor

American Community Gardening Association
US, Canada; Building community by increasing community gardens. www.communitygarden.org

American Jewish World Service
Supporting communicating-based development to alleviate poverty, hunger, disease throughout Africa, Asia, the Americas. www.ajwsconnect

Architecture for Humanity
Design solutions for humanitarian crises. www.architectureforhumanity.org

Asheville Integrative Medicine
Reversing chronic diseases. www.docbiddle.com

Be the Change Earth Alliance
Vancouver, BC, Canada; International network of study/action/support circles. www.bethechangeearthalliance.org

Berkeley Community Gardening Collaborative
Berkeley, CA; Urban agriculture and healthy food. www.ecologycenter.org/bcgc

Blue Ridge Forever
Collaboration of 13 land conservancies. www.blueridgeforever.info

Brower Youth Awards
Promoting youth environmental leadership. www.broweryouthawards.org

Building Green
For environmental protection and a healthy indoors. www.buildinggreen.com

Campaign for a Commercial Free Childhood
Boston, MA; Limiting impact of commercial culture on children. www.commercialfreechildhood.org

CARE Action Network
Atlanta, GA; Humanitarians fighting global poverty, putting women at center of community efforts. www.care.org

Center for Transit-Oriented Development
Integrates transportation systems to include transit, walking. www.reconnectingamerica.org

Center for Wise Democracy
Dynamic Facilitation is used for Wisdom Councils. www.wisedemocracy.org

Co-Intelligence Institute
How to tap wisdom together.
www.co-intelligence.org

CommonDreams.org
Internet news and activism for progressive community. www.commondreams.org

Community Solutions
Empowering survival of peak oil and climate change. www.communitysolution.org

Creative Problem Solving Institute
Sponsors training in creative problem solving.
www.cpsiconference.org

Culture Shapes Community
Turning neighborhood tensions into opportunities for interaction.
www.cultureshapescommunity.org

David Suzuki Foundation
Conserving environment through science-based education, advocacy, policy work.
www.davidsuzuki.org

Dictionary of Sustainable Management
Project of the Presidio School of Management.
www.sustainabilitydictionary.com

Dynamic Facilitation
For great meetings, resolving conflicts, co-creating solutions and fostering true democracy.
www.tobe.net

Earth Charter Initiative
San Jose, CA; Costa Rica; Promotes ethical principles for building a just, sustainable, peaceful global society.
www.earthcharterinaction.org

Earth Island Institute
Oakland, CA; Supports people and groups creating solutions to protect the planet.
www.earthisland.org

Earthaven
NC; Intentional community offering short term experiential sustainable living training.
www.earthaven.org

Ecology Center
Berkeley, CA; Sustainable living models, tools, training, referrals, strategies, infrastructure.
www.ecologycenter.org

Energy Star/Green Star
US Environmental Protection Agency and Dept. of Energy promote energy efficiency.
www.energystar.gov

Environmental Protection Agency, Sustainability
Portal to urban sustainability, built environment, climate change programs.
www.epa.gov/sustainability

Equality Now
Working to end violence, discrimination against women, girls, globally. www.equalitynow.org

Fair Vote
Transforming elections for universal access to participation, and a full spectrum of ballot choices. www.fairvote.org

Farm Animal Reform Movement
Bethesda, MD; Advocating plant-based diet, humane treatment of farm animals.
www.farmusa.org

Fistula Foundation
Sponsor life-transforming surgery for women injured in labor. www.fistulafoundation.org

Flex Your Power
California's award-winning energy efficiency outreach campaign. www.fypower.org

Food Not Bombs
Working to end hunger and stop economic and environmental exploitation.
www.foodnotbombs.net

Food Not Lawns
Community transformation and ecological urban living via gardening, shared resources.
www.foodnotlawns.net

Friends of Edna Maternity Hospital
Help support the work of remarkable Somali activist Edna Adan. www.ednahospital.com

Gentle Teaching International
Teaches skills of being kind, nurturing, and loving toward marginalized children and adults.
www.gentleteaching.com

Girls Learn International
Pairs US classrooms with spartan classrooms in Africa, Asia, Latin America. www.girlslearn.org

Global Ecovillage Network
Supporting ecovillages via expanding education, demonstration programs. www.gen.ecovillage.org

Global Fund for Women
Provides grants, advances human rights.
www.globalfundforwomen.org

Global Green USA
US arm of Green Cross Int'l; creating green buildings/communities, drinkable water.
www.globalgreen.org

Global Living
Connects donors to projects that need support.
www.globalgiving.com

Global Oneness Project
Film project to show how interconnectedness can be lived. www.globalonenessproject.org

Global Sufficiency Network
Getting out the message—there is enough for all. www.globalsufficiency.org

Good Works
National directory of social change organizations, alternatives to corporate employment. www.goodworksfirst.org

Green America
Green Business Network; the go-to place for new economy resources.
www.greenamericatoday.org

Green Casket Company
Providing "green" caskets handcrafted by locals, local timber, sawmills. www.greencasket.net

Green Cross International
Cultivating global interdependence and shared responsibility, clean drinking water. www.gci.ch

Green Festivals
San Francisco, CA; Gatherings to accelerate the emergence of a new economy.
www.greenfestivals.com

Green For All
Lifting people out of poverty by building inclusive green economies. www.greenforall.org

GreenerCars
Rating the environmental friendliness of every vehicle on the market. www.greenercars.com

GreenHOME
Working to make affordable housing and neighborhoods green in DC.
www.greenhome.org

Greensburg, Kansas
Rebuilding a green Greensburg, Kansas after 2007 tornado devastated town.
www.greensburggreentown.org

Grist
Monitors and reports on environmental news since 1999; website forum. www.grist.org

Habitat for Humanity
Americus, GA; Ecumenical housing ministry seeking to eliminate homelessness.
www.habitat.org

Hale Akua Garden Farm
Maui, HI; Educational retreat center and certified organic farm. www.sunrise-center.org

Haute Couleur
Women restoring health to Earth's life support systems. www.hautecouleur.org

Healthy Built Homes
NC; Support for small green home builders. www.healthybuilthomes.org

The Heritage Institute
Clinton, WA; Distance, on-line, and on-site sustainability related continuing education for teachers. www.hol.edu

Housing and Urban Development
US support for affordable housing. www.hud.gov

Hybrid Center
Consumer resources for hybrid vehicles with reviews, comparisons, detailed specifications. www.hybridcenter.org

Imago Therapy and Education
Transforms relationships and the world through dialogue. www.gettingtheloveyouwant.com

Institute for Sustainable Communities
Montpelier, VT; ISC trains and mentors communities in sustainability. www.iscvt.org

Institute for Transportation and Development Policy
Lancaster, UK; Promoting environmentally sustainable and socially equitable transportation worldwide. www.itdp.org

Institute of Noetic Sciences
Petaluma, CA; Research on the potential and power of consciousness. www.noetic.org

Intentional Communities
Information and directory of IC's, with related links. www.ic.org

International Council on Clean Transportation
Lancaster, UK; Improving air quality and transporation issues around the world. www.theicct.org

International Dark Sky Association
Washington, DC; Promotes light pollution education and prevention. www.darksky.org

IPAS
Safe abortion can save women's lives. See the film. www.notyetrain.org

Land Trust Alliance
Unites local communities working to save natural areas. www.landtrustalliance.org

Los Angeles Ecovillage
Re-inventing how we live in cities at a lower environmental impact. www.laecovillage.org

Make It Right Foundation
Actor Brad Pitt's project to rebuild New Orleans green. www.makeitrightnola.org

Marin Conservation Corp
San Rafael, CA; Develops youth and conserves natural resources for strong, sustainable community. www.marincc.org

Matrona
Promoting midwifery and undisturbed birth. www.thematrona.com

National Capital Institute
Serving pathways of change with books, research reports and tools. www.naturalcapital.org

National Complete Streets Coalition
Promoting "complete streets" with safe access for all users. www.completestreets.org

New Dimensions Radio
Ukiah, CA; Striving to provide listeners with practical knowledge and perennial wisdom. www.NewDimensions.org

New Roadmap Foundation
Seattle, WA; Practical tools and innovative approaches to personal and cultural change. www.newroadmap.org

NextGEN
Youth working towards sustainability. www.nextgen.ecovillage.org

Noise Pollution Clearinghouse
Resources for reducing noise pollution. www.noisepollution.org

North American Eco-Municipalities Network
Creating sustainable communities by sharing expertise, resources and experiences. www.1kfriends.org

North Carolina Integrative Medical Society
Promotes natural healing. www.ncims.org

Occidental Arts and Ecology Center
Occidental, CA; Programs on permaculture, hydrology and bioremediation. www.oaec.org

Omega Institute for Holistic Studies
Rhinebeck, NY; Offering year-round lectures, workshops, library; summer work and camping. www.eomega.org

One World USA
Washington, DC; Global info network for nonprofits helping create a better world. www.oneworld.net

Open Space Technology
Guidelines for highly effective meetings, conferences addressing complex problems. www.openspaceworld.org

Pachamama Alliance
San Francisco, CA; Empowering indigenous rainforest people, promoting new global vision. www.pachamama.org

Partners for Livable Communities
Providing information and leadership that help communities help themselves. www.livable.com

Pathfinder International
Working for women's right to contraception, quality reproductive health care. www.pathfind.org

Peace Action
Silver Spring, MD; Mobilizing for peace and disarmament. www.peace-action.org

Peace Alliance / Department of Peace
Center Line, MI; Education and activism to make peace central to society. www.thepeacealliance.org

Plan USA
Grassroots programs in health, education, water, sanitation, income-generation, cross-cultural communication. www.planusa.org

Planetwork
San Francisco, CA; Digital technology for democratic, socially just, ecologically sane future. www.planetwork.net

Positive Futures Network
Bainbridge Island, WA; Education, resources and publications on building a just and sustainable world. www.futurenet.org

Roberta Vogel

Environmental Service Learning Initiative (eslisf.org)

Post Carbon Institute
Sebastopol, CA; Transition from fossil fuels: research and education. www.postcarbon.org

Project for Public Spaces
Central hub for those striving to make public spaces better. www.pps.org

Right Livelihood Award
"Alternative Nobel prize" given annually to pioneers in creating a just and sustainable future. www.rightlivelihood.org

Shift in Action
Online resources for advancing new perspectives. www.shiftinaction.com

Save the Children
Creating lasting, positive change in the lives of children in need. www.savethechildren.org

ShoreBank International
Chicago, IL; Invests in communities toward economic equity and healthy environment. www.sasbk.com

Silicon Valley Toxics Coalition
San Jose, CA; Coalition concerned with health problems caused by high-tech electronics industry. www.svtc.org

Sirius Community
A Massachusetts intentional community in it's 30th year reflecting reverence for all Life. www.siriuscommunity.org

Small Planet Institute
Cambridge, MA; Strives to bring to light the emergence of "living democracy." www.smallplanetinstitute.org

SmallPlanet.org
Positive stories about participatory democracy and sustainability. www.smallplanet.org

Smart Communities
Education for technology and innovation in new global economy. www.smartcommunities.org

SpaceShare
Oakland, CA; For carpooling, greening your events, and more. www.spaceshare.org

Surface Transportation Policy Project
Coalition for equitable, smart communities. www.transact.org

Sustain Dane
Creating communities that deeply enjoy their unique environment. www.sustaindane.org

Sustainability Institute
Hartland, VT; Understanding the root causes of unsustainable behavior. www.sustainabilityinstitute.org

Sustainable Communities Network
Online resources for livability. www.sustainable.org

Sustainable Jersey
Certification program for municipalities in New Jersey that want to go green. www.sustainablejersey.com

Sustainable Lexington
Inspiring systemic changes to create sustainable cities. www.sustainlex.org

Sustainable Seattle
Citizen-based indicators and great resource list;leaders since 1991. www.sustainableseattle.org

Sustainable Urban Transport Project
Helping developing world cities achieve their sustainable transport goals. www.sutp.org

Tapestry Institute
Elizabeth, CO; Research, scholarship and education emphasizing kinship with the Earth. www.tapestryinstitute.org

Transaction Net
Web collaboration for technology and monetary systems. www.transaction.net

Transition Towns
Broad international community of groups and individuals basing work on Transition Model. www.transitiontowns.org

Transition Whidbey
"Transitional town" working towards greater food, energy, and economic self reliance. www.transitionwhidbey.org

Tree Hugger
Media outlet; clearing house for green news, solutions and products. www.treehugger.com

U.S. Green Building Council
Enabling an environmentally responsible built environment via LEED, training, conferences. www.usgbc.org

Union of Concerned Scientists
Works towards securing changes in policy, corporate practices, consumer choices. www.ucusa.org

Urban Land Institute
Research and education org providing leadership in responsible, thriving communities. www.uli.org

Urban Permaculture Guild
Oakland, CA; Inspiring communities to creatively transform how and where they live. www.urbanpermacultureguild.org

Venus Project
Blueprint that maximizes technology to benefit humans and environment. www.thevenusproject.com

Virtual Library on Transportation
Washington, DC; Dept. of Transportation compilation of information links. www.bts.gov/external_links/index.html

Weatherization Assistance Program (WAP)
Federal program assisting low-income families improve energy efficiency of homes. www.waptac.org

Western North Carolina Green Building Council
Promoting environmentally sustainable and health conscious building practices in western NC. www.wncgbc.org

What's Your Tree?
Creating an international network of small groups that heal the world. www.whatsyourtree.org

Wisdom of the World
Novato, CA; Creating intelligent delivery systems for universal, inclusive wisdom. www.wisdomoftheworld.com

Wiser Earth
Connecting people, nonprofits, businesses for a just and sustainable world. www.wiserearth.org

Women for Women
Helping women survivors of war gain stability and self-sufficiency. www.womenforwomen.org

World Green Building Council
Transforming building practices for thriving environment, economy and society. www.worldgbc.org

World Resources Institute Center for Sustainable Transport
Lancaster, UK; Implementing sustainable solutions to urban mobility problems. www.embarq.org

World Transport Policy and Practice Journal
Lancaster, UK; Initiatives that bring reduction in global dependency on cars, lorries, aircraft. www.eco-logica.co.uk/worldtransport.html

YES! Youth for Environmental Sanity
Soquel, CA; Connects, inspires, educates and facilitates change-makers. www.yesworld.org

GETTING PERSONAL

Action for Solidarity, Equality, Environment, and Development (A SEED)
The Netherlands; Promoting small, local organic farms. www.aseed.net

American Farmland Trust
Promoting farms, healthy practices to stop the loss of productive farmland. www.farmland.org

Awakening Earth
Resources/change indicators in global consciousness, voluntary simplicity, media activism. www.awakeningearth.org

Awakening the Dreamer, Changing the Dream Symposium
San Francisco, CA; Inspiring environmentally sustainable, spiritually fulfilling, socially just human life around the world. www.awakeningthedreamer.org

Better World Handbook
Davis, CA; Tips for living for everyone! Excellent sustainability overview. www.betterworldhandbook.com

Better World Shopping Guide
US; 1000+ company database for eco-conscious consumers. www.betterworldshopper.org

Beyond Pesticides
Protecting public health and the environment. www.beyondpesticides.org

BigPictureSmallWorld
Media, PA; Education to empower student leaders. www.bigpicturesmallworld.com

Biodegradable Products Institute
Scientifically based standards; education; promote commercial composting. www.bpiworld.org

Bioneers
Santa Fe, NM; Great conference, education, solutions to restore Earth communities; support youth leadership. www.bioneers.org

Car Sharing
Car sharing info. and links. www.carsharing.net

Care2
Redwood City, CA; Online advocacy programs in environment, human rights, women, animals and more. www.care2.com

Center for a New American Dream
Takoma Park, MD; Helps Americans consume responsibly. www.newdream.org

Center for Food Safety
Promotes organic and sustainable agriculture. www.centerforfoodsafety.org

Center for Teen Empowerment
Inspires young people to handle difficult social problems, create positive change. www.teenempowerment.org

Challenge Day - Youth
Concord, CA; Experiential programs for youth. www.challengeday.org

Circle of Life
Oakland, CA; Find a way of life that honors diversity, interdependence. www.circleoflifefoundation.org

Common Cause
Washington, DC; Vehicle for citizen voices in holding elected leaders accountable to public interest. www.commoncause.org

Community Food Security Coalition
Coalition to build strong, sustainable local, regional food systems. www.foodsecurity.org

Daily Acts
Petaluma, CA; Inspiring choices that matter; sustainability education. www.daily-acts.org

Daily Green
Green news and information. www.thedailygreen.com

Democracy School
New organizing model for citizens. www.celdf.org/DemocracySchool

Dream Change Coalition
Whately, MA; Shifting consciousness and lifestyles through education; w/ John Perkins, Llyn Roberts. www.dreamchange.org

Earth Policy Institute
EPI's sustainable future plan comes with a roadmap; founded by Lester Brown. www.earth-policy.org

Eckhart Tolle groups
Teaches spiritual awakening as next step in human evolution. www.eckharttolle.com

Ecological Footprint
Ecological Footprint Quiz: estimate your daily use of earth resources. www.myfootprint.org

Eco-Troubadour
Rock n Roll eco-education assemblies/cd's for nearly 800,000 youth. www.stanslaughter.com

Evangelical Environmental Network
Inspiring and mobilizing Christians to care for God's creation. www.creationcare.org

Focus the Nation
Portland, OR; Young leaders for a clean energy future. www.focusthenation.org

Food Not Lawns
Turning yards into gardens and neighborhoods into communities around the world. www.foodnotlawns.com

Forum for Food Sovereignty
A global network of NGOs/CSOs concerned with food sovereignty issues. www.foodsovereignty.org

Free Child Project
Advocates, informs, celebrates social change led by young internationals. www.freechild.org

Funders' Collaborative on Youth Organizing
Substantially increasing philanthropic investment in youth groups. www.fcyo.org

Generation Waking Up
The awakening youth movement of the 21st century. www.generationwakingup.org

Lizzy Ziogas

Green Yoga Association
Resources for doing yoga and being green.
www.greenyoga.org

Global Youth Action Network
Brooklyn, NY; Facilitates youth participation and intergenerational partnership.
www.youthlink.org

Global Youth Connect
Empowering youth to advance human rights and create a more just world.
www.globalyouthconnect.org

GratefulnessPractice.org
Provides resources for living in gratefulness to heal our Earth. www.gratefulness.org

Green Guide for Everyday Living
A green guide consumer website and blog.
www.thegreenguide.com

HeartMath
Practical and science-based research on heart-based living. www.heartmath.org

Initiative on Children's Environmental Health
Eliminating environmental exposures that undermine health. www.iceh.org

Institute of Interfaith Dialog
Promotes community service, and study of traditions. www.interfaithdialog.org

Institute for Responsible Technology
Fairfield, IA; Features the Non-GMO Shopping Guide. www.responsibletechnology.org
www.nongmoshoppingguide.com

Integrative Spirituality
Universal science is part of the life-affirming Eco-spirituality center.
www.integrativespirituality.org

Interfaith Youth Core
Bridges campuses to cooperative relationships in local communities. www.ifyc.org

Land Institute
Revolutionary ag research in hybridizing perennials for food. www.landinstitute.or

Landmark Education
San Francisco, CA; A powerful, accelerated learning experience affecting quality of life.
www.landmarkeducation.com

Lifestyles of Health and Sustainability
Green living tips for businesses and consumers.
www.lohas.com

Low Carbon Diet
US; Lose 5000 pounds of household carbon in 30 days. www.empowermentinstitute.net/lcd

Monterey Bay Aquarium
Monterey, CA; Provides excellent links to resources and info on seafood internationally.
www.montereybayaquarium.org

Move On
Online progressive activism and news.
www.moveon.org

National Campaign for Sustainable Agriculture
Coalition of farmers, environmentalists, and consumer advocates.
www.sustainableagriculture.net

National Coalition for Pesticide-Free Lawns
Pesticide reform groups and concerned individuals. www.beyondpesticides.org/pesticidefreelawns

National Family Farm Coalition
Organizing national projects to preserve and strengthen family farms. www.nffc.net

New Road Map Foundation
Promotes financial integrity, and helps people transform their relationship with money.
www.newroadmap.org

Next Generation
San Anselmo, CA; Offers numerous programs in leadership development among youth, teachers.
www.gonextgeneration.org

Nonviolent Communication
Living and teaching Nonviolent Communication.
www.cnvc.org

Nourishment
CA; Programs in cleansing, fasting, Raw Living Foods education. www.innourish.com

One World Now - Youth
Providing global leadership opportunitites for youth. www.oneworldnow.org

Organic Consumers Association
Online and grassroots campaigns. www.organicconsumers.org

Permaculture Institute of Northern California
Bolinas, CA; Teaching the skills necessary to live a more sustainable life on the planet.
www.regenerativedesign.org

Jim Embry

Pioneers of Change - Youth
Young practioners network.
www.pioneersofchange.net

Population Connection
Washington, DC; Advocating to stabilize world population at sustainability level.
www.populationconnection.org

Reconnecting America
Advocating redeveloping communities around transit, walking and biking.
www.reconnectingamerica.org

RenewableEnergyInstitute.org
Changing the way the world does energy by providing research and development.
www. RenewableEnergyInstitute.org

Resources for Spirituality Journeys
Spotlights people of different religious, spiritual traditions. www.spiritualityandpractice.com

Roots and Shoots
Berkeley, CA; Promotes understanding of all cultures and beliefs, and inspires action.
www.rootsandshoots.org

Simple Living Network
Provides tools and examples, and database of voluntary simplicity study circles/groups, with related links, and 3000 resource pages.
www.simpleliving.net

Slow Food Movement
Italy; Reviving threatened seed varieties and regional food specialties. www.slowfood.com

Square Foot Gardening
Natural, high-yield garden method using less space, and water than conventional methods.
www.squarefootgardening.com

Story of Stuff
Berkeley, CA; Video exposing problems with production and consumption patterns.
www.storyofstuff.com

Sunrise Center
Corte Madera, CA; Compassionate Communication, health seminars, interfaith spiritual gatherings. www.sunrise-center.org

Surface Transportation Policy Partnership
Nationwide coalition working to ensure smarter transportation choices. www.transact.org

Taking It Global - Youth
Toronto, ON, CAN; Collaborative learning on line. www.tigweb.org

Transmilenio
Bogota, Colombia; Model urban passenger-transportation services.
www.transmilenio.gov.co

What Kids Can Do
Voices and work from the next generation.
www.whatkidscando.org

World Changing
Independent thinkers covering innovative solutions to planet's problems. www.worldchanging.com

World Health Organization
The directing and coordinating authority for health within the United Nations.
www.who.int

World Spirit Youth Council
Starting spot for young spiritual seekers.
www.worldspirityouthcouncil.org

Young and the Restless
TN; Addressing the most pressing social, environmental and economic problems in the South. www.highlandercenter.org

YouthActionNet
Supporting young social entrepreneurial leaders around the world. www.youthactionnet.org

Claus Wawzinek

DOCUMENTARY VIDEOS & FILMS

A Convenient Truth
How Curitiba, Brazil transformed itself into one of the most livable cities in the world.
www.mariavazphoto.com/curitiba_pages/curitiba_dvd.html

Addicted to Plastic
About plastic pollution.
www.crypticmoth.com/plastic.php

Burning the Future: Coal in America
Challenges the notion of "clean coal."
www.burningthefuture.org

HOME (2009)
Aerial footage of Earth's fragile beauty and manmade problems. www.home-2009.com

Crude
Profiles an Ecuadorian environmental lawsuit against Chevron. www.crudethemovie.com

Division Street
Explores wildlife corridors and "green" highways. www.divisionstreetmovie.com

End of the Line
Explores the impact of over-fishing on Earth's oceans. www.endoftheline.com

Fighting Goliath: Texas Coal Wars
Texans fight the construction of coal-fired power plants. www.fightinggoliathfilm.com

Food Inc.
The lowdown on where are food really comes from and the implications for human and planetary health. www.foodincmovie.com

Forces of Nature
Profiles six Brower Youth Awards winners. shop.nationalgeographic.com/product/170/2513/104.html

Forever Wild
Profiles modern American wilderness heroes.
www.foreverwildfilm.com

Garbage!
How households contribute to environmental degradation. www.garbagerevolution.com

GREEN
About tropical rainforest destruction.
www.greenplanetfilms.org

How to Save the World
About modern industrial agriculture and biodynamic, sustainable farming.
www.greenplanetfilms.org

Mama Earth: Eco-Econ 101
Being eco-friendly is an economic necessity.
www.earthwalkmedia.com/projects.htm

PetroApocalypse Now?
How oil prices are bankrupting the world.
www.petroapocalypsenow.com/film.html

Power Paths
Hopi and Navajo force closure of a Nevada coal plant. www.powerpaths.org

River of Renewal
Profiles a battle over Klamath River Basin resources. www.aifisf.com/aiff/2008

Scarred Lands & Wounded Lives
Explores the ecological impact of war.
www.scarredlandsfilm.org

Tapped
About the bottled water industry.
www.tappedthemovie.com

The Future of Food
Investigates the controversy over genetically engineered foods. www.thefutureoffood.com

The Next Industrial Revolution
Architectural design for both ecology and humans. www.bullfrogfilms.com

The Power of Community: How Cuba Survived Peak Oil
How Cuba came to thrive after losing half their oil imports from the USSR collapse
www.powerofcommunity.org

The Real Dirt on Farmer John
Profiles creation of the largest Community Supported Agriculture farm in the US.
www.greenplanetfilms.org

DOCUMENTARY SOURCES

Bullfrog Films
Ecological and social justice documentary films. www.bullfrogfilms.com

Green Planet Films
Ecological and social justice documentary films. www.greenplanetfilms.org

Media Education Foundation
Documentary films on the impact of American mass media. www.mediaed.org

The Video Project
Ecological and social justice documentary films. www.videoproject.com

ENDNOTES

Key

CBD = Center for Biological Diversity
NRDC = Natural Resources Defense Council
RAN = Rainforest Action Network
RMI = Rocky Mountain Institute
SOTW = State of the World Report, published annually by the Worldwatch Institute
WWF = World Wildlife Fund
UCS = Union of Concerned Scientists
UN = United Nations

Part One: SETTING THE CONTEXT

~ Quotes and figures sourced from The Pachamama Alliance website, www.pachamama.org.

1. Symposium website; http://www.awakeningthedreamer.org
2. Earth under severe stress; stats from sites below listed:
   ozone: http://www.livescience.com/environment/080612-ozone-warming.html
   forest: http://www.un.org/earthwatch/forests/forestloss.html
   land: http://www.worldometers.info/ and
   http://www.fao.org/docrep/t0667e/t0667e04.htm
   fish: http://overfishing.org
3. UN, Section 3, #27 of Our Common Future, 1987;
   http://www.un-documents.net/wced-ocf.htm
4. Charts and stats available on http://www.footprintnetwork.org
5. Extinction research by professor David Ulansey;
   http://www.well.com/~davidu/extinction.html
6. Environmental displacement info;
   http://environment.about.com/od/globalwarming/a/envirorefugees.htm
7. Stats relayed in larger context at
   http://www.globalissues.org/TradeRelated/Facts.asp
8. If the Earth had 100 people, ratio description; http://miniature-earth.com

"When the well is dry, we learn the worth of water."
—Benjamin Franklin

Part Two: ENVIRONMENT

Climate Change

1. The Pew Center for Global Climate Change, "Overview," www.pewclimate.org
2, 3. The Pew Center, "Mythbusters" pdf, www.pewclimate.org, accessed Aug 09. At note 2 the article is referencing the IPCC 2007 report.
4. NASA 2009, "Global Temperature Trends: 2008 Annual Summation" www.data.giss.nasa.gov/gistemp/2008
5, 6. Worldwatch Institute, State of the World Report (SOTW) 2009
7. As reported by Natural Resources Defense Council, http://docs.nrdc.org/nuclear/nuc_08042301A.pdf
8. GHG sources: www.ipcc.ch/pdf/assessment-report; www.fao.org/newsroom/en/news; The Revolution Project
9. Peter Galvin, CBD, personal communication, Sept 09
10. See International Climate Bonds Proposals—Draft from the Network for Sustainable Financial Markets at www.ethicalmarkets.com. Sourced on Hazel Henderson's website, July 09, www.calvert-henderson.com/current.htm
11. Transition Towns and Post Carbon Institute, for starters. See also "Energy," note 3 (below), and the Resource Directory.

Sidebar (Terminology sources): The Pew Center for Global Climate Change, www.pewclimate.org; The Intergovernmental Panel on Climate Change, www.ipcc.ch; International Rivers, www.internationalrivers.org

Oceans

12. *Science Daily* (Aug 13, 08); www.sciencedaily.com/releases/2008/08/080813144405.htm
13. SOTW 2009
14, 15. The Center for Biological Diversity, www.biologicaldiversity.org
16. Sustainable Fisheries Initiative, a project of the New England Aquarium; www.neaq.org/conservation_and_research/projects/fisheries_bycatch_aquaculture/sustainable_fisheries
17, 18. Ben Block, "Scientists Sound Alarm on Ocean Acidification," Worldwatch news reports (Jan 30, 09)
19. "Window to Prevent Catastrophic Climate Change Closing; EU Should Press for Immediate US Action," Worldwatch news reports (Sept 13, 07)
20. *SOTW 2008*
21. *SOTW 2009*
22. "Window...," see note 19 above
23. CBD, see note 14
24. Brian Haldell, "Ocean Pollution Worsens and Spreads," Worldwatch news reports (Nov 8, 07); www.worldwatch.org/node/5474
25. *SOTW 2008*
26. Ocean Futures Society, headed by Jean-Michel Cousteau; www.oceanfutures.org
27, 28. Brian Haldell, see note 24

Coral Reefs

29. CDB, see note 14
30. Ben Block, "Coral Reef Loss Suggests Global Extinction Event," Worldwatch news reports (Dec 12, 08)
31. CBD, see note 14
32. Ben Block, see note 30
33. Recommended by WWF, The Nature Conservancy, and Conservation International

Fresh Water

34. *Drinking Water Week*, accessed Sept 09 on the Occidental Arts and Ecology website, www.oaec.org
35. http://water.org/facts/
36. The Species Alliance, http://speciesalliance.org
37. International Rivers, www.internationalrivers.org
38. Sara Grusky and Maj Fiil-Flynn, "Will the World Bank Back Down? Water Privatization in a Climate of Global Protest," a special report by Public Citizen's Water for All program (April 04)
39. Robert Engleman, "Population and Sustainability: Can We Avoid Limiting the Number of People?" *Scientific American* (June 09); www.scientificamerican.com/article.cfm?id=population-and-sustainability
40. To mention a few: Public Citizen, www.citizen.org and www.wateractivist.org; Food & Water Watch, www.foodandwaterwatch.org; Occidental Arts and Ecology Center, www.oaec.org
41, 42, 43. Sara Grusky and Maj Fiil-Flynn, see note 38
44. For example, see www.rainwaterharvesting.org; www.raingardens.org; www.internationalrivers.org/en/node/3475#rainwater; Salmon Protection and Watershed Network, www.spawnusa.org
45, 46. Food & Water Watch, www.foodandwaterwatch.org

Sidebars

(a) www.washingtonpost.com/wp-dyn/content/article/2005/09/19/AR2005091901295.html
(b) True Thirst. Statistics from Jean-Michel Cousteau, "Seas the Day: Water is World's Key Security Issue," Ocean Futures Society, June 2004 feature story, www.oceanfutures.org
(c) Bottled Water Consumption. Statistics (except for *National Geographic* stat) from *Water Follies: Groundwater Pumping and the Fate of America's Fresh Waters* by Robert Glennon (2002); sourced on www.oaecwater.org

Forests

47. USDA-FS 2000, accessed Sept 09 on www.ran.org, site of the Rainforest Action Network
48. www.ran.org
49, 50. Elisabeth Rosenthal, "In Brazil, Paying Farmers to Let the Trees Stand," *The New York Times* (Aug 22, 09), front page
51. Peter Galvin, CBD, personal communication
52. UN Global Forest Resource Assessment 2005 on www.ran.org

53. Posted on RAN's blog by Jennifer Krill (Oct 2, 09)
54. Marc Gunther, "Eco-police find new target: Oreos," *Fortune* magazine (Aug 13, 08)
55. The World Wildlife Fund's Jason Clay, author of *World Agriculture and the Environment*
56. See www.lesscars.org, www.culturechange.org and/or search "paving moratorium" on the Web.
57. New American Dream offers links to certified sustainably harvested wood and recycled products,http://www.newdream.org/marketplace/wood.php. Follow links to both FSC-certified wood (www.fscus.org) and Smartwood-certified (www.smartwood.org) reused, reclaimed, recycled and salvaged wood products. Also find good wood and "WoodWise" products at Green America, http://www.greenamericatoday.org/programs/woodwise/consumers/whatyoucando/goodwood.cfm

Biodiversity
~ Chief Seattle quote sourced on www.ecoera.org
~ E.O. Wilson quote from *The Creation: An Appeal to Save Life on Earth* (2006), p. 31

58. Center for Biological Diversity, www.biologicaldiversity.org
59. E.O. Wilson, *The Creation: An Appeal to Save Life on Earth* (2006)
60. Extinction research by professor David Ulansey; http://www.well.com/~davidu/extinction.html
61. Trish Andryszewski, Mass Extinction (2008)
62. http://www.conservation.org/LEARN/SPECIES/Pages/overview.aspx; info@sierraclub.bc.ca, and www.sierraclub.bc.ca/quick-links/media-centre/media-clips/armageddon-of-extinction
63. International Union for the Conservation of Nature (IUCN), 2009, Red List, sourced on www.biologicaldiversity.org
64, 65, 66. Trish Andryszewski, *Mass Extinction*, see note 61
67. http://dotearth.blogs.nytimes.com/2008/09/29/ecuador-constitution-grants-nature-rights/
68. CBD, www.biologicaldiversity.org; see also note 57

Waste, Pollution, and Toxics
~ Captain Charles Moore quoted from *Earth Island Journal*; see note 69 below

69. Project Kaisei, radio news reports sent from the gyre, Aug 09; www.projectkaisei.org. See also *Earth Island Journal* (Spring 09): http://www.earthisland.org/journal/index.php/eij/article/charles_moore/
70. Algalita Marine Research Foundation, www.algalita.org/pelagic_plastic.html
71, 72. Brian Halwell, "Ocean Pollution Worsens and Spreads," see note 24
73. www.projectkaisei.org

Sidebar
(d) Plastic Stats: California Integrated Waste Management Board, www.zerowaste. ca.gov/PlasticBags/default.htm; US Environmental Protection Agency (2008), Municipal Solid Waste: Generation, Recycling, and Disposal–Facts & Figures for 2007; third stat based on US Census data for 2005, and US EPA (2006) Municipal Solid Waste report for 2005.

74. Mushroom info gathered from the following: www.fungi.com (Stamets' own site); *Mycelium Running*, one of the books by Paul Stamets; www.youtube.com/PaulStamets; the TED video "Six Ways Mushrooms Can Save the World" on TED.com; radio interview with Sue Supriano, www.SueSupriano.com/audio/paulstamets.mp3
75. For living machines, start with www.oceanarks.org; also www.yesmagazine.org/article.asp?ID=673
76. Quoting Captain Charles Moore; see note 69

No matter how far you have gone on the wrong road, turn back.
—Turkish proverb

Creative Commons/Center for American Progress Action Fund

Part Three: **ENERGY**

1. Christopher Flavin, Worldwatch Report: "Low-Carbon Energy—A Roadmap," http://www.worldwatch.org/node/5945 (download free report using this URL)
2. See "Portland Leads the Way in Preparation for Peak Oil" at www.worldwatch.org
3. To become a Transition Town and wean your community from fossil fuels, see Part Six, *Communities*, of this book, as well as: http://transitiontowns.org/TransitionNetwork/Criteria; and http://transitionus.org (United States); www.citiesgogreen.org; www.greencities.com; www.summitgreen.org; www.postcarbon.org

Renewable Energy
Sidebar
(a) What Is Renewable Energy? boxed definition from www.RenewableEnergyInstitute.org
Sidebar
(six major groups of energy sectors) NRDC, Fig 1 in http://docs.nrdc.org/nuclear/nuc_08042301A.pdf

4. Christopher Flavin, "Low-Carbon Energy," see note 1
5. "Renewables Global Status Report, 2007 Update," Renewable Energy Policy Network, accessed through http://www.worldwatch.org/files/pdf/renewables_exec_sum_2007.pdf. Also SOTW 2008, noting a UN report that investments in renewable energy reached the $100 billion mark in 2006.
6. Worldwatch Institute, SOTW 2009
7. Renewable Energy Institute, www.RenewableEnergyInstitute.org
8. Matthew L. Wald, "Wind Energy Bumps into Power Grid's Limits," *The New York Times* (Aug 26, 08), Business section
9, 10. *National Geographic*, "Plugging into the Sun" (Sept 09)
11. *SOTW 08*
12. NRDC, http://www.nrdc.org/air/energy/renewables/solar.asp
13. Sierra Club, www.sierraclub.org

Sidebar
(b) Christopher Flavin, "Low-Carbon Energy," see note 1 above
(c) National Geographic, "Plugging into the Sun" (Sept 09)

14. www.WindEnergyInstitute.com
15. Rocky Mountain Institute, www.rmi.org, "Forget Nuclear" by Amory Lovins et al.
16. NRDC, http://www.nrdc.org/air/energy/renewables/wind.asp
17. US Geological Survey (USGS), "Geothermal Energy: Clean Power from the Earth's Heat," accessed Aug 08 at www.nonukes.org/library/usgs_2003_report_on_geothermal_energy.pdf
18. Sierra Club, www.sierraclub.org
19. USGS, see note 17
20, 21. Renewable Energy Institute, www.RenewableEnergyInstitute.org
22. Rocky Mountain Institute, www.rmi.org

Sidebar (Renewable Energy DIY)
(d) Condensed from "Producing Your Own Renewable Energy" by Andy Karnitz, published in *Humboldt Coalition for Property Rights Newsletter* (Summer 09)
Sidebar (Sweden)
(e) www.RenewableEnergyInstitute.org
(f) *SOTW 2008*

Hydroelectric, Coal, Nuclear Energy
23. NRDC, www.nrdc.org/air/transportation/hydrogen/contents.asp
24, 25. www.InternationalRivers.org among others
26. NRDC, http://docs.nrdc.org/nuclear/nuc_08042301A.pdf
27. www.sierraclub.org/cleanair/factsheets/power.asp#return4
28. *SOTW 2008*
29. Rocky Mountain Institute, www.rmi.org
30. *SOTW 2008*

~ "Ten Strikes" list and quote beginning "New nuclear power is so costly..." from "Forget Nuclear," by Amory B. Lovins, Imran Sheikh, and Alex Markevich of the Rocky Mountain Institute; accessed on www.rmi.org/sitepages/pid467.php

Energy Conservation

31. Christopher Flavin, "Low-Carbon Energy," see note 1
32. McKinsey Climate Change Special Initiative 2007, found on NRDC website
33. Amory B. Lovins, commissioned paper, "Energy End-Use Efficiency," accessed Aug 09 at www.rmi.org/images/PDFs/Energy/E05-16_EnergyEndUseEff.pdf
34. Jeff Goodell, "Look West, Obama," *Rolling Stone* (Feb 19, 09)
35, 36. Pie charts: US chart from Energy Information Administration, AER 2008; Global chart from British Petroleum, annual report on energy production, 2008
37. Chart: US Energy Consumption by Sector, US Energy Information Administration, 2007

"You may say I'm a dreamer, but I'm not the only one.
I hope someday you'll join us, and the world will live as one."
—"Imagine" by John Lennon

Part Four: A JUST SOCIETY

~ Cynthia McKinney quoted from her acceptance speech (GA Congress) in Nov 04. Eleanor Roosevelt quoted from remarks at a UN presentation, 1958.
~ E.O. Wilson quote from *The Creation: An Appeal to Save Life on Earth* (2006), p. 75

Global Challenges

1. End Poverty 2015 Millennium Campaign, press release (June 23, 09); www.endpoverty2015.org
2. *Overcoming Barriers: Human Mobility and Development*, Human Development Report 2009, UN Development Program, http://hdr.undp.org
3. Michael Renner, "Environment a Growing Driver in Displacement of People," Worldwatch news reports (Sept 17, 08)
4. *Overcoming Barriers*, see note 2
5. Robert Engleman, "Population and Sustainability: Can We Avoid Limiting the Number of People?" *Scientific American* (June 09); this is also the source of the boxed text in the right margin: www.scientificamerican.com/article.cfm?id=population-and-sustainability. Engleman is VP for programs at the Worldwatch Institute and author of *More: Population, Nature, and What Women Want* (Island Press). See current numbers on the federal government's "population clocks" site, www.census.gov/main/www/popclock.html
6. "Population Challenges: The Basics," published by The Population Institute and available as a downloadable pdf from their website: www.populationinstitute.com.
7. Robert Engleman, *Scientific American*, see note 5
8. "The Population Taboo," posted by Lisa Stiffler on *Sightline* (June 17, 09), accessed July 09, http://daily.sightline.org/daily_score/archive/2009/06/17/the-taboo-of-population growth
9. Nicholas D. Kristof and Sheryl WuDunn, "Why Women's Rights Are the Cause of Our Time," *The New York Times Magazine* (Aug 29, 09)
10. Hillary Clinton quoted by interviewer Mark Landler in "A New Gender Agenda," *The New York Times Magazine* (Aug 29, 09)
11. Kristof and WuDunn, see note 9
12. Robert Engleman, *Scientific American*, see note 5 above
13. Optimum Population Trust and the London School of Economics, "Fewer Emitters, Lower Emissions, Less Cost" www.optimumpopulation.org/reducingemission.pdf
14. Chris Maser, "To Control Our Population, We Must Honor Women," essay from *The Perpetual Consequences of Fear and Violence: Rethinking the Future* (2004)

The UN: Envisioning a Better World

15. UNDP Human Development Report, 1997
16. United Nations, "Human Rights and Poverty: 60 Years Later," www.un.org/works/sub3.asp?lang=en&id=63
17. UNPFII (2005), Report on the Fourth Session (E/C.19/2005/9)
18. Bonney Hartley, UN Permanent Forum on Indigenous Issues. "MDG Reports and Indigenous Peoples: A Desk Review," No. 3 (Feb 08) www.mdgmonitor.org/factsheets.cfm
19, 20. Millennium Promise website: www.millenniumpromise.org
21. Teach a Man to Fish website: www.teachamantofish.org.uk

Indigenous Rights

22. "Resource Kit on Indigenous Peoples' Issues," UN Permanent Forum on Indigenous Issues, 2008; www.un.org/esa/socdev/unpfii/.../resource_kit_indigenous_2008.pdf

23. UN Declaration on the Rights of Indigenous Peoples, Article 20.1; www.un.org
24. Bonney Hartley, see note 16
25. Seventh Generation Fund newsletter, March 06; www.7genfund.org
26. Nellis Kennedy and Winona LaDuke, "Opportunity knocks but it's not Desert Rock," *Navajo Times* (June 18, 09); http://www.honorearth.org/news/opportunity-knocks-it039s-not-desert-rock
27. "White Earth Land Recovery Project Receives...Award," Jessie Smith Noyes Foundation press release; http://www.foundationcenter.org/pnd/news/

Honoring Diversity

~ Nobel Prize references: http://nobelprize.org/nobel_prizes/peace/laureates/2009/press.html (Oct 9, 09); "Nobel economics prize goes to woman who studies natural resources" by Grist contributor Agence France-Presse (Oct 12, 09); www.grist.org/article/2009-10-12-nobel-economics-prize-goes-to-woman-who-studies-natural-resource

28. www.huffingtonpost.com/2008/03/18/obama-race-speech-read-th_n_92077.html
29. *In These Times*, "20 Questions with Grace Lee Boggs," www.inthesetimes.com/community/20questions/4060/grace_lee_boggs/
30. Congressional Black Caucus Foundation, *African Americans and Climate Change: An Unequal Burden* (2004); www.cbcfinc.org
31. Hayes Morehouse, Ella Baker Center for Human Rights blog (Aug 21, 09); www.ellabakercenter.org/blog
32. Denver-based Sisters of Color for Education; www.sistersofcolor.org
33. Census data Immigration Policy Center; www.immigrationpolicy.org/sites/default/files/docs/American_Roots_in_the_Immigrants_Experience_101909.pdf
34. Charu Chandrasekhar, "Flying While Brown: Federal Civil Rights Remedies to Post-9/11 Airline Racial Profiling of South Asians," *Asian Law Journal*, Vol 10 (May 03)
35. Asian American Justice Center, www.advancingequality.org
36. Asian Pacific Environmental Network, http://apen4ej.org/building.htm

Pathways to an Equitable Future

37. US Department of Labor, "DOL Announces Green Jobs Grants—$150 Million Available for Pathways Out of Poverty" (June 09); www.doleta.gov/grants/find_grants.cfm
38. Joel Warner, "Urbavore's Dilemma: Blue and Yellow Logic hopes to mix up a new form of green," *Denver Westword* (Aug 4, 09); www.BlueandYellowLogic.com
39. The Corps Network, www.corpsnetwork.org/index.php?option=com_content&view=article&id=87&Itemid=54
40. Ellis Jones, Ross Haenfler, and Brett Johnson, *The Better World Handbook* (2007)

Part Five: ECONOMICS

1. Peter M. Senge, Joe Laur, Bryan Smith, Nina Kruschwitz, and Sara Schley, *The Necessary Revolution* (2008). Excerpt, "Seeing the Whole Picture" in Sustainable Systems at Work, Discussion Course by Northwest Earth Institute, 2009; www.nwei.org
2. Peter Senge et al., *The Necessary Revolution* (2008). List slightly abridged for space.

Global Crisis

3. David Korten, "Living Wealth: Better Than Money," *Yes!* Magazine (Fall 07); www.yesmagazine.org/issues/stand-up-to-corporate-power/1834
4. The New Economy Working Group, www.neweconomyworkinggroup.org
5, 6. David Korten, "Living Wealth," see note 3 above
7. The New Economy Working Group (in process)
8. David Korten, "What do you mean by 'Money is a System of Power'?" www.davidkorten.org/MoneyPower
9. The New Economy Working Group website: www.neweconomyworkinggroup.org

Globalization

10. "Global Marshall Plan, Balance the world with a eco-social market economy," www.globalmarshallplan.org/the_initiative/strategy/index_eng.html
11. Laura Carlsen, "Americans Policy Report the Mexican Farmers' Movement: Exposing the Myths of Free Trade (2003); www.ifg.org/analysis/wto/cancun/mythtrade.htm International Forum on Globalization

12. Tao Wang and Jim Watson, "Trade, Climate Change, and Sustainability." In 2009 *State of the World*–Into a Warming World, Report by Worldwatch Institute; www.worldwatch.org

Global Solutions

13, 14. Joseph Stiglitz, "Reform is needed. Reform is in the air. We can't afford to fail," *The Guardian* (27 March 09); http://guardian.co.uk/commentisfree/2009/mar/27/global-recession-reform

15. List compiled from the following sources: Henderson (2002, 2003), Jubilee USA, Redefining Progress, Global Policy Forum, and the Global Marshall Plan Initiative's "Five Elements of an Eco-Social Economy"

16. Citizens Trade Campaign 2009 "Trade Reform, Accountability, Development and Employment (TRADE) Act" had 75 US Congressional co-sponsors in 2008.

17. Hazel Henderson, "Re-defining Economic Growth and Re-shaping Globalization Toward Sustainability 2009," International Conference on Concerted Strategies to Meet the Environmental and Economic Challenges of the 21st Century. Vienna, Austria (April 2009); http://www.cluboferome.org/eng/meetings/vienna_2009/presentations.asp

18. Rachel Dixon, "'Teach us how to fish—do not just give us the fish'; Does buying Fairtrade products really make a difference to people's lives?" www.guardian.co.uk/environment/2008/mar/12/ethicalliving.lifeandhealth/print

19. Norwegian Nobel Committee, Oct 06. Accessed at www.grameen-info.org/index.php?option=com_content&task=view&id=197&Itemid=197

Enterprise Economics

20. David Suzuki with Faisal Moola, "Life-altering planetary experience," *Science Matters* (Oct 2, 09), email newsletter

21. David Korten, "Why This Crisis May Be Our Best Chance to Build a New Economy," *YES!* Magazine (Summer 09)

22. Chris Maser explains in detail in *Earth in our Care* (2009)

23. Janine Benyus, *Biomimicry: Innovation Inspired by Nature* (1997)

24. Definition of sustainable development: 1987, United Nations World Commission on Environment and Development

25. Joyce Marcel, "Seventh Generation buys itself," *Vermont Business Magazine* (July 1, 2000); http://findarticles.com/p/articles/mi_qa3675/is_200007/ai_n8903496/

26. Hazel Henderson, *Ethical Markets: Growing the Green Economy* (2006)

27. Ray Anderson, plenary speaker, Bioneers conference 2008; www.bioneers.org/presenters/ray-anderson

28. John R. Ehrenfeld, "The Roots of Sustainability," *MIT Sloan Management Review* (Winter 05). IN Sustainable Systems at Work, Discussion Course 2009, Northwest Earth Institute

29. "What's Wrong with Corporate Social Responsibility?" *Corporate Watch Report* (2006). Downloadable pdf from www.corporatewatch.org.uk/?lid=2693

30. www.climatebiz.com/news/2008/11/17/verizon-ups-cox-fleets?page=0%2C1

31. www.climatebiz.com/news/2008/11/13/fedex-ibm-and-office-depot-report-green-progress

32. John Elkington, Chapter 1 Enter the Triple Bottom Line (Aug 17, 04); www.johnelkington.com/TBL-elkington-chapter.pdf

33. John Talberth, "A New Bottom Line for Progress." Chapter 2, SOTW 08 by the Worldwatch Institute. Dr. John Talberth is Director of the Sustainability Indicators Program at Redefining Progress.

34. Earth Charter International. "The Earth Charter, GRI, and the Global Compact: Guidance to Users on the Synergies in Application and Reporting" (2008), (c) Global Reporting Initiative, downloadable pdf from www.globalreporting.org

35. Global Reporting Initiative, "Number of companies worldwide reporting on their sustainability…," press release (July 15, 09); www.globalreporting.org/NewsEventsPress/PressResources/PressRelease_14_July_2006_1,000GRIReports.htm

36. "What's Wrong with Corporate Social Responsibility?" Corporate Watch Report, see note 29

37. Kenny Bruno, [50] "The UN's Global Compact, Corporate Accountability and the Johannesburg Earth Summit," Corporate Watch (Jan 24, 02); www.corpwatch.org/article.php?id=1348 IN "What's Wrong with Corporate Social Responsibility?" Corporate Watch Report (2006). Downloadable pdf from www.corporatewatch.org.uk/?lid=2693

38. RiskMetrics Group, "Corporate Governance and Climate Change: Consumer and Technology Companies." A Ceres Report (Dec 08); http://www.ceres.org/Page.aspx?pid=1002

39. Carl Frankel, "Putting the Brakes on Fast Money: An Interview with Woody Tasch," *Chronogram Magazine* (April 27, 09); http://www.chronogram.com/issue/2009/5/Community+Notebook/Putting-the-Brakes-on-F...8/27/2009

Sidebar Notes (40)

(a) Ellen Brown, "The Public Option in Banking: How We Can Beat Wall Street at its Own Game" (Aug 5, 09); http://www.webofdebt.com/articles/public_option.php

(b) Ellen Brown, "But Governor, You Can Create Money! Just Form Your Own Bank" (May 26, 09); http://www.webofdebt.com/articles/but_governor.php

41. See also Sourcewatch wiki: www.sourcewatch.org for info on Greenwashing

42. www.ChevronToxico.com

43. Brian Goldberg, "In the US, the Federal Trade Commission Takes on Environmental Marketing Claims." Posted on Environmental Law Resource (July 8, 09); http://www.environmentallawresource.com/2009/07/articles/sustainability/in-the-us-the-fe...

44. "Learn more about corporate power," http://www.foei.org/en/what-we-do/corporate-power/nominations-wanted-worst-corporate-climate-lobbyists/?searchterm=corporate%20lobby

45. Larry Lohmann, "When Markets are Poison: Learning about Climate Policy from the Financial Crisis" (Sept 09); www.thecornerhouse.org.uk/pdf/briefing/40poisonmarkets.pdf

46. Stacy Mitchell, "The Corporate Co-Opt of Local" (July 9, 09); www.newrules.org/retail/article/corporate-coopt-local

47. Stacy Mitchell, "Local Where? Big corporations are finding ways to sell themselves as the folks next door" (July 22, 09); published on Seven Days www.7dvt.com

Local Solutions

48. Chris Maser, from "True Community is Founded on a Sense of Place, History and Trust" (2008), Social Essay 28; and from "The Commons Usufruct Law" (2009), Social Essay 31; www.chrismaser.com

49. Michael Shuman, "Local Stock Exchanges and National Stimulus," posted on Sept 2, 09; www.small-mart.com/home

50. Michael Shuman, *The Small-Mart Revolution: How Local Businesses Are Beating the Global Competition* (2006)

51. Doug Pibel, "Communities Take Power: The Citizens of Barnstead, New Hampshire, Used Local Law to Keep Corporate Giants Out of Their Water," *YES!* Magazine (July 07); http://www.yesmagazine.org/issues/stand-up-to-corporate-power/1828

52. Michael Shuman, "Local Stock Exchanges…," see note 49

53. www.community-wealth.org/strategies/panel/cdcs/index.html

54. "Models & Innovations in Ownership," on National Center for Economic & Security Alternatives website: www.ncesa.org/html/thirdway.html

55. David Korten, "The World We Want," presentation to the Consumer Cooperatives Management Association, June 08

Cooperatives

56. Living Young & Free website quote: www.livingyoungandfree.com/

57. "Resilience of the co-operative business model in times of crisis" and statistical information on the International Co-operative Alliance website: www.ica.coop/coop/statistics.html

Innovative Community Banks

58. "Our Story" about Development Deposits^sm; www.shorebankcorp.com

59. "Our Story," www.shorebankcorp.com/

60. Chris Maser, "True Community is Founded on a Sense of Place, History and Trust" (2008), Social Essay 28; www.chrismaser.com

"The future belongs to those who understand that doing more with less is compassionate, prosperous, and thus more intelligent, even competitive."
—Paul Hawken

"Mindfulness must be engaged. Once there is seeing, there must be acting. Otherwise, what is the use of seeing?"   —Thich Nhat Hanh

Part Six: COMMUNITY

1. http://transitionus.org (United States)

Growing Communities

2. "Cook One Meal, Eat for a Week…," http://www.greenamericatoday.org/pubs/realgreen/articles/cooperativemeals.cfm
3. Phone interview with Bruce Davidson in Shutesbury, MA, Sept 23, 09
4. Bill McKibben, "A Place that Makes Sense: On Not Living Too Large," Sept 23, 08; www.christiancentury.org/article.lasso?id=5225
5. Stephanie Hemphill, "Swedish Town Takes Sustainability to New Level," Minnesota Public Radio, Morning Edition (July 8, 09); http://minnesota.publicradio.org/display/web/2009/07/07/sustainable_sweden/
6. Alison Pruitt, "Hammarby Sjöstad, Stockholm Becomes Model of Sustainability," July 13, 09; www.energyboom.com/policy/Hammarby_Sjostad_Stockholm_Becomes_Model_of_Sustainability

Green Building

7. A simple formula: Add the number of hours each day you are at work/school, in transit (vehicle), eating, using TV/computer, shopping/errands inside, sleeping, and average the numbers.
8. www.baosol.com/
9. Visionary: http://weburbanist.com/2008/07/08/15-more-future-wonders-of-green-technology/
10. When you grab your keys to go, turn off all nonessentials with a single switch: www.jackgodfreywood.co.uk/switch.htm; www.diylife.com/2007/10/02/power-off-the-whole-house-with-a-single-switch/; www.ccogeek.com/component/content/article/958
11. Architects Steven Kieran and James Timberlake are profiled in "Treehugger." The transparent Cellophane house is designed to be disassembled, re-used, and recycled. www.treehugger.com/files/2008/07/wrapping-up-with-the-cellophane-house.php; www.kierantimberlake.com
12. The pride of the Midwestern green building community, Greensburg was flattened by a tornado of historic intensity, now being reconstructed from the ground up. Planet Green covers the process, reality-TV style; www.greensburggreentown.org/; www.nytimes.com/2009/09/23/realestate/commercial/23kansas.html?_r=2&scp=1&sq=greensburg&st=cse. Germany's Eco City is profiled in Inhabitat, www.inhabitat.com/2009/08/19/eco-city-seeking-highest-rating-from-the-three-major-major-green-rating-systems/; www.ecocity.de/
13. "The State of Green Building," a White Paper; published by ThermaTru, a door manufacturer; www.thermatru.com/pdfs/WhitePaper.pdf
14. A thorough report from Environment America: www.environmentamerica.org/uploads/qk/zy/qkzycNV75kmR8g8HlAR7rw/AME_BBA_web.pdf
15. Global Footprint Network expands on the carbon footprint concept, www.footprintnetwork.org
16. US Green Building Council, Green Building Research, www.usgbc.org
17. Pat Murphy, "The Energy Impact of Our Buildings," www.communitysolution.org
18. Andrew Michler, "Seven steps to a sustainable building, a performance path" (April 16, 09); www.igreenbuild.com
19. On outgassing/indoor air pollution: dkmommyspot.com/what-is-outgassing; www.outgasreport.com/
20. Each of these sites has energy audit links: www.cbpca.org/homeowners; www.energystar.gov/; www.mygreenclement.com/category/environmental-footprint/
21. Get stimulated! Find weatherization programs at www.waptac.org/; apps1.eere.energy.gov/weatherization/
22. Just a few: www.jetsongreen.com/2008/01/greenmobile-ult.html; www.greenpoddevelopment.com/; greeninc.blogs.nytimes.com/2009/02/11/reinventing-modular-housing-as-green/; www.weehouse.com; www.motherearthnews.com/Green-Homes/Green-Modular-Homes.aspx
23. Architect Sarah Susanka brings to light a new way of thinking about what makes a place feel like home: www.notsobighouse.com
24. LEED: www.usgbc.org/DisplayPage.aspx?CategoryID=19; BREEAM: www.breeam.org; www.thegbi.org/news/news/2009/GBI-Testimony-and-Background-info-to-Senate-Energy-Committee.pdf
25. State tax incentives, www.dsireusa.org/; federal incentives, www.energystar.gov
26. "The State of Green Building," see note 13 above

27. Tassafaronga is registered for LEED for Homes with a goal of Platinum certification, www.dbarchitect.com
28. Brad Pitt's Make It Right Foundation plans 150 new homes for New Orleans' 9th Ward, www.makeitrightnola.org/
29. New Orleans: www.globalgreen.org/neworleans/holycross/; www.helpholycross.org
30. www.hud.gov/recovery. Watch HUD Secretary Donovan talk green.
31. "Architecture for Humanity brings design, construction and development services to communities in need globally," www.architectureforhumanity.org
32. World Habitat Day, US-hosted in 2009, www.hud.gov/whd/
33. Arthur Schendler, "Getting Green Done," www.thebigmoney.com/articles/judgments/2009/03/12/losing-money-through-walls
34. Tom Whipple covers peak oil in the Falls Church News-Press, www.fcnp.com
35. *Environmental Building News*, "Passive Survivability: A New Design Criterion for Buildings," www.buildgreen.com
36. USGBC on Langston High School, leedcasestudies.usgbc.org; *Washington Post* on green schools, www.washingtonpost.com/wp-dyn/content/article/2007/09/10/AR2007091002310.html
37. www.ecoschools.com/Energy/Energy_wSidebar.html
38. Nevada's "model for a sustainable regional energy economy," www.energynevada.com
39. *NY Times* blogs green schools: greeninc.blogs.nytimes.com/2009/05/28/shining-a-natural-light-on-green-schools/
40. A Green White House: www.inhabitat.com/2009/09/15/the-white-house-takes-aim-at-leed-certification/; www.huffingtonpost.com/2008/11/28/obama-i-want-to-make-the_n_146951.html
41. "Teach, don't just lock up," www.grist.org/article/2009-08-19-washington-state-prisons-pursue-sustainable-practices-green-jobs/; blogs.evergreen.edu/sustainableprisons/
42. ADPSR's Prison Alternatives Initiative supports community-based alternatives to incarceration, www.adpsr.org

Greening Cities

43. David Owen, "Is Manhattan one of the greenest cities around?" *The New Yorker*, www.newyorker.com/online/blogs/newsdesk/2009/09/david-owen-green-metropolis.html
44. Rocky Mountain Institute, Clinton Climate Initiative, and partners, www.rmi.org
45. New York City's PlaNYC provides a comprehensive set of sustainable objectives: www.nyc.gov/html/planyc2030; volunteer.nycservice.org
46. North Carolina: www.ncprojectgreen.com/; Texas: www.txgreenenergyaudits.com
47. DC's websites go deep: www.greenhome.org; www.green.dc.gov.
48. "High Point…," www.seattlehousing.org
49. Watch Greensburg rebuilding: www.planetgreen.discovery.tv/greensburg. More great shows include Greenovate, World's Greenest Homes, Focus Earth, Invention Nation, Renovation Nation, and scolding Wa$ted!
50. Sundance Channel, www.sundancechannel.com, "White Roofs Can Cool Homes, Businesses and the Planet;" Target Center: livegreentwincities.com/news/newsitem.aspx?newsid=1072&newsitemid=7006; Chicago's City Hall: www.cityofchicago.org; www.greenroofs.org
51. "Green walls—go vertical!" www.eltlivingwalls.com/; www.g-sky.com/; www.cnn.com/2009/TECH/science/06/29/green.walls/index.html; www.mnn.com/business/commercial-building/blogs/pnc-unveils-six-story-green-wall; www.mnn.com/the-home/building-renovating/stories/green-walls-of-china; www.treehugger.com/files;/2008/09/11-buildings-wrapped-in-green-walls.php

52. The Humanure Handbook: A Guide to Composting Human Manure, www.weblife.org/humanure/
53. www.igreenbuild.com/cd_3218.aspx
54. Sleek style for a greywater workhorse: www.inhabitat.com/2009/09/28/sinktoilet-combo-is-an-all-in-one-greywater-recycling-system/
55. www.grist.org/article/single-stream-dream
56. "Green Building Retrofits Represent a Potential $400B Market," www.environmentalleader.com/2009/06/18/green-building-retrofits-represent-a-potential-400b-market/
57. "Insulation gets stimulated!" http://apps1.eere.energy.gov/weatherization
58. Environmental Leader: www.environmentalleader.com; State Government reps: www.usa.gov's; DC names you need: www.congress.org

Transportation

59. Senator John Kerry, "We Can't Ignore the Security Threat from Climate Change," *The Huffington Post* (Aug 31, 09)

60. Toronto Transportation Services, Idling Control Bylaw, www.toronto.ca/transportation/onstreet/idling.htm

61. United for a Fair Economy, www.faireconomy.org

62. Toronto Transportation Services, see note 60

63. The Idle-Free Zone, http://oee.nrcan.gc.ca/transportation/idling/why-idle.cfm?attr=28

64, 65. Entrepreneur, "Unnecessary Engine Idling Causes Air Pollution," www.entrepreneur.com/tradejournals/article/128712592.html

66. "Redesigning Urban Transport," *Earth Policy News*, adapted from Ch. 10, "Designing Cities for People," in Lester R. Brown, Plan B 3.0: Mobilizing to Save Civilization (2008)

67. "Restructuring the US Transport System: The Potential of High-Speed Rail," Earth Policy News, adapted from Ch. 11, "Raising Energy Efficiency," in Lester R. Brown, see note above

68, 69. See note 66

70. Lloyd Alter, "They are Building Bicycle Superhighways in Copenhagen" (Aug 21, 09); www.treehugger.com/files/2009/08/copenhagen-bicycle-superhighways.php

71. See note 66

72. Rocky Mountain Institute, "Transformational Trucking, How the Trucking Industry Can Avoid the Automotive Industry's Fate," accessed at http://www.treehugger.com/files/2009/03/transformational-how-trucking-industry-avoid-automotive-fate.php. See also CSR Wire, The Corporate Social Responsibility Newswire, July 7, 09, press release, "EA Logistics Publishes White Paper on Green Transport," www.csrwire.com

73. Sierra Club, www.SierraClub.org

74. See, for example, Union of Concerned Scientists, "Clean Vehicles," http://www.ucsusa.org/clean_vehicles/technologies_and_fuels/hybrid_fuelcell_and_electric_vehicles/battery-electric-vehicles.html; "Automakers Go Electric" by Ben Block (Dec 9, 08), Worldwatch Institute, www.worldwatch.org/node/5956; Honda Corp., http://automobiles.honda.com/fcx-clarity/; and Tesla Motors, www.teslamotors.com. To compare hybrid vehicles: www.hybridcenter.org

75. Toyota Green Road to Growth, "Making Manufacturing Sustainable," www.toyota.co.jp/en

76. UCS, www.ucsusa.org/clean_vehicles/technologies_and_fuels/gasoline_and_diesel/ucs-vanguard-2009.html

77. The Rocky Mountain Institute, www.rmi.org

78. Vandana Shiva paraphrased from Soil Not Oil (2008), pp. 2, 77-89.

79. For more on Univ of Florida efforts, see www.sustainable.ufl.edu

80. List based on Sierra Club material, with additional suggestions toward the end. See www.sierraclub.org

81. The Surface Transportation Policy Project, www.transact.org, is a nationwide coalition working for safer, smarter transportation choices that enhance the economy, improve public health, promote social equity, and protect the environment. RE: Connecting jobs to public transit, see http://goodjobsfirst.org/smart_growth/connecting_jobs.cfm

Part Seven: GETTING PERSONAL

Food

1. India Environment Portal: Food and Water Watch, www.indiaenvironmentportal.org.in/category/publisher/food-water-watch

2. Univ of Minnesota studies: C.F. Runge and B. Senauer, "How Biofuels Could Starve the Poor," Foreign Affairs (May/June 07), referenced in "Why GM Crops Will Not Feed the World," by Bill Freese, *GeneWatch* magazine

3. www.localharvest.org/buylocal.jsp

4. Union of Concerned Scientists, *The Consumer's Guide to Effective Environmental Choices* (1999), p. 58

5. www.sierraclub.org/factoryfarms/factsheets/antibiotics.asp

6. David Wolfe, *Eating for Beauty* (2009)

7. Andrew Martin, "Is a Food Revolution Now in Season?" *The New York Times* (March 22, 09), Business section

8. India Environment Portal, see note 1

Sidebar

(a) GHGs per US Food Sector chart: US Institute for Agriculture and Trade Policy, http://www.iatp.org/iatp/publications.cfm?accountID=258&refID=105667

9. Food and Agriculture Organization of the United Nations, "Livestock's Long Shadow: Environmental Issues and Options," Rome (2006), p. 272

10. Robert Goodland and Jeff Anhang, "Livestock and Climate Change," Worldwatch (Nov/Dec 09), p. 11

11. USGS, "Estimated Use of Water in the United States in 2000," authored by Hutson et al. (2005)

12. Gidon Eshel and Pamela Martin, Univ of Chicago study (2006), "Vegan Diets Healthier for Planet, People Than Meat Diets," *Environmental Science and Technology* (2008)

13. *Journal of the American Dietetic Association* (June 03), Vol 103, No 6: pp. 748–65

14. Trathen Heckman contributed his unique and passionate writing to this section.

Sidebar

(b) Sidebar: Is Seafood a Good Choice? From Helen Olsson, "Eco Eating," in Delicious Living Magazine, Whole Foods Market (April 09), Vol 25, No 4. For responsible seafood choices, go to the Monterey Bay Aquarium's website at: www.montereybayaquarium.org/cr/seafoodwatch.aspx; see also New England Aquarium, www.neaq.org

Home Sweet Nontoxic Home

15. *Rachel's Environment and Health Weekly* #538 (March 20, 97)

16. *Yes!* Magazine (Summer 98), p. 13

17. "A Greener Future, Part 1," *Los Angeles Times* (Sept 14, 08)

18. Elise Miller, ED of the Institute for Children's Environmental Health, at a Bioneers panel on "Protecting Our Most Vulnerable" (Oct 18, 08)

19. American Cancer Society

20. Sightline Institute, www.sightline.org/research/sust_toolkit/solutions/precautionary

21. Bioneers panel, see note 18

22. US Consumer Product Safety Commission, Children's Sleepwear Regulations, 1, 16 CFR Parts 1615 & 1616

23. Food Not Lawns (landscaping)

Sidebar

(c) Improving Appliances: DOE site; www1.eere.energy.gov/consumer/tips/water_heating.html; From Treehugger.com, "Repair or Replace (and Recycle) Your Hot Water Heater," by Colin Dunn, posted March 23, 2008. See www.oaecwater.org for solar water-heating tips from the Occidental Arts and Ecology Center's Water Institute.

Ecological Footprint

Info contributed by the Global Footprint Network; www.footprintnetwork.org

The Consumption Conundrum

24. Adam D. Sacks, "The Fallacy of Climate Activism" (Aug 23, 08), www.grist.org/article

25. See regular Worldwatch Institute reports called Vital Signs for statistical evidence

26, 27. Juliet Schor, "Forget commercialism! The new realities of consumption and the economy" (posted Nov 18, 08); see also "The Politics of Consumption," Boston Review (Summer 99). www.simpleliving.net is a good place to start thinking about your own consumption.

28. "Population Challenges: The Basics," www.populationinstitute.com

Spirituality

Thanks to Rev. Kelly Isola, MDiv, for this section.

The Way is long—let us go together. The Way is difficult—let us help each other. The Way is joyful— let us share it. The Way is ours alone—let us go in love. The Way grows before us—let us begin.

—Zen Invocation

Leah Beck